Learn to Paint

WITH
Watercolours, Oils, Pastels and Acrylics

Alwyn Crawshaw, FRSA
Peter John Garrard, PRBA, RP, NEAC
and John Blockley, ARWS

This edition published 1994 for Aurora Publishing
First published in this edition by
William Collins Sons & Co., Ltd 1985

Photography by Michael Petts

Printed and bound in Italy
by New Interlitho, Milan

ISBN O 261 66414 X

CONTENTS

INTRODUCTION

Whether you are a complete beginner or an artist with some experience in one medium but anxious to experiment with others, this book will help you discover the fascinating and absorbing world of painting. For the first time four of the most popular titles in the highly successful *Learn to Paint* series are presented here together, offering in one volume all the information the amateur artist needs to know about the most common media – watercolours, oils, pastels and acrylics.

The only qualifications required for learning to paint are a desire and willingness to try, and perhaps a little patience. Even as a complete novice you can express yourself in paint in an individual way, and it is never too late to start. For some people painting becomes a relaxing hobby; for others it is a means of expressing their innermost thoughts and feelings; and for many it offers an enjoyable escape from everyday pressures, resulting in a creative work of art.

It is easy for a beginner to feel daunted by the enormous range of painting equipment on the market, and confused by the variety of techniques used in each medium, but this need not be the case. In each section of this book all the materials for the relevant medium are fully discussed and described, and early chapters are devoted to explaining basic techniques. Once these have been mastered, the reader is encouraged to put them into practice by working on a series of exercises, each on a different subject, with the aid of simple instructions and advice, and in most cases detailed step-by-step illustrations. A variety of subjects are included in each medium, ranging from still life compositions, portraits and figures to landscapes, snow scenes, seascapes, boats and buildings. This choice of subjects, and media, offers many possibilities for developing different styles and techniques, but the main emphasis in the book is on enjoying what you paint and gaining satisfaction out of each achievement.

The three authors of this book are all professional artists with a great love of painting, and their enthusiasm for their art will inspire all those who long to paint. Each author offers here the necessary advice, encouragement and direction to see the amateur artist through the early stages of learning to paint so that he too will be captivated and share that enthusiasm. Learning to paint can be fun, exciting and rewarding, and this book shows you how.

PORTRAIT OF AN ARTIST ALWYN CRAWSHAW FRSA

Alwyn Crawshaw was born in 1934 at Mirfield, Yorkshire: he now lives in Devon with his wife and three children. During his earlier years he studied the many facets of watercolour and oil painting and, more recently, acrylic painting. Now a successful painter, author and lecturer, his work has brought him recognition as one of the leading authorities in his field.

Crawshaw paints what he terms realistic subjects and these include many English landscape scenes which are frequently the subject of favourable articles and reviews by the critics. In most of Crawshaw's landscapes there can be found a distinctive 'trademark' – usually elm trees or working horses. His paintings have a feeling of reality about them, an atmosphere which at times succeeds in transmitting to the onlooker a faint memory, as if he had been there before.

The widespread popularity of Crawshaw's work developed after his painting *Wet and Windy* had been included among the top ten prints chosen by the members of the Fine Art Trade Guild in 1975. Fine art prints of this well-known painting are still very much in demand throughout the world. Another now famous painting was completed during Queen Elizabeth's Jubilee Year in 1977 when, after lengthy and painstaking research and hours spent working at the location, he finished *The Silver Jubilee Fleet Review 1977*.

Crawshaw's paintings are sold in the UK and many other countries throughout the world. He is a Fellow of the Royal Society of Arts, a member of the Society of Equestrian Artists, and is listed in *Who's Who in Art*. He demonstrates his painting techniques to members of many art societies throughout Britain and has had numerous one-man exhibitions. He has also discussed his techniques on radio and television.

According to Alwyn Crawshaw, there are two attributes necessary for success as an artist: dedication and a sense of humour. The need for the first is self-evident; the second 'helps you out of many a crisis'.

PORTRAIT OF AN ARTIST
PETER JOHN GARRARD PRBA, RP, NEAC

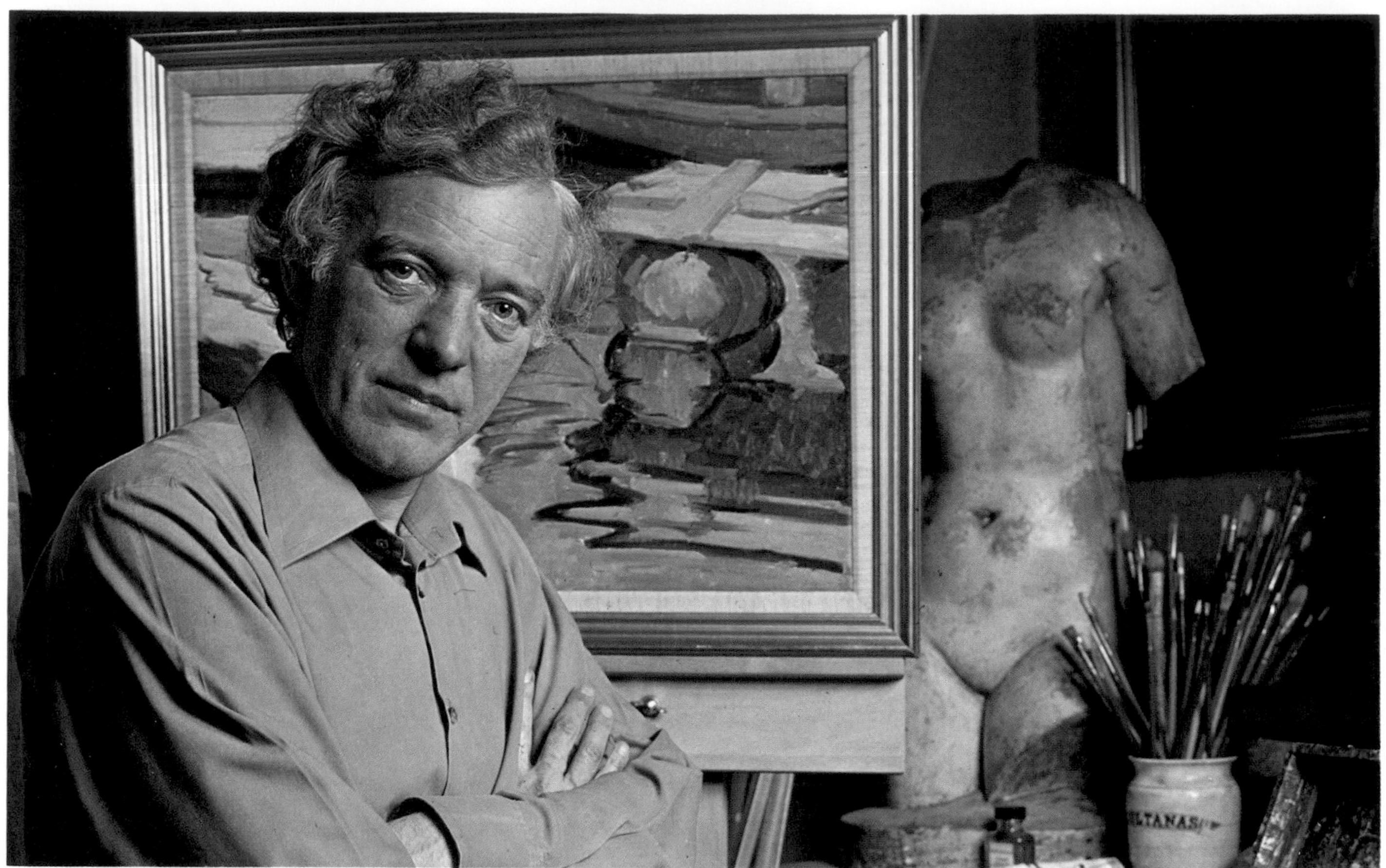

Peter John Garrard was born in Peterborough, Cambridgeshire, and now lives in London with his wife, Patricia, and their three children. A well-known teacher and painter, he is aware of the problems that face beginners and has played a part in the development of art education for adults.

After leaving school, Garrard taught Latin and rugger at Summerfields, Oxford, the famous prep school, and during this period he studied art at local adult evening classes. He then joined the army and served with the Suffolk Regiment in Greece during the civil war. When he returned to England, he studied at the Byam Shaw School of Painting and Drawing in London.

While a student, he won the Knapping Prize and twice won the David Murray Landscape Scholarship. In his final year he was commissioned to paint several landscapes and portraits. After leaving art school he worked for a firm of restorers and this gave him an abiding interest in the technicalities of paint. Although he does a lot of drawing and watercolour painting, oils have always been Peter Garrard's favourite medium, and he continues to paint mostly realistic portraits and landscapes.

The appeal of Garrard's paintings is international. His work is on display in public and private collections all over the world, including the Royal Academy in London. He has taken part in three representative exhibitions of British painting overseas, and has held four large one-man exhibitions in London, where he has also had pictures in most of the major mixed exhibitions.

He was editor of *The Artist* from 1972 to 1979, and has written articles on painting and drawing for numerous magazines. He was also the author of the ninth edition of *The Artist Guide*, published in 1976.

Peter Garrard is a governor of the Mary Ward Settlement and runs the Mary Ward Centre Art Workshop part-time. He is also the President of the Royal Society of British Artists and a member of the Royal West of England Academy, the Royal Society of Portrait Painters, the New English Art Club and the Art Workers Guild. In 1977 he was awarded the de Laszlo Medal by the Royal Society of British Artists.

PORTRAIT OF AN ARTIST JOHN BLOCKLEY ARWS

John Blockley was born in Knighton, Shropshire, on the Welsh border, and for some years lived and worked in the north of England.

He now lives in Lower Swell, a small village in the Cotswolds, where he has established a painting centre, running courses which attract students from all parts of Britain and abroad. At the time of writing, he is also planning the conversion of another sixteenth-century building in nearby Stow-on-the-Wold, to create a gallery displaying his own work, and that of his close associates.

Blockley sums up his attitude to painting as a continuing exploration; always looking for new ideas and interpretations. His work is based on constant observations of everything around him. He is not interested in merely a photographic likeness of the subject, whether it is a landscape, people or buildings. Nor is he concerned with distortion or contrived effects – his interest is in seeking out some special mood or quality of the subject, such as light, surface textures of buildings, or patterns of rocks, the ground and tree trunks.

These interests have evolved through many years of painting landscapes throughout Britain. While living in the north, he painted mostly mountains, moors and industrial subjects. He frequently painted large landscapes, but also small, intimate studies of corner shops and shoppers with their baskets. He deliberately moved to the Cotswolds to work in a new environment, leaving an area where he was completely settled. He now paints the totally different architecture of mellow Cotswold buildings, woodlands and rolling landscapes of the upper wolds.

His work is widely sought and there is always a demand for his paintings in the few selected galleries where he exhibits. His paintings are in collections the world over.

John Blockley paints mostly in pastel and watercolours. He is a Council member and Past President of the Pastel Society, and exhibits annually at the society's main exhibition at the Mall Gallery, London, and at other exhibitions arranged by the society in other parts of Britain. He is also an Associate of the Royal Society of Painters in Water-Colours.

WATERCOLOURS

ALWYN CRAWSHAW FRSA

WHY USE WATERCOLOURS . . . AND WHAT ARE THEY?

I am constantly asked why I paint in more than one medium. The reasons are varied. An artist sometimes uses a medium because he has been commissioned to do so or because he likes one medium more than another but more important is the fact that each medium has its own mystique and, of course, a particular quality. There is also the restraint of size. For instance, watercolour paper isn't made large enough for a 76 × 152cm (30 × 60in) painting and neither is pastel paper so the medium can determine the size of the painting. Finally, the subject matter has to be considered. When I am out looking for possible subjects I see one as a subject for an acrylic painting, another as a perfect watercolour, and so on.

Whatever *your* reason for choosing watercolour, even if it's the obvious one – you like it! – *you* have made the choice and we will work together over the next forty-one pages, from simple beginnings to more serious exercises later.

First, a word of caution. Because your earliest recollection of painting – probably when you were at infant school – is associated with the use of water-based paint (poster paint, powder colour or watercolour) you may have the impression that it is easy. Well, of course, to enjoy painting and get favourable results is relatively easy. However, to get the desired results through deliberate *control* of watercolour needs *a lot* of practice and patience but the more you learn, the more you will enjoy using watercolour.

Watercolours are so called because the adhesive that sticks the pigment powder to the paper is soluble in water. The paint is a finely ground mixture of pigment, gum arabic (the water-soluble gum of the acacia tree), glycerine (to keep the colours moist) and glucose (to make the colours flow freely).

When water is loaded on to a brush and added to the paint on the palette, the paint becomes a coloured, transparent liquid. When this is applied to the white surface of the paper, the paper shows through and the paint assumes a transparent luminosity unequalled by any other medium. You buy the colours either in a half pan, a whole pan or a tube (see **fig. 1**). I will explain more about this in the equipment section. One great advantage of watercolour is that it requires no complicated equipment. For painting out-of-doors, for instance, your basic essentials are a box of paints, a brush, paper and water.

You will find that the paint dries within minutes of its application to the paper as the water evaporates, leaving the dry colour on the surface. This process can be seen when working. While the paint is shiny on the paper, it is still

Fig. 1

wet and you can move it about or add more colour with the brush, but as soon as the shine goes off the paper (the paint is now in an advanced drying stage) you must leave it alone and *let it* dry. If you try to work more paint into it, you will get nasty streaks and blotches. Because the paint dries quickly – especially if you are under a hot sun – watercolour painting does not favour faint hearts. If you think you are in that category, don't worry; you will gain confidence as you read and *work* through these pages.

Before you start a painting you need to have a plan of campaign in your mind. Naturally, as you progress, this will become second nature to you. When I was at art school I was taught to look and observe and, ever since, I have always looked at the sky as if it were a painting and considered how it had been done – in which medium, with which brush, which colour was used first, and so on. I see things as shapes and colours, and techniques of painting. The strange thing is that I see most things as watercolour paintings. I think this is because of the very nature of the medium: you have limited time, you are painting from light to dark (more about that later), a bad mistake can't be over-painted (in true watercolour) and, therefore, it all comes down to observation and planning. Nevertheless, you will have to accept the fact that not every watercolour painting is a success – *not to you*, the artist, that is. You will find that you paint a beautiful picture, everyone likes it and it is worthy of being put into an exhibition, but there will be passages of that painting where the watercolour was not completely under your control and it made up its own mind about the final effect. Well, this is an accepted characteristic of *watercolour* painting – only the artist knows how he made the paint behave or misbehave. But when you paint a good picture with plenty of watercolour effect and it was *all* under your control, then you will have achieved a small, personal ambition which will no doubt elevate you into that special band of dedicated watercolourists.

Opposite is a list of the available colours. The colours illustrated are those that I use, set out in my palette order, and will be referred to throughout. This colour chart is produced within the limitations of printing and is intended as a guide only.

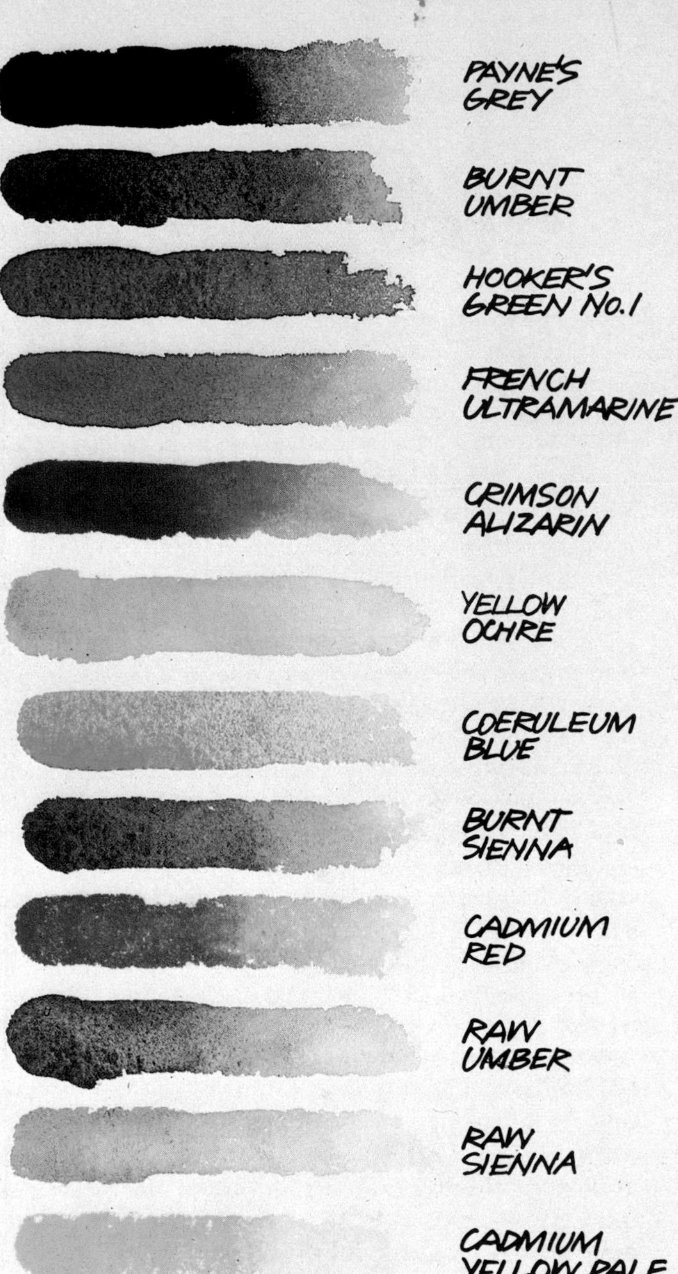

Additional colours available

Chinese White
Chrome Lemon
Chrome Orange
Chrome Orange Deep
Chrome Yellow
Hooker's Green No 2
Indian Red
Ivory Black
Lamp Black
Light Red
Naples Yellow
Olive Green
Permanent Blue
Permanent Magenta
Permanent Mauve
Prussian Blue
Sap Green
Terre Verte
Vandyke Brown
Venetian Red
Alizarin Green
Brown Madder (Alizarin)
Brown Pink
Crimson Lake
Indian Yellow
Indigo
Monestial Blue
Permanent Red
Permanent Sepia
Permanent Yellow
Purple Lake
Purple Madder (Alizarin)
Rose Dore (Alizarin)
Scarlet Alizarin
Scarlet Lake
Violet Alizarin
Aureolin
Cobalt Blue
Cobalt Green
Cobalt Violet
Gamboge (Hue)
Lemon Yellow
Viridian
Cadmium Orange
Cadmium Yellow
Cadmium Yellow Deep
Permanent Rose
Carmine
Scarlet Vermilion

WHAT EQUIPMENT DO YOU NEED?

Every professional artist has his favourite brushes, colours, and so on. In the end, the choice must be left to you, to make from your personal experience.

In the last chapter I gave you a list of the colours that I use. I suggest that you, too, use these as you work through these pages because I shall refer to them to describe different colour mixes. You may find that you prefer to drop a couple of colours or change some once you have made some progress – this will be fine and, of course, it also applies to other materials used in the exercises.

To get the best results, you should use the best materials you can afford. The two main distinctions between different watercolour paints are cost and quality. The best quality watercolours are called *Artists' Quality Water Colours* and those a grade lower are called *students' water colours*, some of which are manufactured under brand names such as *Georgian Water Colours*. Watercolour paints can be bought in a water colour box, empty or ready filled with colours (see **fig. 2**), or in separate pans which you can use as refills or to fill an empty box with your own choice of colours. **Fig. 2** shows one box of half pans, one of whole pans and a very small box that contains eighteen quarter-pans of colour, measures only 13 × 5cm (5 × 2in) and has a leatherette case. This last box is ideal for keeping in your pocket or handbag to use for impromptu sketching. The last two boxes illustrated carry tubes of paint – you have to squeeze the colour on to the palette (the open lid of the box) and use the paint as if you were working from pans. Colours in tubes are ideal for quickly saturating a brush in strong colour, using less water, but I do not advise beginners to use tubes because it is difficult to control the amount of paint on the brush. You can buy additional palettes for mixing your colours and you can see these on page 15 in the illustration of my studio working area. This has been over-crowded intentionally, to accommodate all the different materials you might require as you progress. At the end of this chapter is a list of basic, beginner's equipment.

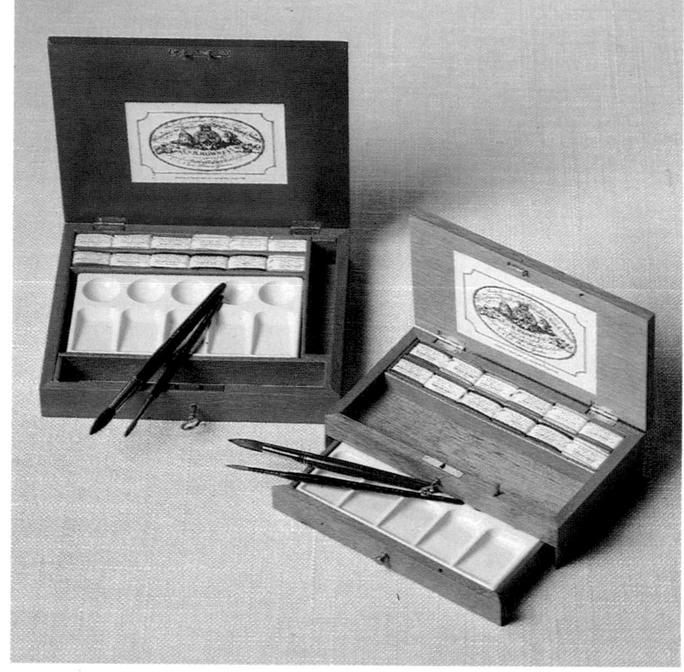

Both these boxes are copies of original Artists' Water Colour Boxes first sold by Thomas and Richard Rowney between 1795 and 1810

Now we come to the tools of the trade – brushes. The best quality, watercolour brushes are made from kolinsky sable. They are hand made and are the most expensive brushes on the market but they give you perfect control over your brush strokes and, if properly cared for, will last a long time. Also in the fine-quality range of watercolour brushes, but less expensive, are those made with squirrel hair, ox-ear hair and ringcat hair. Man-made fibres are also used in the manufacture of artists' brushes and an excellent range of white nylon brushes became available in the mid-1970s. Remember, brushes are the tools with which you express yourself on paper. It is only your use of the brush that reveals your skill to the onlooker and this applies to watercolour more than any other medium. *One brush stroke* can express a field, a lake, the side of a boat, and so on; therefore, you must know your brushes and what to expect from them. There are two basic types: a round brush and a flat brush. If you look at **fig. 3** you will see brushes of different shapes, made from different hairs. Usually, the handles of watercolour brushes are short but where the brush can also be used for oil or acrylic painting, the handle may be longer – the flat, ox-ear-hair brush, Series 62, is a good example. The round brush is a general purpose one: both a wash and a thin line can be obtained with this shape. The flat brush is used mainly for putting washes over large areas or where a broad brush stroke is called for. Naturally, the width of these strokes is determined by the size of the flat brush. Usually, round brushes are graded from size No. 00 to size No. 12 and some manufacturers make a No. 14 size. This scale can be seen in **fig. 3** and the brushes are reproduced actual size. Flat brushes and very large brushes, such as the squirrel-hair wash brush, have a name or size of their own.

Watercolour paper, of course, is a very important piece of equipment – so important, in fact, that I have put it in a section of its own on pages 16 and 17.

Other items you need are pencils – start by getting an HB and 2B (the other grades up to 6B, the softest, I will leave to your own choice); a good quality, natural sponge for wetting the paper or sponging off areas you want to repaint; blotting paper for absorbing wet colour from the

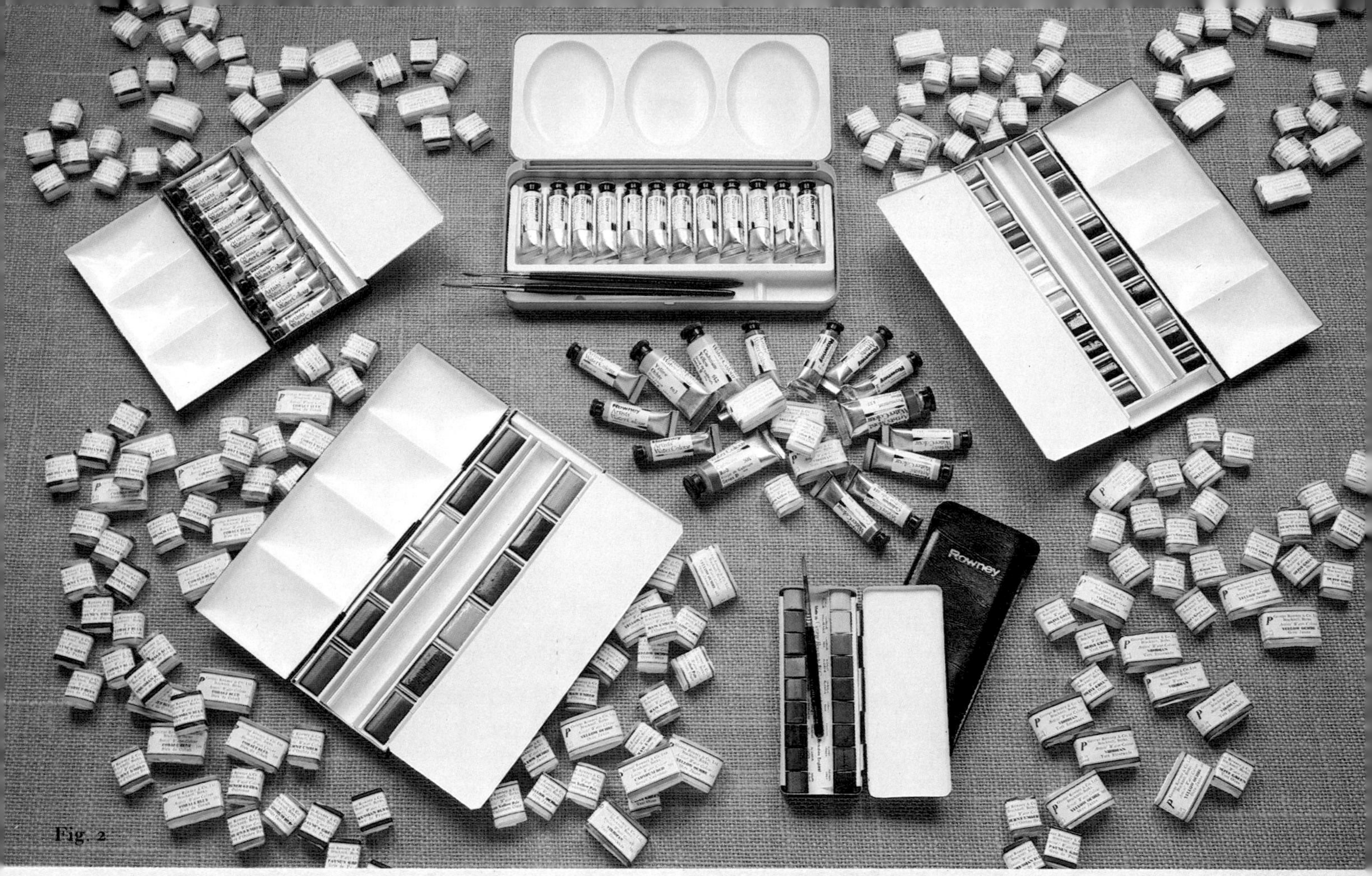

Fig. 2

Round brushes

00

0

1

2

3

4

5

6

7

8

10

12

Series 40 Round Brush Sable Hair size No. 12

Series 66 Squirrel Hair Wash Brush (extra large round)

Series 63 Squirrel Hair Wash Brush (large flat)

Series 62 Flat Ox Ear Hair Brush 1in

Series 133 Thin Flat Bright, Sable and Ox Ear Hair Brush size No. 12

Series 103 Rigger Brush, Sable Hair size No. 3

Series 270 White Nylon Brush size No. 12

Fig. 3

All brushes are shown actual size. Some brush series have additional sizes to those shown, i.e. 9, 11 and 14

surface of the paper in order to lighten a passage that is too dark; and a brush case, very necessary when you are painting outside (see **fig. 4**) to avoid damaging your brushes.

You need a drawing board on which to pin your paper. You can make one from a smooth piece of plywood or you can buy one from your local art shop. A container to hold your painting water can be anything from a jam jar to a plastic cup but make sure that it is big enough to hold plenty of water, and *keep changing* the water so that it is always clean. A kneadable putty rubber is the best type to use for erasing as it can be used gently on delicate paper without causing too much damage to the surface. When you are using a pen and wash technique in the exercises, you will require a mapping pen and black Indian ink.

A watercolour is never painted right up to the edge of the paper so it is a good idea to have some mounts for offering up to a finished watercolour. You will then be able to see where the painting will be masked when it is framed. Cut mounts of various sizes from cartridge paper or thin card and when you have finished a painting, put a mount around it to see what you think. This will help you decide whether you think your picture looks finished or not.

Now for your essential equipment: you will see what you need in **fig. 5**. You can start with only three brushes: a size No. 10 round brush (the quality you get will depend on the price), a size No. 6 round brush for general detail work and either a squirrel-hair wash brush or a one-inch, flat, ox-ear-hair brush for covering extra-large areas with washes. You need a paint box to hold 12 colours in half pans or whole pans, HB and 2B pencils, a kneadable putty rubber, a drawing board, paper, blotting paper, a sponge and a water jar. I haven't included an easel because it is not an essential piece of watercolour equipment; when you are working outside, your painting is usually small enough to manage on a drawing board or watercolour block (see page 16) resting on your knees.

This short list represents the advantages of watercolour: its equipment, its approach and its execution are simple. However, although you can have a lot of fun with it, you can achieve complete control over watercolour only after a great deal of experience.

Back to the drawing board – or easel. You can work very comfortably at a table, with the top edge of your drawing board supported by a book or piece of wood about 8–10cm (3–4in) high so that the washes can run down correctly. If you want to work on an easel, choose one from the variety on the market.

Fig. 4 **Brush case**

Fig. 5 **Beginner's basic equipment**

A STRETCHED PAPER
B VARIOUS BRUSHES & PENCILS
C MIXING PALETTES
D WATER CONTAINER
E SPONGE
F WATER COLOUR BOX WITH TUBES
G WATER COLOUR BOX WITH WHOLE PANS
H BLACK INK
I PUTTY RUBBER
J PENCILS & MAPPING PENS
K TUBES, WHOLE PANS & HALF PANS
L MIXING PALETTES
M POCKET SIZE WATER COLOUR BOX (5"x2")
N VARIOUS BRUSHES WITH BRUSH CASE
O CARD MOUNTS
P OUTDOOR STOOL
Q STUDIO EASEL
R BLOTTING PAPER
S WATER COLOUR BLOCK
T VARIOUS PAPERS ON DRAWING BOARD

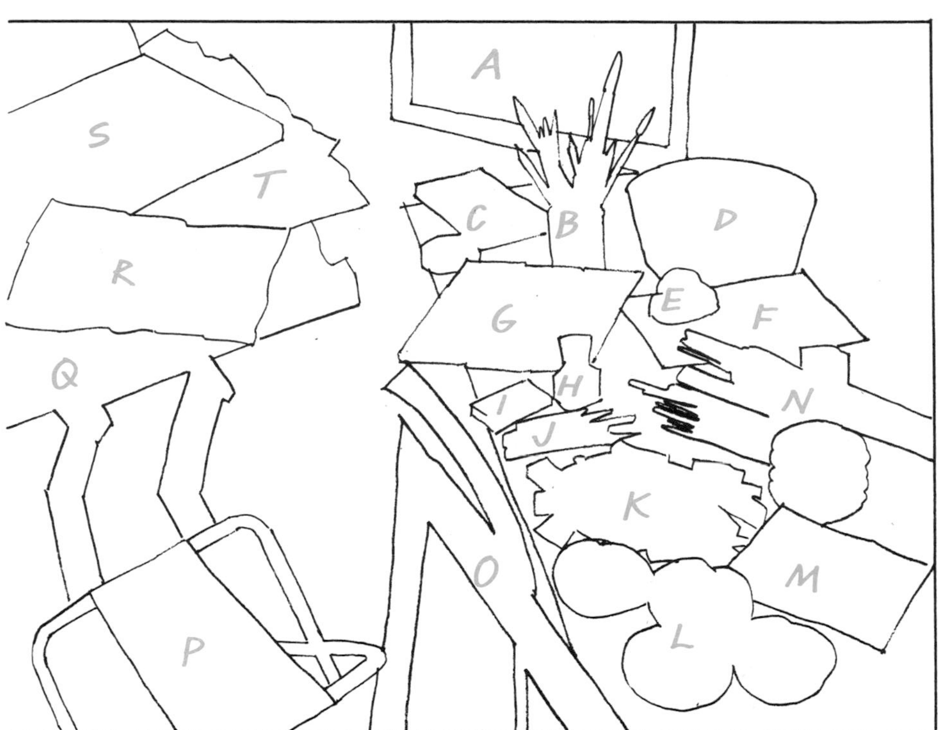

WHICH PAPER?

You can paint with watercolour on almost any type of paper. You can work on drawing paper, on the inside of a cardboard carton, or even on the back of a roll of wallpaper. Naturally, there are problems in using any old paper. Firstly, if the paper is too absorbent, the liquid will be sucked into the surface like ink on blotting paper and secondly, if the surface is non-absorbent, the paint will run completely out of control. The answer, then, is to use paper that has been specially made for the watercolour artist. The finest quality papers are made by hand, by craftsmen whose skills have been handed down over the centuries. Up to the beginning of the nineteenth century, even the cheapest wrapping paper was made by hand but then, machinery took over a great proportion of the production. Because the best quality, watercolour paper is still made by hand it is very expensive. However, in comparison with a ready-stretched canvas of equivalent size, top-quality paper is far cheaper – and each of them produces only one picture.

Watercolour papers have a unique, surface texture that is sympathetic to the brush – artists usually refer to it as a tooth. It is this tooth that responds to the brush and helps create the unique, watercolour effect. The paper also has just the right amount of absorbency to hold the liquid colour under manageable control. There are many types of paper on the market but they all have two things in common: they are all finished with one of three kinds of surface texture and they are all graded by weight (this tells us the thickness of the paper). The surfaces are: *Rough*, *Not* (the Americans call this *Cold Pressed*) and *Hot Pressed* (HP). Paper with a Rough surface has a very pronounced texture (tooth) and is usually used for large paintings where bold, vigorous brush work is required. The Not surface has less tooth and this is the one most commonly used by artists; it is also ideal for the beginner. The Hot Pressed surface is very smooth, with very little tooth, and before you try this paper you need to know how to handle your watercolour: if you use the paint very wet, it can easily run, concerned only for its own destination and your downfall!

Usually, you buy watercolour paper in an Imperial size (approximately 31 × 22in) but hand-made paper sizes can vary by a few inches.

The weight of the paper is arrived at by calculating how much a ream (480 sheets) weighs. For instance, if a ream weighs 300lb (which is about the heaviest paper you can use) then the paper is called (with its manufacturer's name and surface title) *Greens Pasteless Board 300lb Not*. You will find that a good weight to work on is a 140lb paper. If this sounds complicated, don't worry. To start with, get used to two or three types of paper. You will learn how the paper reacts to the paint and what you can and can't do. This is as important as getting used to your brushes and colours. When you first buy paper, pencil the name, size and weight in each corner for future reference. On the opposite page are pieces of watercolour paper, reproduced their actual size. I have put some paint on each one and I have also given its full description.

Paper tends to cockle when you put wet paint on it and the thinner the paper the more it will cockle. I have explained below how to get over this problem by stretching the paper. (Heavy and thick papers do not need stretching.) Paper can also be bought in sheets stuck together on the edges of all four sides to prevent cockling. These are called water colour blocks, they come in various sizes and are excellent for use out-of-doors. When the painting is finished, you simply tear off the sheet and work on the next one.

When you have practised and have become confident in handling your colours without spoiling too much paper, buy the best paper you can afford and stick to that one until you know it like the back of your hand. The better you know your brushes, your paints *and* your paper, the more you will enjoy painting – and the better your results will be.

How to stretch your paper

Cut a sheet of paper the size you need but *smaller* than your drawing board, submerge it in a sink full of water or hold it under a running tap and *completely soak* both sides. Hold it up by one end, let the surface water drain off, then lay it on a *wooden* drawing board. Use a roll of brown, gummed paper to stick the four sides down, allowing the gummed paper to fall half over the paper and half over the board. Now leave it to dry naturally, overnight. In the morning, it will be as tight as a drum and as flat as a pancake, and it will stay flat while you work. The finished result is shown in the photograph at the top of the page. It is heaven to work on.

GREENS PASTELESS BOARD 300lb Rough

GREENS PASTELESS BOARD 300lb HP

GREENS PASTELESS BOARD 300lb Not

GREENS TURNER GREY 72lb Not

GREENS DE WINT 90lb Rugged

GREENS CAMBER SAND 72lb Not

FABRIANO CLASSICO 5 281 lb Rough

FABRIANO CLASSICO 5 140lb HP

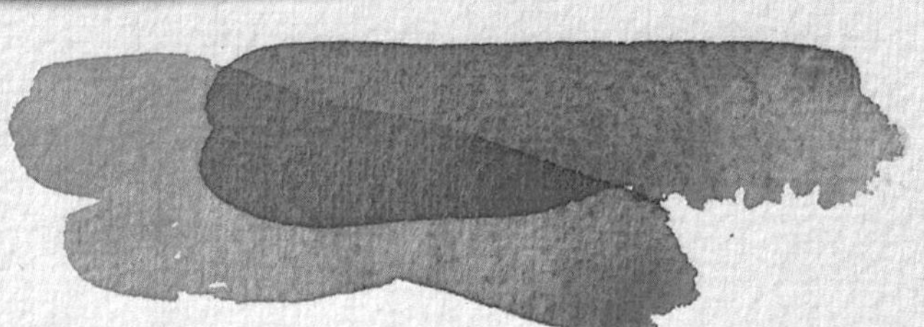

FABRIANO CLASSICO 5 281 lb Not

'GEORGIAN' WATER COLOUR PAPER 140lb

ARTISTS SUPERIOR QUALITY BOCKINGFORD
WATER COLOUR PAPER 300 gm^2

GREENS R.W.S. 140lb Rough

LET'S START PAINTING

PLAYING WITH PAINT

At last, you can start painting. A lot of people who have not painted before find this the most difficult bridge to cross – to actually put some paint on paper. Unfortunately, we are all self-conscious when doing things we have never tried before and our families don't help either! I have often come across the case of a member of the family who sees someone's first efforts at painting. Remarks such as What's that! and Oh well, never mind, are never meant to hurt or be unkind, but, unfortunately, they can put off a sensitive beginner – sometimes for ever. Well, this is how we will get over that problem, if it arises. It's human nature for us all to strive to do better and if we try to run before we can walk, then this is when disaster will strike and cause those humorous comments from the rest of the family. So we will start at the very beginning and take things in a steady, progressive order – I'll see you don't run first.

Let us take colours as our first step. A beginner may find the hundreds of colours that exist somewhat overwhelming. But the choice can be simplified: there are only three basic colours, *red*, *yellow* and *blue* which are called primary colours (see the illustration opposite) and all other colours, and shades of colour, are formed by a combination of these three. In painting, there are different reds, yellows and blues which we can use to help recreate nature's colours. Look at the illustration again and you will see that there are two of each primary colour. As I have explained earlier, these colours, plus another six, are the ones I use, for all my watercolour painting.

Before you start mixing colours, get yourself a piece of watercolour paper or cartridge paper and *play* with the paint on this. See what it feels like, try different brushes, add more water, less water, mix colours together. You will end up with a funny-looking, coloured piece of paper. Incidentally, if the family laugh at this one, laugh with them, show them my doodles on paper and laugh at that! What you have done is to experience the feel of watercolour paint. You will have noticed that if you add more water, you make the colour lighter. This is the correct method for making watercolours lighter, not by adding white paint. The paint isn't a stranger to you any more, nor are your brushes or paper. You have now broken the ice and will feel much more confident in tackling the next section. Good luck.

MIXING COLOURS

As we progress through the exercises, I will help you as much as I can but you must first spend some time practising mixing different colours. Look at the illustration opposite. I have taken the primary colours and mixed them to show you the results. In the first row, Cadmium Yellow Pale mixed with French Ultramarine makes green. In the second row, Cadmium Yellow Pale mixed with Cadmium Red makes orange. To make the orange look more yellow, add more yellow than red and to make it more red, add more red than yellow. Add more water to make the orange paler.

You may have noticed that my colours do not include black. Some artists use black and others don't. I am one of the don'ts. I don't use black because I believe it is a dead colour, too flat. Therefore, I mix my blacks from the primary colours and I suggest that you do the same. Remember that, in general, if you want a colour to be cooler, add blue and if it is to be warmer, then add red.

Practise mixing different colours on white cartridge paper. Mix the colours on your palette with a brush and paint daubs on to your white paper. Don't worry about shapes at this stage, it's the colours you're trying for. Experiment and practise – that is the only real advice I can give you, here. When you're next sitting down, look around you, pick a colour that you can see and try to imagine what colours you would use to mix it.

One last, important point: when there are only three basic colours it is the *amount* of each colour that plays the biggest part. You can easily mix a green as in the second line opposite, but if it is to be a yellowy green, you have to experiment on your palette; you have to mix and work in more yellow until you have the colour you want. This lesson of mixing colours is one that you will be practising and improving upon all your life – I am, still.

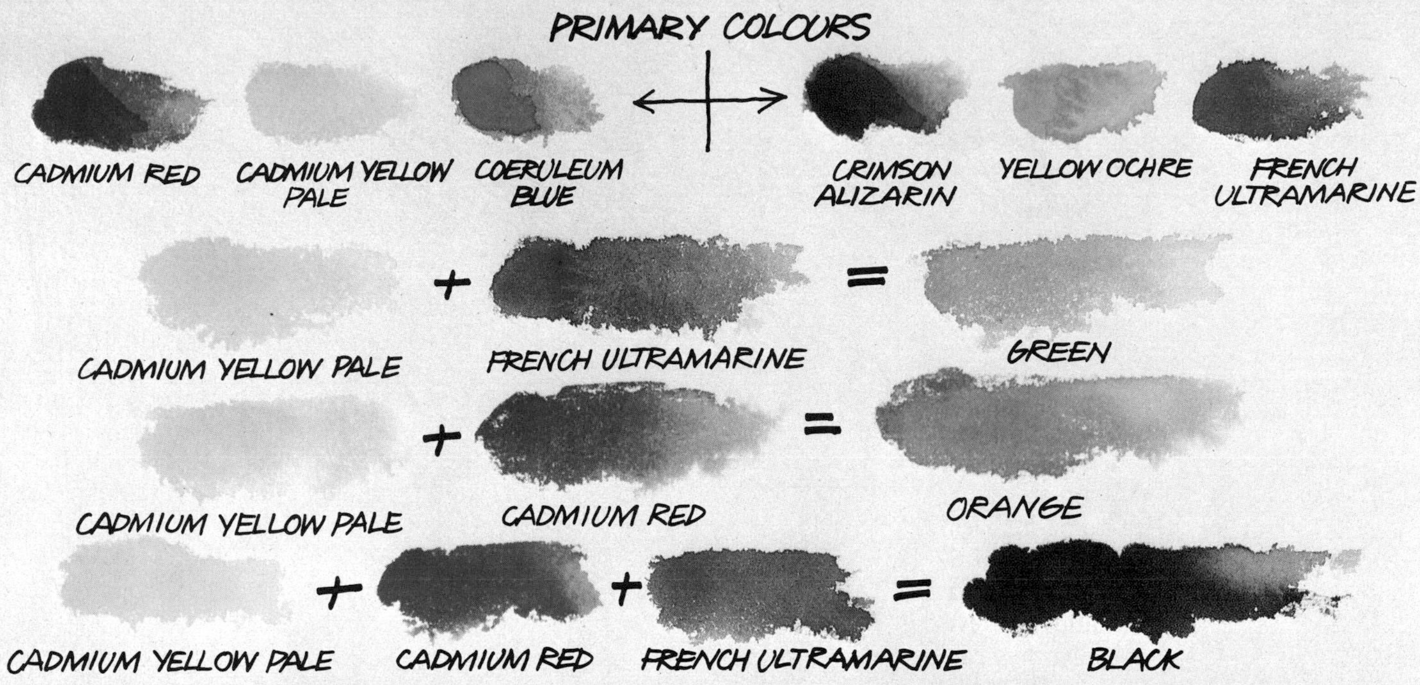

PRIMARY COLOURS

CADMIUM RED | CADMIUM YELLOW PALE | COERULEUM BLUE ↔ CRIMSON ALIZARIN | YELLOW OCHRE | FRENCH ULTRAMARINE

CADMIUM YELLOW PALE + FRENCH ULTRAMARINE = GREEN

CADMIUM YELLOW PALE + CADMIUM RED = ORANGE

CADMIUM YELLOW PALE + CADMIUM RED + FRENCH ULTRAMARINE = BLACK

NOW JUST DOODLE AND SEE WHAT HAPPENS

DOODLE!

Fig. 6

BRUSH CONTROL

Now you must learn to control the paint brush. Like all things, when you know how, it is much easier than you had thought. A lot of control is required when painting edges of areas that have to be filled in with paint, such as the outline of a pair of scissors (**fig. 6**).

Take a pair of scissors, or anything handy that has round shapes, and draw round it with an HB pencil. You can do this on cartridge paper or watercolour paper. Use your round sable brush with plenty of water. When you start to fill in the curved shapes, start at the top and work down the left side, to the bottom (**fig. 6**). Let the bristles follow the brush, i.e. pull the brush down. Try to do this in two or three movements. When you paint the right side of the handle, your brush will cover some of the pencil lines and you will feel slightly awkward. The answer is to accept that it feels a bit awkward but the more you use your brush like that, the more natural it will feel – practise!

Now, let's go on to straight lines. This time, draw a square, like the side of a box. Try this one freehand, don't draw around anything. Here is a *very important* rule to remember: when you draw straight lines (unless you are drawing very short ones), always move your wrist and arm – not your fingers. Try this with a pencil – first, draw a straight line downwards, moving only your fingers. You will find that you can draw only a few centimetres before your fingers make the line bend. Now do the same exercise but keep your fingers firm and move only your hand, bending your arm at the elbow. The result will be a long, straight line.

You can paint the edges of the box with the round sable brush again. Use this same brush for filling in the square with the rest of the paint (see **fig. 7**).

Draw another two squares like the one in **fig. 7** and paint both up to the outside edges. Then, paint another box inside the bottom box, without drawing it first. Also, change the colour as you paint, working from the top box to the bottom one. This one will keep you busy!

Now draw your own shapes and fill them in, mixing your own colours. Look around and choose a colour, perhaps the colour of your carpet or a cushion, then try to mix a colour like it to use for painting in your shapes. You are practising all you have learned so far, in one exercise: well done – but keep at it, enjoy it and keep practising.

Fig. 7

SIMPLE PERSPECTIVE AND DRAWING

Drawing, or the knowledge of drawing, comes before painting and, therefore, we will take a little time to practise simple perspective. If you believe you can't draw, don't let this worry you. Some artists can paint a picture but would have difficulty in drawing it as a drawing in its own right. It is the colours, the tones and the shapes of the masses that make a painting.

Over the centuries, artists have always invented and used drawing aids. Today, there is a very simple, but very effective, aid to drawing on the market, called a *Perspectograph* – it sorts out the perspective for you. But it is not too difficult to do this yourself.

When you look out to sea, the horizon will always be at your eye level, even if you climb a cliff or lie flat on the sand. So the horizon is the eye level (E.L.). If you are in a room, naturally, there is no horizon but you still have an eye level. To find this, hold your pencil horizontally in front of your eyes at arm's length: your eye level is where the pencil hits the opposite wall. If two parallel lines were marked out on the ground and extended to the horizon, they would come together at what is called the vanishing point. This is why railway lines appear to get closer together and finally meet in the distance – they have met at the vanishing point (V.P.).

First, look at **fig. 8A**. I have taken our box, the square you drew in the previous section, and put it on paper. Then I drew a line above to represent the eye level. Then, to the right-hand end of the E.L., I made a mark, the V.P. With a ruler I drew a line from each of the four corners of the box, all converging at the V.P. This gave me the two sides, the bottom and the top of the box. To create the other end of the box, I drew a square parallel with the front of the box and kept it within the V.P. guide lines. The effect is that of a transparent box drawn in perspective. Incidentally, we are looking down on this box because the eye level is high. In **fig. 8B** I have shaded the box with pencil to show the light direction.

Figs. 8C, D and **E** show the same box, the first one painted all over with a wash of Hooker's Green No. 1; the second box painted with a second wash over two sides when the first wash had dried; the third one painted with an additional wash on the darkest side, which made the box appear solid. The last one (**fig. 8F**) shows the same drawing painted to represent a hollow box.

This is a simple exercise but it is the most important exercise you will ever do. You are creating on a flat surface the illusion of depth, dimension and perspective; in other words, a three-dimensional object.

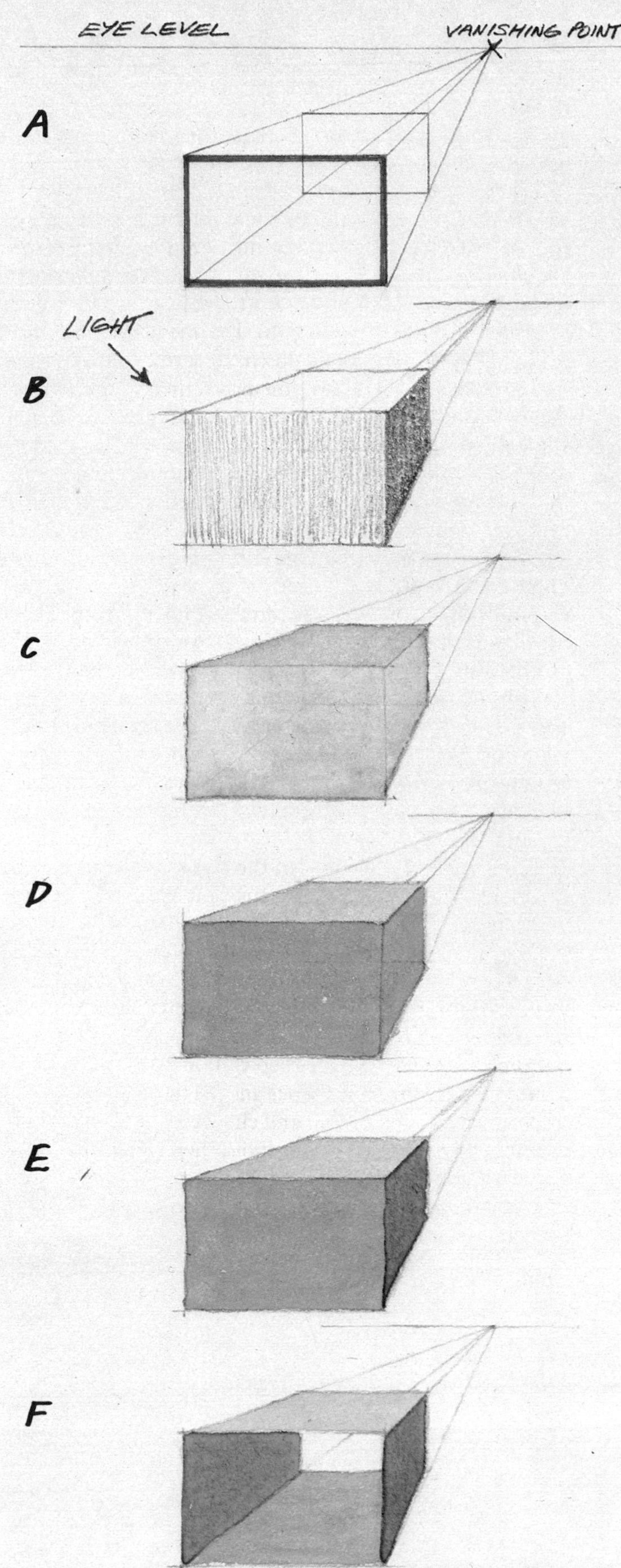

Fig. 8

BASIC WATERCOLOUR TECHNIQUES

Before you start these basic techniques, read the next three paragraphs carefully.

When you put the first wash on the box (**fig. 8C**) did you notice that, although the box was drawn in perspective, it looked flat? This is because there was no light or shade (light against dark). It is this light against dark that enables us to see objects and understand their form. If we were to paint our box red, on a background coloured the same red, without adding light or shade (light against dark) we would not be able to see it. If light and shade were added, it could then be seen. You must always be conscious of light against dark whenever you are painting. When you are painting a still life or outside, it will help you to see shapes if you look at the scene through half-closed eyes. The lights and darks will be exaggerated and the middle tones will tend to disappear: this will enable you to see simple, contrasting shapes to follow.

You will see that while your colour is wet, it appears dark and rich but when it is dry, it is slightly lighter. You will learn from experience how to adjust the density of your colours in order to achieve the desired effect. In the meantime, don't worry – it won't spoil your paintings. Don't get too depressed if you feel a painting has gone wrong or out of control. It happens to the best of watercolour artists – it's part of watercolour painting. Remember: you can learn a lot from your mistakes.

When using colours, you must always work to one *very* important rule: your colours must always be in the same position in your paint box and you must always use the box the same way round. You will have enough to think about, without wondering where your colours are, when you are in the middle of painting a wash. The position of the colours in my box is shown on page 14 and I have my box with the deep wash pans (in the lid) on the left of the box. I was taught to work this way at art school and I have done so ever since.

Now, we can study the most basic technique of watercolour painting – *the flat wash.*

In all instructive illustrations I have used arrows to help you understand the movement of the brush. The solid-black arrow shows the direction of the brush stroke and the outline arrow shows the direction in which the brush is travelling over the paper. For example, **fig. 9** shows the brush stroke moving horizontally, from left to right, and the brush moving down the paper after the completion of each horizontal stroke.

For a flat wash you need *plenty* of watery paint in your palette. *Load* your largest brush and start at the top, left-

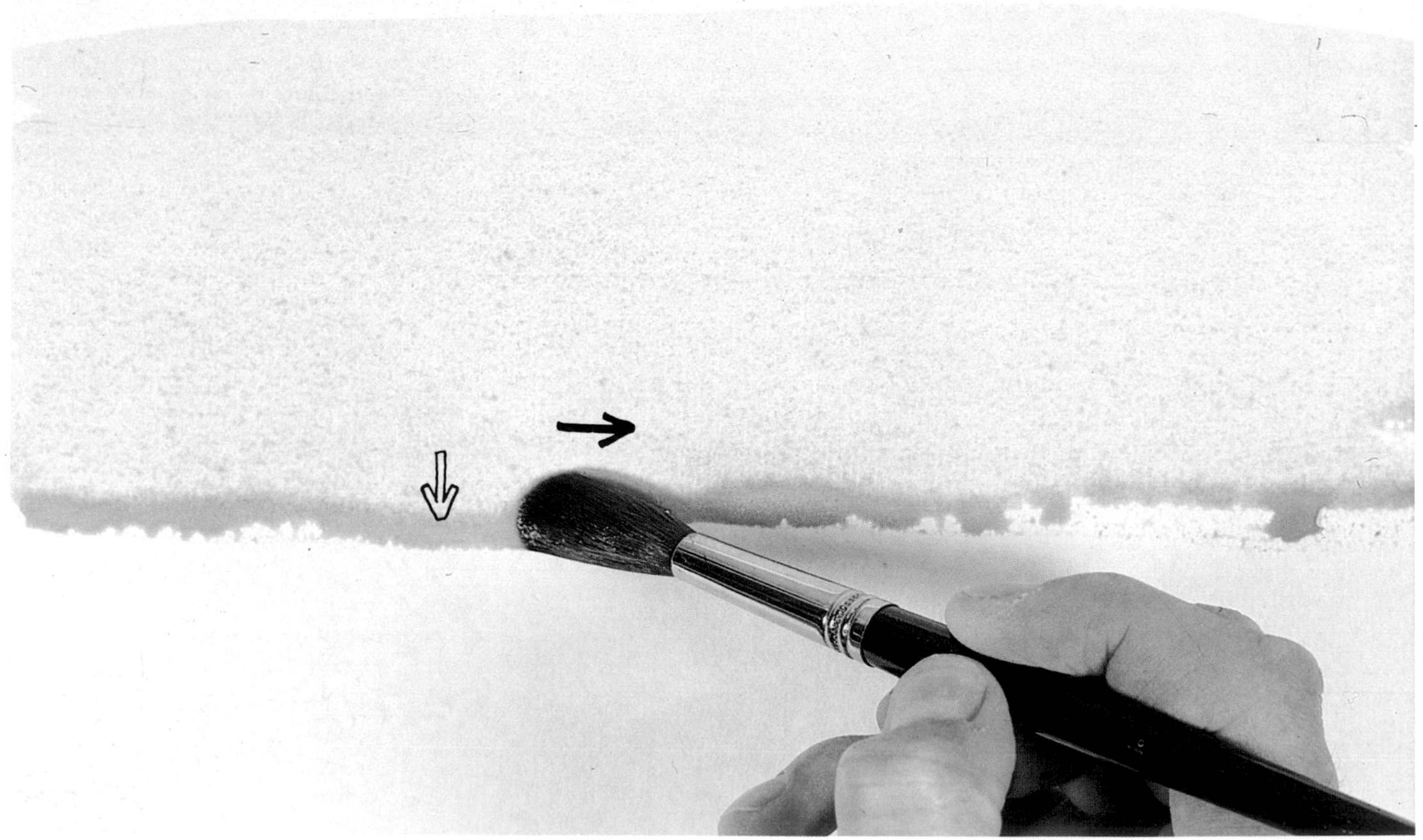

Fig. 9

Fig. 11

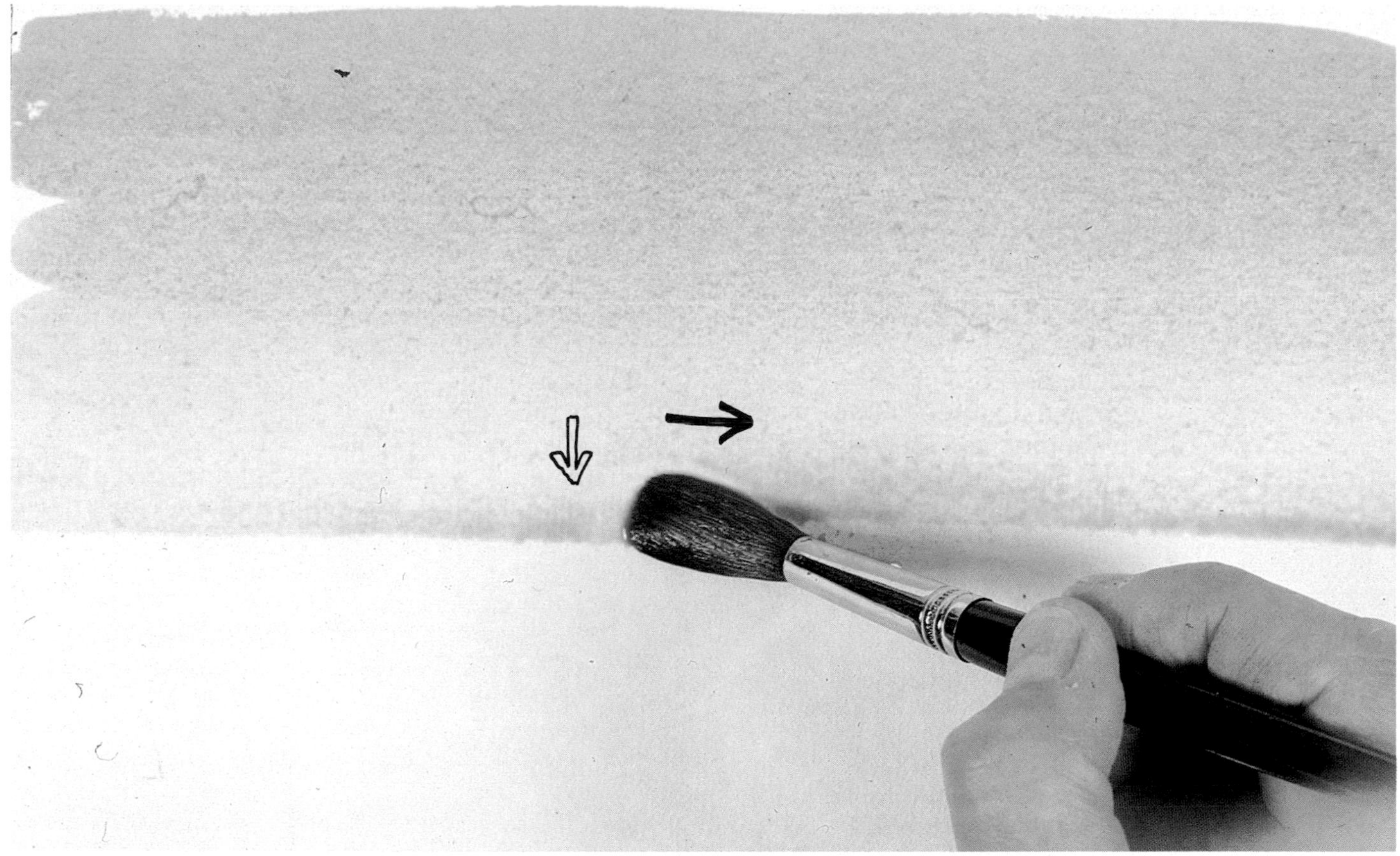

Fig. 10

hand side of the paper, taking the brush along in a definite movement. Don't rush. When you get to the end, bring the brush back, run it slightly into the first wet stroke and make another brush stroke like the first. You will, of course, add more paint to your brush when you need it. Because the colour was mixed before you started the wash and you have added no more water, the colour density of the wash should be the same all the way down. Let this wash dry, then paint another one over it, using the same colour but leaving about one centimetre (half an inch) at the top of the original wash. If you repeat this process at least six times, you will begin to get the knack of putting on a wash, you will practise the watercolour technique of applying transparent colour over and over again, and you will see that the more washes you apply, the darker the colour becomes (see **fig. 10**).

Graded wash

A graded wash is produced in exactly the same way as a flat wash except that, as you travel down the paper, you add more *clean* water to the colour in your palette. This weakens the density of the colour, with the result that the wash gets progressively paler from top to bottom (see **fig. 11**).

Fig. 12

Wet on wet

The term wet on wet is common to all painting mediums and means that wet paint is applied over existing wet paint. It is one of the most intriguing, watercolour techniques. It is impossible to predict exactly what will happen when you put wet paint on top of a wet wash (see **figs. 12** and **13**). This is precisely why it is such a fascinating technique. You will create some fantastic effects – some of them dramatic, others subtle.

You can see one of my experiments in **fig. 12**. I painted Coeruleum Blue first, very wet. Then, I added a mix of Payne's Grey and Burnt Umber, very wet, in the middle. When this was dry, I lightly sponged it with clean water, then attacked the middle again with a mix of Payne's Grey, French Ultramarine and Burnt Umber – this is very strong colour. Immediately, I added more water to the mix and put a daub on each side of the centre.

If you wait until the first wash is drying, you will have more control over the paint and you will also achieve a slightly different effect. You can get good skies, using the wet on wet technique, by sponging your paper first with clean water, then painting your sky colours and letting them run together.

You need to experiment with this technique and practise control. The overall effect is planned – it's the unpredictable wanderings of the paint that add interest and beauty. When it is dry you might see an area that, by happy accident, needs only a brush stroke to make it read better: if the brush stroke is applied correctly, this passage could be a little gem in the painting.

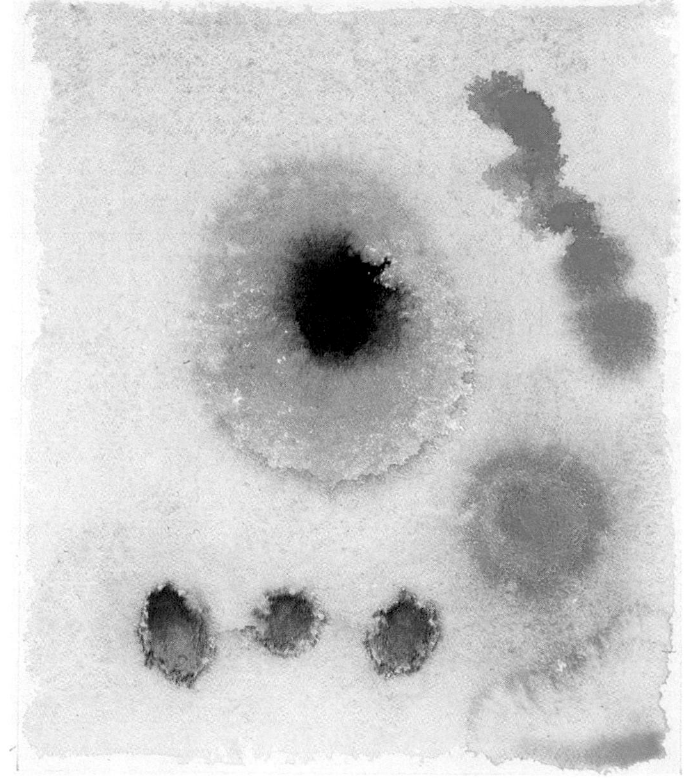

Fig. 13

Fig. 15

Fig. 14

Dry brush

Dry brush is another technique that is used in most types of painting. It simply means that a brush is damp-dried before being dipped into the paint or else a wet brush is loaded with paint, dried out to a damp consistency on a piece of blotting paper and then applied to the watercolour paper. The technique is used to achieve a hit-and-miss effect. If you try this on rough watercolour paper, it is relatively easy but on a smooth-surfaced paper it needs a little more practise. The chances are that you accidentally produced a dry brush effect when you were doodling or painting the boxes earlier on – you were probably annoyed because you were running out of paint – but it was unintentional and, therefore, uncontrolled.

The best way to get used to the dry brush technique is to use long brush strokes, from left to right, with only a little paint (see **fig. 14**). You will find that your brush runs out of wet paint and finishes the stroke with a dry brush effect. Try to control the amount of wet paint you load on to your brush and take it over, say 30cm so that the stroke is finished with a dry brush. When you can do this, you have gone a long way towards controlling your watercolour brush-work. In **fig. 15** I used a size No. 6 Series 220 nylon brush for the dry brush strokes.

DIFFERENT WAYS TO PAINT

Watercolour is a very versatile medium. It can be used in different ways by different artists. For instance, six artists could paint the same subject, using the same technique, but each painting would be different. In other words, each artist would have his own style. But my wet on wet watercolour, opposite, is painted in a completely different style to my pen and wash watercolour on page 29. Therefore, an artist's style is, to some extent, altered by the technique. To avoid confusion, in this chapter the word style refers to the individual artist's way of painting and the word technique refers to the method of using the paint.

On the following pages are six pictures I have painted of the same subject, using a different technique each time, to show you the versatility and beauty of watercolour. My purpose is to enable you to compare several versions of the *same subject* so that you can see the difference between each technique. The actual size of each painting is 34.4 × 23cm ($13\frac{1}{2}$ × 9in) and the type of paper I used is indicated below each one.

I must point out that some subjects do not necessarily lend themselves to a particular technique and, on the other hand, some subjects cry out for just one technique. Therefore, you must choose your subject and technique carefully. Naturally, a pencil-and-wash or pen-and-wash drawing can be tackled only if you have a reasonable knowledge of drawing because this plays a large part in these two watercolour techniques.

Whatever the technique, the basis for the painting is still the wash – whether it be flat, graded or wet on wet. I mention this at this stage because you just can't practise them enough – the wash *is* watercolour. When you can master it on all scales, small and large, you will be much more relaxed when you work and you will find that fewer disasters come off the brush. Keep practising.

Flat wash and graded wash — Greens Pasteless Board 300lb Not

Flat wash and graded wash

I regard the flat wash and graded wash as basic, traditional ways of using watercolour. Having thought out the moves very carefully beforehand, you work up the effect with washes. Remember to use the lightest colours first and work gradually to the darker tones.

Here, I feel I must make an observation about the buildings. It has always been thought that something old – especially a building – has plenty of character and is a perfect subject for the painter. I agree with this. When television boomed in the 1960s, artists avoided the old buildings that had TV aerials fixed to them, or just left the aerials out. The strange thing is that, when I found the buildings for the pictures on the following pages, I felt that the TV aerials *added to their character and charm*. It is amazing how things gradually become accepted.

Wet on wet

The wet on wet technique is a very exciting way of using watercolour but it can be also very nerve-racking. The freedom, the apparent ease and the sheer audacity of letting colours make their own way around the paper excites artist and onlooker alike. But although the finished result looks natural and unlaboured, you have to put in many hours of patient practice. Both these paintings were done on Greens Pasteless Board 300lb Not.

Wet on wet — Greens Pasteless Board 300lb Not

Body colour Greens Turner Grey 72lb Not

Body colour

You can strengthen your colours by using the body colour technique. Simply add White to the paint and this will immediately take away the transparency of the colour. Generally speaking, instead of water, White is used in this technique to make the colours lighter.

I painted the picture, above, on a Greens Turner Grey 72lb Not paper. I made the sky dark for a dramatic effect and I used pure White where the sun catches the window frame. When you are next painting a watercolour, if you find you have lost it, try using White with your colours and turn it into a body colour painting. Remember that light can be added over dark.

Open wash

This painting looks a little flat when compared with the others but it demonstrates a crisp, clean watercolour technique. I have called the technique open wash because white paper is left between each wash. Apart from its own charm, open wash has a very valuable application. When you are painting outside, it is often impractical to wait for each wash to dry before applying the adjacent one. If you use this method, you can carry on almost without stopping.

The paper I used for this painting, below, is Fabriano Classico 5 281lb Not.

Open wash Fabriano Classico 5 281lb Not

Pencil and wash Greens Camber Sand 72lb Not

Pencil and wash

I used Greens Camber Sand 72lb Not paper for this painting, above. Pencil and wash is one of the most delicate ways of using watercolour. It can be very sensitive and detailed. First, I did the drawing – as though it were to be a drawing in its own right. Naturally, the amount of detail you put in depends upon your drawing ability. All the shading was done with a pencil. Washes of colour were applied after the drawing was completed. Incidentally, this fixes the pencil and stops any smudging.

Pen and wash

A very popular technique, pen and wash is used at some time or another by many watercolour artists. The addition of the pen gives a sparkle to the painting. I painted the picture first, then added the pen work, but you can work the other way round – pen first – if you find it suits you better. Like body colour, the use of the pen is another method of saving a watercolour. Next time you want to put a bit more sparkle into a painting, try using a pen – you could transform a mediocre painting into a masterpiece.

Pen and wash Greens Pasteless Board 300lb HP

SIMPLE EXERCISES

No doubt you have had a few funny experiences with the paint. At times, you may have lost control or found that runs of paint have broken away from the main wash and run down the paper on to the table or the floor. However, you will have learned a lot and now, you can use this knowledge to do some real painting.

If you have been using cartridge paper or thin water-colour paper and have not yet tried stretching any paper, now is the time to do so. It makes an incredible difference, especially to cartridge paper. You will need to refer to the instructions on page 16.

Before you start a watercolour painting, you must always have *clean* water in your container. Remember, the paint stains the water to make the colour. If the water is dirty, obviously, you will not get a true, clear colour.

To avoid breaking my rhythm when I am painting in the studio, I sometimes speed up the drying time of a wash by using my wife's hair drier to blow dry my wash. If you do this, *don't hold the drier too close* – what you are trying to achieve is a *quicker*, *natural* way of drying your wash.

I have chosen a potato for the first exercise. The drawing is not too difficult and if you put a bump in the wrong place, it will not look wrong. Also, although the colour isn't bright or exciting, it can be easily matched. The colour of potatoes varies, so if you don't match it exactly, your painting will still look right. You may now have the impression that if an object isn't represented correctly, it doesn't matter. Of course, this is not true. What I am trying to do is to make sure that your first painting of an object looks correct to your family and friends so that you will receive their praise and congratulations. This will boost your confidence which, in turn, will improve your work. Now you can understand why I chose a potato for you – because it has no specific shape or colour.

First, draw the potato with your HB pencil. Using your large, round brush, paint the background as a wash. When this is dry, paint the potato and add more colour on the shadow side as you paint down. Before this paint is dry, use the same brush and darker colour to work the dark blemishes. Because the paint is still slightly wet, these marks will run a little and the edges will be soft. While the paint is still wet on the potato, dry out your brush and wipe out some highlights. These are only subtle effects but they help to give the object form. Finally, put in the shadow. Don't be fussy with the detail and, if it doesn't work out the first time, keep trying. When you can paint that potato, you will have come a long, long way. Try some more vegetables – you will find that you enjoy painting them.

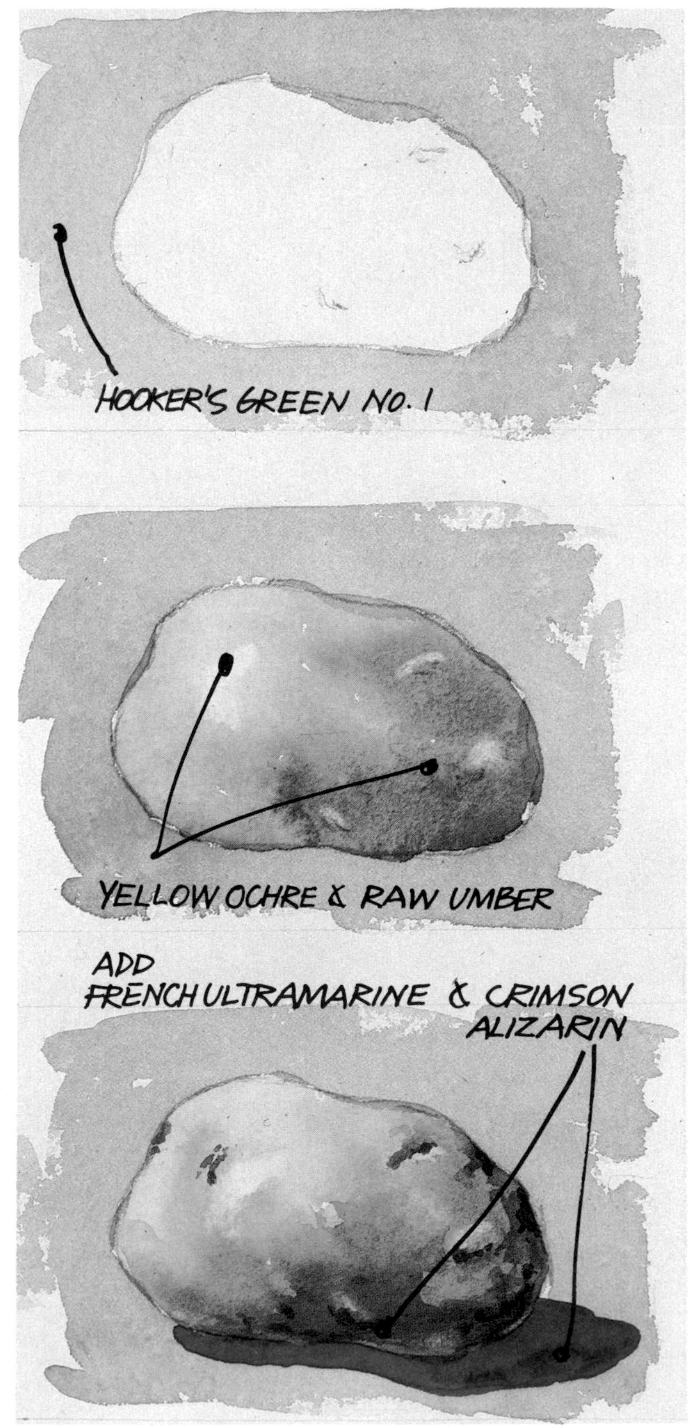

Complicated subject and simplified painting

Below is a complicated, pencil sketch I made of the River Hamble in Hampshire. I put quite a lot of drawing into this but, if you only wanted to paint it, you could manage by sketching only the key positions – the horizon, the wooden quay and a couple of the main boats – the brush could do the rest. I used a rough surface for this, a lot of dry brush, and I scratched out the light on the middle-distance water with a blade.

Complicated subject

Simplified painting

LET'S TRY A BANANA – USE THESE COLOURS

CADMIUM YELLOW PALE
BURNT UMBER
CRIMSON ALIZARIN
FRENCH ULTRAMARINE

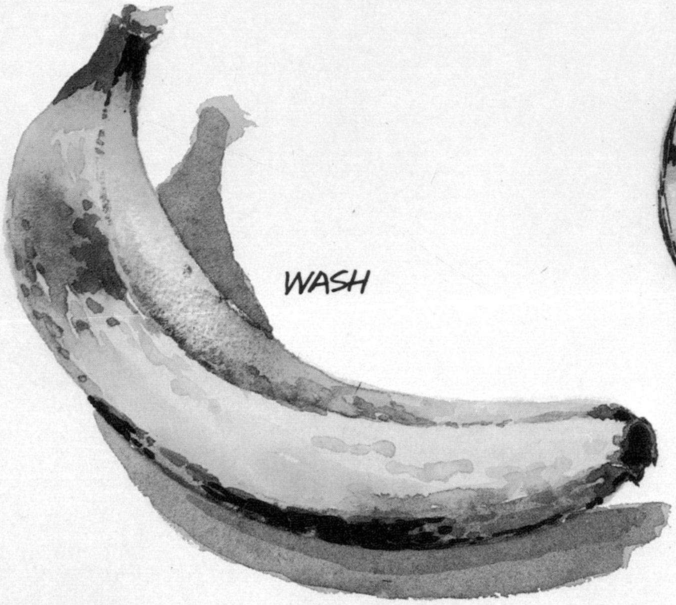

WASH

PEN & WASH

PENCIL & WASH

BODY COLOUR

WET ON WET

Let's try a banana

This time, try a *very simple approach* to five of the techniques I described earlier. First, draw five bananas on the same sheet of paper with your HB pencil.

Now, paint the banana shapes, using the same colours for all five. Paint the first one, using your large, round brush and the colours shown. Let the brush strokes follow the shape of the banana. When the paint is almost dry, put on a darker wash and add some darker marks on top of this. Then, paint a dark shadow wash to show up the banana (light against dark). Put in a few dark accents with your small, size No. 6 brush to crispen it up.

Paint the pen and wash banana in the same way. When the wash is dry, use a mapping pen and black Indian ink to draw the banana. Experiment to find your natural style. You can try drawing the banana with pen and ink first before putting coloured washes over the top.

The next one is pencil and wash. Draw and shade the banana with your HB and 2B pencils as if you were doing a pencil drawing. Pencil leads are graded up to 6B (the softest, or blackest) so if you want darker shading on your drawing, use a softer pencil. Next, paint it in the same way as the first one but this time, over your pencil shading. Now, use the wet on wet technique. Use your sponge or large brush to wet the paper then, while it is still quite wet, paint the banana with the same brush. The colours will run over the edges of your pencil drawing. Then paint the darker side and add some dark blemishes. When this is nearly dry, use the same brush to paint your background. Start at the left, above the banana, follow its top shape in one brush stroke, then work underneath it.

Finally, we will use the body colour technique, i.e. we will use White to make the paint lighter and opaque. Usually, poster colour or tubes of gouache colour are used and you must *wash it off your palette* when you have finished with it. If white paint gets accidentally mixed with watercolour and applied to paper, and you *put a wash* over the top (or even a very watery brush), it will run and ruin your work. Now, paint your banana; using the same colours as before but adding White to them – don't use a lot of water. You will find that the paint does not flow so easily and you have to work it more than usual.

Now a rose

Use your size No. 6 brush to put a wash of Crimson Alizarin and Cadmium Red on the flower. While this is still wet, wipe out some of the paint for highlights with a damp brush. Paint the stem and leaves and, while the leaves are still wet, add some Cadmium Red with the point of the brush. Paint the petals with stronger colour and, when dry, scratch out some highlights. With the same brush, paint the background – very wet. Be definite when painting up to the leaves – let the brush stroke make the shape. Add some shadow on the stem and leaves under the flower.

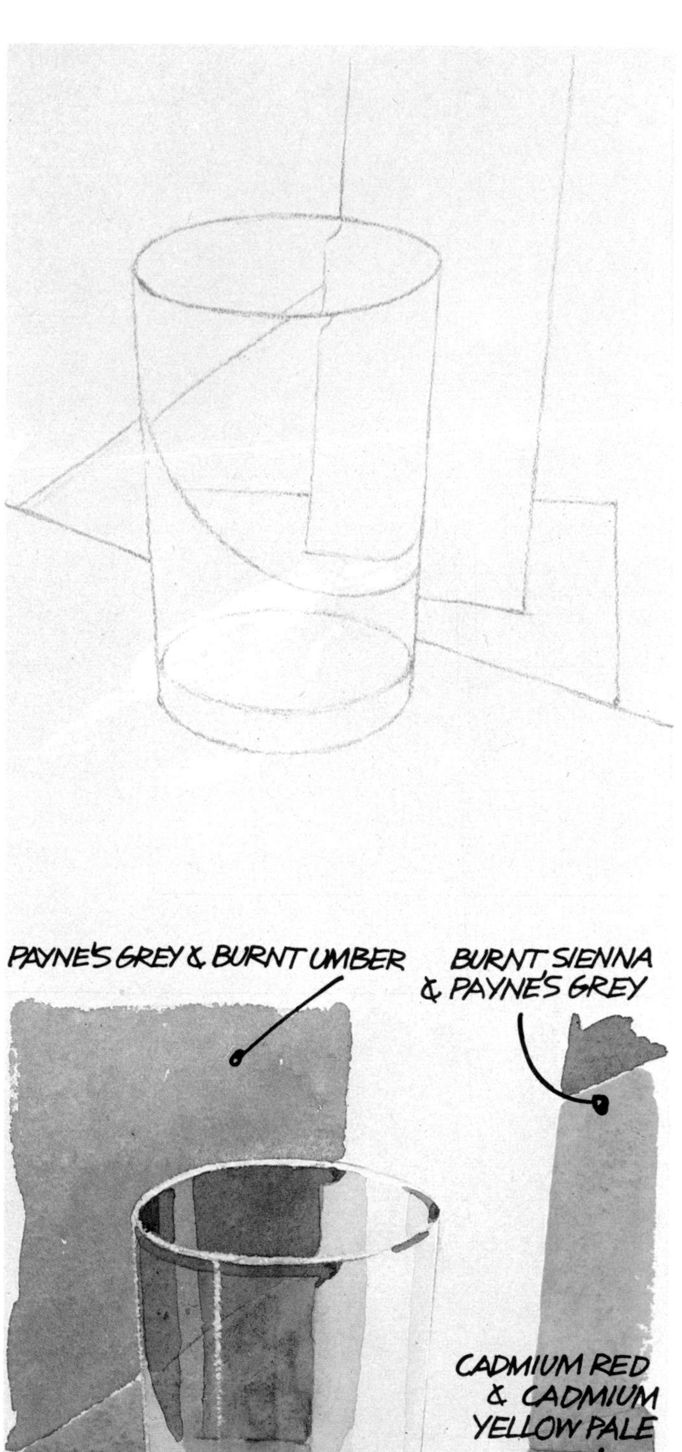

A drinking glass

I find that most students fight shy of painting glass and I am often asked how to make it look like *glass*. The answer, as always, is by *observation*. Look right through the glass and analyse the shapes behind it. Then, draw the glass and simplify these shapes. If you look at my drawing, you will see that definite shapes are formed *in* the glass. Use a large brush to paint the top-left, dark area first – leave the rim of the glass and paint into the glass. Then paint the orange areas. Next, use a very pale wash for the white areas, leaving some unpainted white paper in the glass. Now, using downward strokes, put a dark wash down the left-hand side of the glass, leaving some areas untouched. When this is dry, go over the area again with even darker colour and add a few dark accents with your small sable brush. Use a sharp blade to scratch out some highlights on the glass.

Set up your own glass and study the background shapes – I am sure you will soon learn the secret of painting a glass.

Now some skies

I have already said that the wash is the basis of all watercolour painting and if you have been practising your basic techniques, you should now be able to handle a wash quite confidently. The last two exercises – a rose and a glass – needed a lot of hard thinking and careful brush work but you can be a little more relaxed when painting skies. After all, if you get the overall shape of a cloud correct, it doesn't matter if you have an extra bump here and there. Skies are one of the best subjects on which to practise washes and large brush work, and although it is an exercise, you can produce a very rewarding painting.

Tackle this exercise for the sheer joy of painting and enjoy the freedom that the paint and the subject matter allow. My six paintings were all done on Greens Pasteless Board 300lb Not but you can try all kinds of paper, surfaces, weights, colours, and so on. I worked them exactly twice the size they are reproduced here, i.e. 18cm (7in) wide – a handy size on which to practise this exercise because you have more control over the paint on a small area.

A

A This was a clear, windy day and the clouds were moving across the sky quite fast. I used dry paper and a size No. 10 brush. First, I painted a wash of Coeruleum Blue and a little Crimson Alizarin for the blue sky then, while it was wet, I added Yellow Ochre to the mix and used it for the shadow of the clouds

B Here, I applied a wash of Payne's Grey, French Ultramarine and Crimson Alizarin to dry paper with a size No. 10 brush, leaving white areas for clouds. While this was wet, I painted the darker sides of the clouds. Then, I added a touch of Yellow Ochre to the dark shadows

C This evening sky has a normal graded wash worked from the top to the horizon, and below the land. The paper was dry and I used Coeruleum Blue, Crimson Alizarin and Cadmium Yellow Pale for the wash, worked with a size No. 10 brush

D These big, full clouds were painted first with a mixture of Yellow Ochre, Crimson Alizarin and French Ultramarine. Before they dried, French Ultramarine mixed with Crimson Alizarin (blue sky) was painted between them, leaving white edges – a silver lining to help merge the clouds. Notice the little silhouette of a cottage at the bottom left and the white lake at the foot of the hills – this gives dimension to the clouds

E A very wet, drizzly day, The paper was soaked with a sponge except at the bottom, right-hand corner. A mix of French Ultramarine, Crimson Alizarin, Payne's Grey and Yellow Ochre was worked on to the wet paper and you can see the result. Where the paper was dry at the bottom right, I let the brush form the cottage – again, to give atmosphere and dimension

F For this evening sky I applied a normal wash of Crimson Alizarin and Cadmium Yellow Pale over the paper. When the wash was dry I painted the clouds, using a size No. 6 brush and with French Ultramarine added to the colour. Before these clouds were dry, I worked a darker wash over them to form the dark clouds just above the horizon

F

B

C

D

E

EXERCISE ONE
STILL LIFE

On the following pages I have taken five subjects and worked them in stages for you to follow, and copy if you wish. I have explained how to do the work and, most important, I have shown the same painting from the first stage to the last (the finished stage). This is important because you see the *same painting* through its stages and you can look back to see what was done earlier. It is also important for you to know the size of the finished painting (not the reproduction) because this gives you a relative scale to adjust to. The actual size is indicated under the finished stage.

The close-up illustrations for each exercise are reproduced the same size as I painted them so that you can see the actual brush strokes and details. Finally, I have used insets to illustrate the method of painting passages that I think you need to see more closely.

For your first exercise I have purposely chosen a still life subject because the objects are easy to find but, above all, they can be painted under your own conditions. This is the beauty of still life: you can control the lighting, size, shape and colour of your subject. If you use inorganic objects, you can paint the same ones for years. To avoid your spending that long on your still life, I have added some fruit.

Before we start, here are one or two important notes on still-life painting. Don't be too ambitious to start with. Set up just a few objects that have simple shapes and colours, and put them on a contrasting background. The best light source is an adjustable desk lamp which can be directed on to your subject to give maximum light and shade (light against dark). Before you set up a still life subject, make sure that none of the objects you use will be needed by you or your family in the near future.

First stage Draw the picture with an HB pencil. Using your large brush, mix Hooker's Green No. 1, Crimson Alizarin and French Ultramarine, and paint a wash down the paper, working around the fruit but painting over the left-hand side of the glass jar. Now, work a wash down the right-hand side of the picture, using French Ultramarine, Crimson Alizarin and Yellow Ochre – again, paint over the jar but leave some white paper for highlights. Paint the table top with the same colour.

Second stage Paint the sultanas in the jar, using Crimson Alizarin, French Ultramarine and Cadmium Yellow Pale. While the paint is still wet, dry your brush and wipe out the two highlights on the jar. Then start putting in the fruit. Load your brush with watery paint and start with the orange – use Cadmium Yellow Pale, Cadmium Red and a touch of French Ultramarine in the shadow area. Next, paint the apple with Hooker's Green No. 1 and Cadmium Yellow Pale. Add the red lines of the apples while the paint is still wet so that they will merge and look softer. Paint the two pears with a wash of Cadmium Yellow Pale and Hooker's Green No. 1. When they are nearly dry, paint the darker, browny-green areas with Hooker's Green No. 1, Crimson Alizarin and Yellow Ochre. The onion is next: use Cadmium Yellow Pale and Crimson Alizarin. With a wash of Yellow Ochre and Burnt Umber, paint all the nuts inside and outside the bowl, except the kernel inside the broken walnut. When these are dry, add Crimson Alizarin to your wash to give more tone to the chestnuts. Dry out the highlights with your brush. Paint the blue dish, using French Ultramarine and a little Hooker's Green No. 1; add more pigment to the wash so that it gets darker to the right of the bowl – make sure you leave a white rim to the bowl.

Third stage By now, all the areas have a wash over them but no detail or depth is apparent. At this stage, darker washes are applied to the painting. Start with the green background, using the same colours but adding more pigment. Paint over the jar again but *do leave some areas of the original wash* showing. As you work on the fruit, use a little more brush work to achieve moulding and shape.

First stage

Second stage

Third stage

Fourth stage

Fourth stage Now your work on the nuts begins in earnest. Use your size No. 6 brush and start with the walnuts. Let the brush do the drawing of the gnarled shells, as if it were a pencil. If you find the line too harsh or too strong, dry your brush and soften the line with it. Work the brazil nuts and the chestnuts in the same way. Whatever you do, keep the highlights on the chestnuts – they are an essential feature of these particular nuts. Now paint the shadows with a wash of Crimson Alizarin, French Ultramarine and Yellow Ochre; when these are dry, add another wash to the bowl. Finally, use one stroke to put a wash down the right-hand side of the jar and over the sultanas.

Finished stage The picture is almost finished at this stage but it lacks that final crispness and a little detail. This work is done with a size No. 6 brush. Start with the jar, adding dark line-work to give it better definition. Wipe some colour off the left-hand side of the apple to accentuate its shape and to separate it from the orange. Then, add the stalk. Paint some thin lines on the onion and work the sultanas in the jar in more detail. Give all the nuts stronger treatment and paint the shadows cast from the apple and pear on the nuts in the bowl. Put some stippling on the orange with your size No. 6 brush for an orange-skin look – use darker paint and work from the dark area into the light, leaving light areas showing through (see below). Finally, paint all the shadows again with a stronger wash.

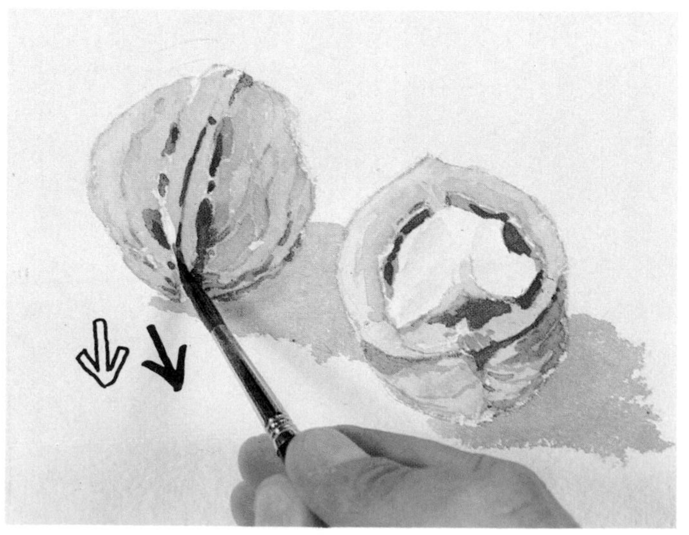

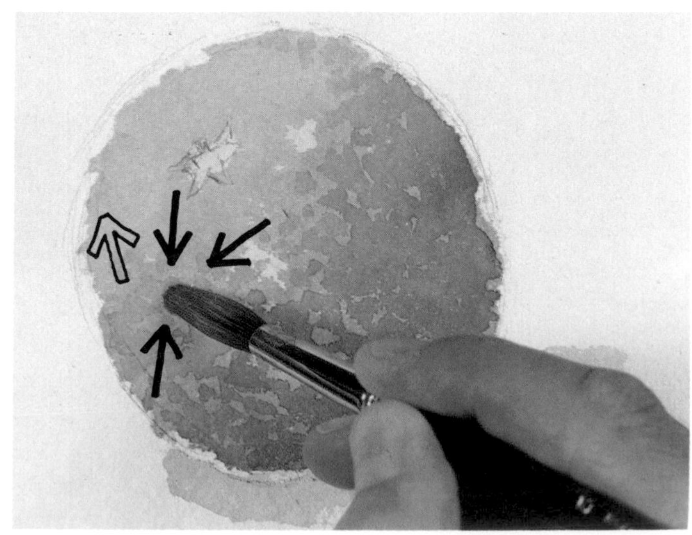

Finished stage 25.3 × 36.8cm (10 × 14½in)

EXERCISE TWO
PORTRAIT

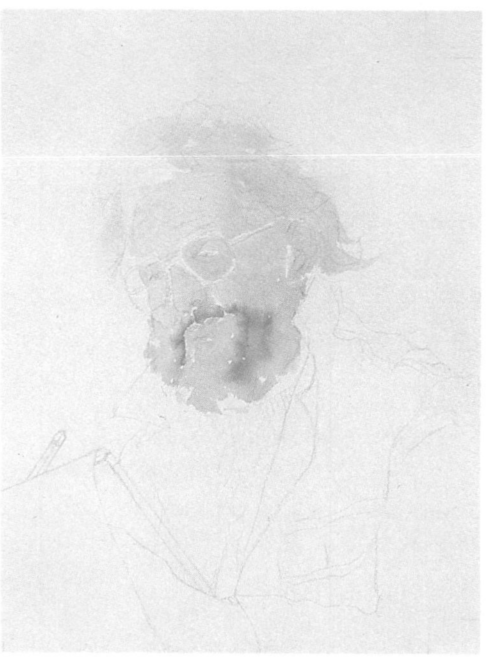
First stage

Second stage

Third stage

For the student, portrait painting has many advantages in common with still life painting. Again, you can dictate the lighting, colour scheme and mood. The painting of a portrait does not depend on the weather but only on your model's availability. But, remember, you always have one model with you – yourself; all you need is a mirror.

Watercolour is not the easiest of mediums to use for portraits but it does have some natural advantages. With watercolour, you can create an impression of the subject that has a very fresh and unlaboured appearance. Also, washes can be used in some very delicate work to give depth to the skin tones. If you find that you start to lose it while working on a portrait, carry on with body colour, or even pen work, and you may find that you have succeeded in painting a good portrait. The likeness can come through as an impression – a feeling. If you want detail, eventually, then you can gradually build up to it through practice and careful observation.

First stage Draw the portait with an HB pencil. Wet the paper with a sponge and wait until it is nearly dry (when the shine has gone). Then, using your large brush, mix Coeruleum Blue and Crimson Alizarin, and paint the hair, leaving an area unpainted above the forehead. While this is still wet, use Cadmium Red and Yellow Ochre to paint the first wash of the flesh tones, letting this colour mix with the hair. Use a stronger wash (add Crimson Alizarin and a touch of French Ultramarine to your first wash) to paint the shadow side of the face. This will mix with the wash underneath and keep the edges soft. While it is still wet, paint the beard, using Payne's Grey and Crimson Alizarin.

Second stage Now, paint the jacket with a mix of Coeruleum Blue and Crimson Alizarin. While it is still damp add Payne's Grey to your wash and put in the shadows. Paint the wrist and the shadow of the sketching pad.

Third stage More detail is to be added to the face in this stage. Use your size No. 6 brush and the same colours as in the first two stages but mix them stronger. If you get a hard line you can soften it by stroking it with a damp brush. If it is difficult to move, wet the area with your brush and blot up the surface water with blotting paper. (Always keep

Finished stage 32.3 × 24.7cm ($12\frac{3}{4}$ × $9\frac{3}{4}$in)

blotting paper at your side – it is invaluable for getting you out of trouble.) When the face is really dry, use French Ultramarine and Crimson Alizarin to paint the glasses, leaving some areas unpainted for highlights.

Finished stage The last stage involves crispening up your painting and adding the jumper. Draw this with a brush, using French Ultramarine, Crimson Alizarin and Yellow Ochre. Now, use your size No. 6 brush and a mix of French Ultramarine, Crimson Alizarin and Yellow Ochre: put the dark accents under the right side of the beard, to the left of the jumper, at the back of the jacket collar, under the jacket lapel; draw some detail around the jacket pocket and put the shadow on the pad. Finally, put a small accent under the hair and paint the pencil.

EXERCISE THREE
LANDSCAPE

Landscape painting holds the romantic promise of a day spent in the countryside painting away, enjoying ourselves to the full. This applies to many artists but not to all: some people worry about painting while strangers look on, others can't get out into the countryside as often as they would like to. If you lack confidence, the best way to start is to tuck yourself away behind a tree, make a quick drawing in your sketch book of a scene you would like to paint and mark the main colours in pencil, then paint it at home. As your confidence grows, take your watercolour box outside with you. Remember that nine out of ten people who take the trouble to come to see you will be full of admiration for you and your work.

Sketching in pencil also applies to the person who can't often get outside. Rather than always *painting* just one scene when you *do* go out, instead make a few different pencil sketches. Six of them could be completed in a day. Take your watercolour box and some water with you, and make some colour notes on these sketches. Then, when it's stay-at-home day, you can use this information to produce six different paintings.

A landscape can be painted from a window, if necessary, but you must sketch and paint outside as much as possible. Always carry a sketch book with you; even if you only have ten minutes to sketch a scene and draw only ten lines, you will have had to observe it. The important factor is *observation*. The knowledge it provides will be committed to your memory and you will find that, in time, you will be capable of painting from memory indoors. Those memory banks must be kept in good condition – take every opportunity to observe and sketch out-of-doors.

I have chosen this landscape for working the wet on wet technique; this gives the real, wet, watercolour look. Remember to thoroughly soak your paper. Incidentally, I should warn you that once you start a painting like this you are committed to continue to the end while it is still wet or damp.

First stage I get a great deal of pleasure from using this watercolour technique, especially when worked to the extreme as it is in this exercise. It has an element of risk – where is the paint going? – and one of great excitement. Although you have planned in your mind what you want to do and you can control it to a great extent, there is the *certainty* of many a happy accident, and even pure surprise, when using this technique. For you to copy this picture, or even for me to copy it, and achieve the same result would be an impossibility. What you have to do is work towards the same composition and if a happy accident occurs, then use it. I will explain what to do, as I have in the other exercises, but remember, your painting will have its own little gems created purely by this wet on wet technique. Draw the picture with your HB pencil, using a minimum of drawing. Soak the paper thoroughly with water. Use your large brush and put on your palette French Ultramarine, Crimson Alizarin, Payne's Grey and Yellow Ochre – *don't* mix these colours all together in the palette; apply them to the wet paper and they will mix on the surface, creating some beautiful effects. Run the sky into the land and notice the unpainted area I left for the puddle.

Second stage Using a wash of Payne's Grey, Crimson Alizarin and Yellow Ochre, paint the middle-distance trees with your large brush. These will run into the sky and lose a bit of shape but don't worry, the impression you are creating is that of a landscape in an early-morning mist. While these trees are wet, paint the main trees into them. Then, using your size No. 6 brush, add some smaller branches. Next, take your large brush on to the now damp

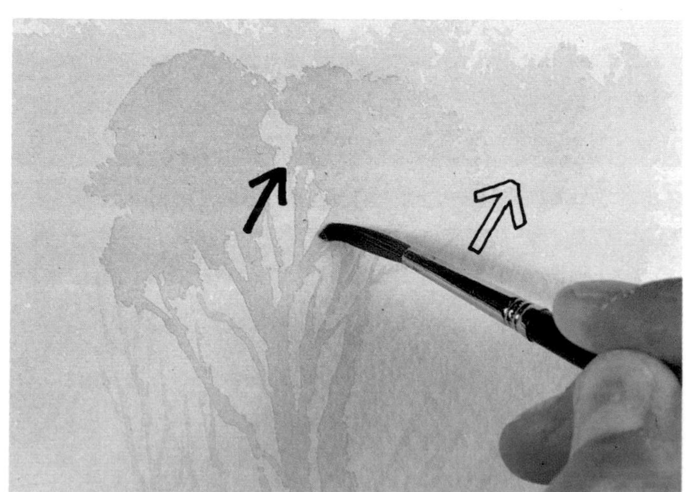

First stage

Second stage

sky and drag the brush down into the wet, small branches (so it all runs together) to form the top of the trees. If at any stage your work dries out too quickly for you, wet the paper again; it may move some of the pigment but if you do it gently, you will get away with it.

Third stage With your large brush and plenty of watery paint – Payne's Grey, Burnt Umber, Hooker's Green No. 1 and Crimson Alizarin – paint the foreground. You will notice that the puddle is more obvious, now that a darker tone has been added.

Third stage

Fourth stage

Fourth stage Work over the main tree again while it is still damp. Use your size No. 6 brush to put in some more branches but keep them light in tone at the top. Also, paint the tree in the left-middle distance. Add the little bit of fence to the right of the main tree.

Finished stage Put another wash of darker colour over the foreground and add any darker accents you feel necessary for your picture. *Don't overdo the detail* when using this technique. I will give you some idea of timing on this type of picture: I took about 45 minutes to complete it. This effect cannot be achieved if you work slowly, the very essence of the technique is speed. Some artists use this technique to start a painting and then, when it has reached this stage (finished stage), they spend a lot of time working it up into a highly detailed watercolour – you could try that, next time.

Finished stage 36.8 × 28cm ($14\frac{1}{2}$ × 11in)

EXERCISE FOUR
BUILDINGS

Buildings can be a tremendous source of pleasure to the artist. You may be inspired by the size and splendour of a building or by the quaint, old-world charm of a village street. Watercolour is a good medium to use for buildings, and buildings are a good subject for the student of watercolour. When you look at buildings with a painting in mind, you will see that the colour areas are broken up into quite definite shapes. In an earlier exercise, you looked through the drinking glass to find the shapes and colours; buildings have already done this for you. The shapes of roofs and walls, windows and doors, are quite definite and these shapes give you the areas on which to work your washes. But these are disciplined washes and different to those you used for the sky exercises.

A great deal of my watercolour training was done outside, sitting on the pavement, just off the main flow of people, painting buildings. If you are worried about sitting at the top of your local high street to paint, you can usually find some little corner where you can tuck yourself away, unnoticed. One of the great advantages of using watercolour to paint buildings is that you need only a small amount of equipment: stool, sketch block or some paper on a drawing board, paint box, brushes, water container, pencil and eraser. In fact, you don't always need a stool: sometimes, you can get a very good view of buildings from your car, in a car park. I have an estate car and I have often worked from that.

The subject of this exercise, I believe, is not too advanced and I have made it a pencil and wash drawing for those who can draw. If you feel you would rather stick to painting as a technique, you can do so. After drawing the main building areas simply work with your washes as you did in the still life exercise. Use the colours I suggest but mix them much stronger (I want the pencil to show through the wash).

First stage Draw the main area of the composition with an HB pencil, then draw the areas that you want to show through the washes. This means all-detail-work areas of tone and shadow. When shading, it is usually best to start at the top of the drawing to avoid working over finished, lower areas and smudging them. Start with the chimney and draw the stones, shading a few of them because some are darker than others. Work down on to the tiled roof, then the lower part of the main building, drawing the stones again as you did on the chimney.

Second stage Continue drawing with your HB pencil, working next the houses at the end of the street – note that no stonework is drawn on these because this would make them appear nearer. Then, put in the house on the right, working plenty of shading on it because it is in shadow. Put plenty of pencil work on the lean-to against the main building, being very careful with the tiles and windows, and the railings in front of it. Draw the three figures and the shadow cast by the man in broad pencil shading. Add some dark accents with your 2B or 3B pencil. Now, you should have a drawing capable of standing in its own right as a pencil drawing.

First stage

Second stage

Third stage For this exercise I used Greens Camber Sand 72lb Not paper. It was not stretched, only pinned to a drawing board. Incidentally, I used a piece of cartridge paper as a backing sheet in order to get a better line with the pencil; if you do not do this, the grain of the drawing board can be felt through the paper and will hinder the pencil lines. Because the paper is not very heavy, don't use very wet washes. Using your large brush, paint the sky with Coeruleum Blue and Crimson Alizarin. Be sure to keep all your washes well diluted so that they do not cover your pencil work. Your pencil must show through in order to achieve the full beauty of this effect. Next, paint the stonework, using Raw Umber, French Ultramarine and Crimson Alizarin.

Third stage

Fourth stage

Fourth stage Use a mixture of French Ultramarine, Crimson Alizarin and Raw Umber on the roofs. Paint the red tiles on top of the roofs with Cadmium Red and Cadmium Yellow Pale. Darken the mixture you used on the roofs and use this to work a wash on the windows. Put in the orange-painted, wooden beams on the main house and use the same colour for the window frames; put a dark stonework-coloured wash over the buildings on the right and, finally, paint the red canopy at the end of the street with a weak wash of Cadmium Red.

Finished stage Paint a wash of Burnt Sienna and Crimson Alizarin over the lean-to extension, then use French Ultramarine and Crimson Alizarin to paint over the windows and the dark wall under the railings. Put a wash on the windows of the left-hand house and add a tone of Yellow Ochre, Crimson Alizarin and French Ultramarine over the front of the house. Put a dark tone on the figure and a broad, dark accent down the right of the two figures against the main house. Apply a wash of French Ultramarine, Crimson Alizarin and Yellow Ochre to the road with your size No. 6 brush, using broad strokes. With the same brush, add any dark accents you feel necessary.

50 50

MEŠTROVIĆ

НАРОДНА БАНКА ЈУГОСЛАВИЈЕ
NARODNA BANKA JUGOSLAVIJE
НАРОДНА БАНКА НА ЈУГОСЛАВИЈА

ДИНАРА
DINARJEV

50

DINARA
ДИНАРИ

ZAMJENIK GUVERNERA-ЗАМЕНИК НА ГУВЕРНЕРОТ
NAMESTNIK GUVERNERJA-ЗАМЕНИК ГУВЕРНЕРА

ГУВЕРНЕР-GUVERNER

БЕОГРАД – BEOGRAD
БЕЛГРАД
12. VIII 1978.

AL 3950544

50 50

ZAVOD ZA IZRADU NOVČANICA-BEOGRAD

50

ПЕДЕСЕТ
ДИНАРА
PETDESET
DINARJEV

SLOVENIJA·SRBIJA·БОСНА И ХЕРЦЕГОВИНА·MAKEДОНИЈА·СЛОВЕНИЈА·СРБИЈА·HRVATSKA·ЦРНА ГОРА·BOSNA I HERCEGOVINA·CRNA GORA·HRVATSKA·MAKEDONIJA·

50

PEDESET
DINARA
ПЕДЕСЕТ
ДИНАРИ

50

ФАЛСИФИКОВАЊЕ СЕ КАЖЊАВА ПО ЗАКОНУ – KRIVOTVORENJE SE KAŽNJAVA PO ZAKONU
PONAREJANJE SE KAZNUJE PO ZAKONU – ФАЛСИФИКУВАЊЕТО СЕ КАЗНУВА СПОРЕД ЗАКОНОТ

50

M. PETROVIĆ FEC.

T. KRNJAJIĆ SC.

SOCIJALISTIČKA
FEDERATIVNA
REPUBLIKA
JUGOSLAVIJA

СОЦИЈАЛИСТИЧКА
ФЕДЕРАТИВНА
РЕПУБЛИКА
ЈУГОСЛАВИЈА

SOCIALISTIČNA
FEDERATIVNA
REPUBLIKA
JUGOSLAVIJA

Finished stage 36.8 × 28cm ($14\frac{1}{2}$ × 11in)

EXERCISE FIVE
WATER

First stage

Second stage

Third stage

A lake or pond (unless discoloured by mud) reflects its immediate surroundings and the sky. In very clear, still water the reflection of a building can be mirror-like; therefore, the water is painted as a building, upside-down. This is important: the reflection goes *down* vertically into the water, not across the surface. It is only the movement of the water that shows as horizontal lines and, remember, any movement breaks up the reflected images. Light on moving water is also seen horizontally. The first, golden rule for painting water is to make sure that all movement lines or shapes are *perfectly horizontal*. If they are not, you will have painted a sloping river or lake.

The illusion of water can be created quite simply with watercolour. Even leaving white paper to suggest water can be very effective (remember example D on page 35 when you were practising skies – the lake with the silhouette of the cottage at the side is white paper). Painting reflections can be approached in the same way as painting the glass. Observe your subject carefully and decide what the main shapes and colours are. Then go ahead.

A very wet on wet technique is usually very descriptive of water. Learn to observe the different moods of water and remember that a reflection immediately creates the illusion of water.

First stage Before you paint water, the surroundings must be painted first because these determine the colour and the shapes on the water. Draw the picture with your HB pencil but don't draw on the water area, these shapes will be created with your brush. Wet the paper with a sponge, then paint a wash of Coeruleum Blue and Crimson Alizarin. Just before it is dry, put in the middle-distance trees with French Ultramarine, Crimson Alizarin and Hooker's Green No. 1. Paint the field underneath, using Cadmium Yellow Pale and a little Crimson Alizarin. Next, paint the roof of the boat-house with Cadmium Red, Cadmium Yellow Pale and Hooker's Green No. 1.

Second stage Paint the mooring posts and side of the boat-house, using Payne's Grey and Hooker's Green No. 1. Then paint the tree trunks, working upwards with your large brush and using Payne's Grey, Hooker's Green No. 1 and Burnt Umber. While the trunks are still wet, paint into these with Cadmium Yellow Pale, Hooker's Green No. 1 and Crimson Alizarin to form the leaves. Do this with your size No. 6 brush, making diagonal strokes from right to left at a flattish angle to the paper. You will get a broad, hit-and-miss stroke which will give the impression of leaves. Paint the boats and bank of the river.

Finished stage 28 × 21cm (11 × 8¼in)

Third stage Now wet the paper again over the water area and, while it is still wet, run in the reflected colours. Before you start, decide roughly where they are going to be; for instance, the tree trunks, the red of the roof, and so on. I often have a dummy run over the paper with my brush to get the feel of where the strokes and colours will go. As you can see from this stage illustration, the colours merge and could even be left as finished. This, remember, was only the first wash but because the colours run into each other and the reflections and colours complement the background, to the eye it suggests water.

Finished stage When the first wash is nearly dry, add more, darker-colour washes and more, definite, reflection shapes to give more detail to the water. Finally, scratch out some horizontal highlights with a blade.

OILS

PETER JOHN GARRARD PRBA, RP, NEAC

OIL PAINTS–WHAT THEY ARE

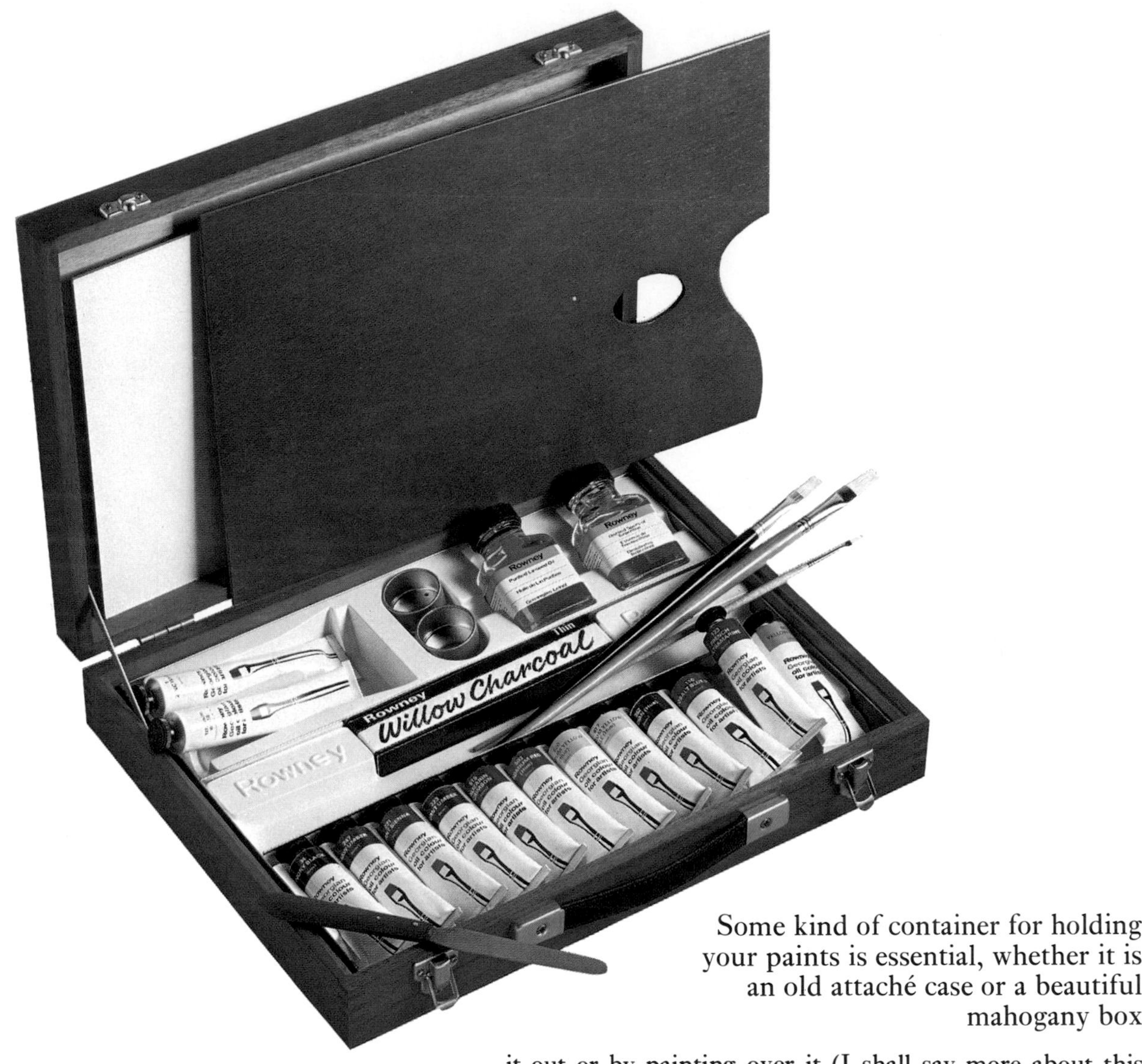

Some kind of container for holding your paints is essential, whether it is an old attaché case or a beautiful mahogany box

Painting with oils is one of the most exciting ways of painting but, to be truthful, for myself at the moment, it is the only way to paint. I like the stuff of oil paint; I enjoy messing about with it; I like the way it can be used thickly and thinly; the way that every touch can be varied, and even the smell pleases me. In short, it is for me the ideal means of expression. I do not mean I do not like to draw, often there are occasions when drawing with a pencil is just what is required, but for sheer personal pleasure I will paint with oils.

As a medium for the beginner it is perfect because it is very easy to correct what you have done either by wiping it out or by painting over it (I shall say more about this later). The great difficulty with other media, such as watercolour, is that correction, when you realize it is necessary, is well nigh impossible. For example, you realize that a colour should be lighter; with oil paint you work over it with the 'right' colour, but with watercolour you can only scrub it down, and this is not easy. Another advantage is that you can place touches of different colours immediately next to each other whilst both are still wet and they will not run into each other. In fact, this is one of the most useful ways of painting, which I will mention often. Oil painting provides you with the greatest range of choices: you can paint rich, dark colours or pale, gentle shades; it lends itself to objective painting, and many abstract painters prefer it above all else. But enough of

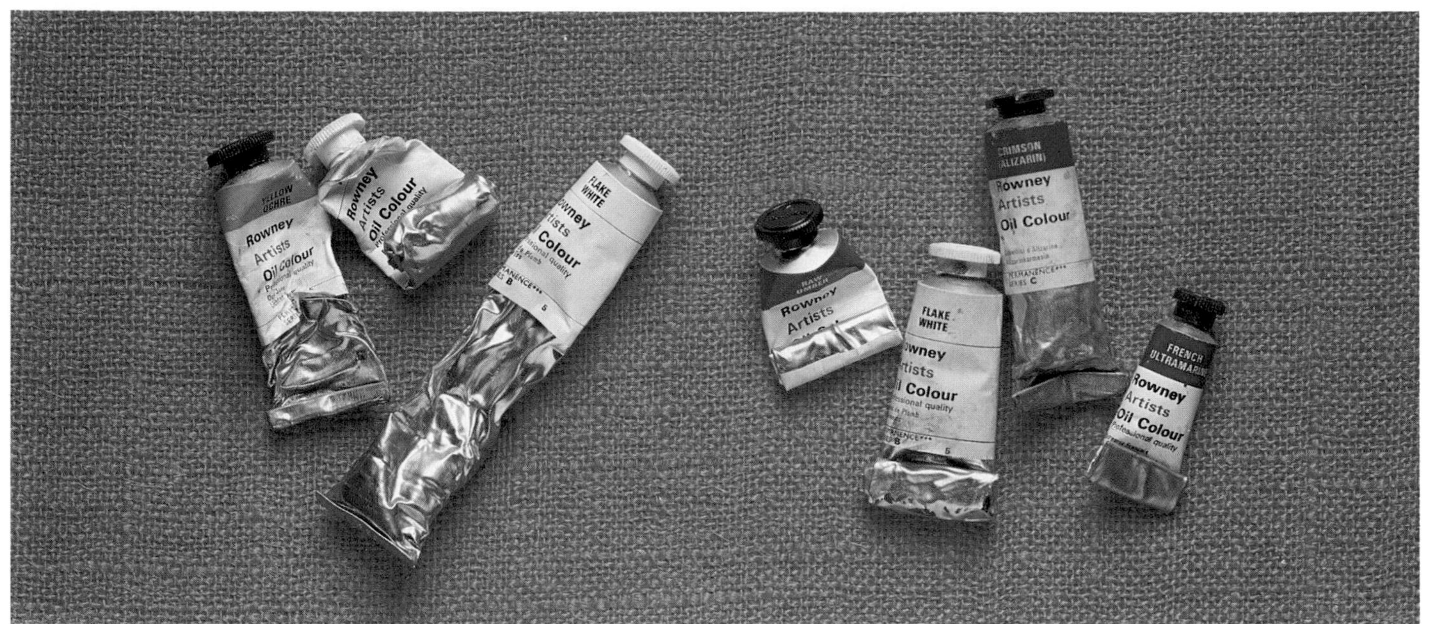

Take care of your tubes of paint. The tubes on the left are badly squeezed, which is wasteful. On the right, what you should do

this; by now you should be finding out some of this for yourself because I hope you have started a painting.

There are some disadvantages in using oil paints. For many people, the fact that they do not dry completely for a long while is, I suppose, the most serious, but for the most part this need not be a great problem. I have found slowness of drying a difficulty only when I have been on a painting trip and have to transport home a lot of wet paintings. Again, this can be overcome: if you paint on canvas, place canvas pins at each corner of the canvas and place another canvas on top. Canvas pins hold apart two canvases. If you have painted on a board, use thin slices of cork and tie the boards together with string.

I imagine that some people would consider the fact that you do have to learn some technical information about the paint a disadvantage. The amount you have to learn can be remarkably small, provided you remember one or two simple rules and do not use too complex a palette of colours. Throughout these pages you will find that I mention rules, or rather, sensible ways of behaviour. The equipment you need is discussed in the next section and a basic set of colours is described on p. 60.

You may well ask why a beginner should bother about such things. A sensible question, but you will mind if a picture you paint today is in a bad state in two months, if it has cracked all over or the colour has changed. A first basic rule: do not do the drawing or underpainting in Ivory Black because it dries much slower than other colours – if an underneath layer dries more slowly than a top layer it will crack when the top layer dries. From a technical point of view, what you require in the short term will also ensure your paintings last for posterity.

It would help at this point if I described the differences between the media. At their simplest, oil paint is pigment ground in oil; acrylic paint is pigment ground with an acrylic polymer resin; watercolour is pigment mixed with gum arabic and several other ingredients; pure tempera is pigment plus egg yolk (there are variations of this), and tempera emulsion is pigment plus egg and linseed oil. Thus, a paint is composed of pigment plus a vehicle (oil or diluent). For example, you want Yellow Ochre paint: Yellow Ochre ground with linseed oil will make a paint. But this simplification is not true of most paints you use, because the shelf life (the time a paint remains in a good state for use) varies considerably from pigment to pigment. For example, Vermilion will harden in the tube in only a fortnight if ground with linseed oil, as I have found to my cost. From early days Vermilion was ground with some kind of wax to stop it drying so rapidly.

Today it is safe to say that the artists' colourman (the manufacturer) has tried to iron out the problems and variations of each pigment so your paints will behave – in terms of drying and shelf life – in the same manner. Of course there will be variations – Ivory Black will remain a slower dryer than other paints – but if you stick to the lists on p. 60 you will encounter few technical problems.

I use Artists' professional quality oil colours, but these are expensive, so I recommend you use Rowney Georgian oil colours. These paints are produced so the quality is as high as possible, whilst the price of different colours remains constant. I used Georgian oil colours for most of the demonstration paintings in this book.

Medium (plural media) refers to the different types of painting you can do, i.e. oil, acrylic or watercolour.
Medium (plural mediums) describes the additives which the artist uses with a paint to make it behave differently (e.g. turpentine is added to make the paint run more easily).

WHAT EQUIPMENT DO YOU NEED?

Your requirements can be very simple. When you choose anything, ask yourself two questions: is it reasonably strong so it will stand up to a lot of wear and tear without breaking down; is it essential, i.e. will it make painting more comfortable or make you more efficient. You will find you will collect endless things which are sometimes useful but you could do without. Every now and again, turn out the room in which you paint – be ruthless. I speak from bitter experience, because I collect far too much which I like to look at and, if I am honest, use once in a blue moon and could well do without.

On p. 54 you can see a paintbox, which you will find very useful. A container for holding your paints is essential; it does not matter if it is an old attaché case or a beautiful mahogany box like that. I have several boxes; the one I like best is an old, cork-lined one which I acquired, full of butterflies, as a child and my father adapted for me when I was a student. It has the minimum number of divisions for brushes, paints, an oil tin and a turpentine tin and a device for saving paint, and it also holds a 25.4 × 35.6cm (10 × 14in) board in the lid. In the division for brushes there are palette and painting knives, two dippers and some drawing pins and a paint rag (there is another rag on top of the tubes of paint). Whatever box you choose, old or new, make sure it is long enough to hold your brushes and not too heavy if you are going to paint outdoors. The combined easel and paintbox is lovely to look at but I find it requires too much hard work if I want to walk some distance.

When I go out painting I sit on a chair or stool. The one I like most is an army surplus chair with a back so I can lean back comfortably. I have tried out most chairs or stools that are available; the only one I do not like is the tiny folding metal stool, because it gives me a cramp in my thighs. Your stool or chair should be strong, easy to carry and not too heavy. Do not choose a comfortable, lightweight garden chair which is fine for sitting on but has arms which restrict your movements when painting.

In the studio I use a tall chair with a back (the sort which was used by counting office clerks). It is comfortable and my head is approximately the same height as when I stand. This means I can do a drawing sitting down, and later, when I stand to paint, I see the objects or my sitter from the same height. I keep my palette beside me on a tall kitchen stool, so it is easy to mix up my paints. Many of my friends use old tea trolleys or have constructed a series of compartments on wheels. The top level of the trolley can make an excellent palette – lay down some white paper and cover it with a sheet of plate glass cut to size. This is easy to keep clean and is a nice surface on which to mix up your paints.

If you like painting people, a 'throne' is necessary so you raise the level of your sitters in relation to yourself and do not always look down on them. Mine is 137.2cm ($4\frac{1}{2}$ft) square, 30cm ($11\frac{3}{4}$in) high and on castors so that it moves easily. An old screen is helpful; you can hang material over it to change the colour of the background behind your sitter.

You may have a spare room which you could convert into a studio. This would be ideal because it means you can leave things about and do not have to go through a clearing up session before you start to work. Also, I believe it is helpful to leave paintings around so that in unguarded moments you can glance at them and see what should be altered. I have worked in many different rooms and have found the only thing I am very concerned about is a good source of light. In the northern hemisphere a window facing north – a north light – is best because it produces the most constant light, whatever time of day you work (in the southern hemisphere the reverse is true). Do not have carpets on the floor, sooner or later you will spill something. I once dropped my palette on an Aubusson carpet with unhappy results! If you have to work in your sitting room or kitchen a large sheet of polythene for the floor is useful.

A EASEL
B PAINTING KNIVES
C PLASTER CAST
D LINSEED OIL
E SPARE CLEAN BRUSHES
F PAINT
G BRUSHES IN USE
H PAINT RAG
I SINGLE DIPPERS
J PALETTE
K PAINT BOX
L T-SQUARE
M RETOUCHING VARNISH
N TURPENTINE
O ADJUSTABLE MAGNIFYING GLASS
P DOUBLE DIPPER

A
B
C
D
E
F
G
H
I
J
K
L
M
N
O

Fig. 1

Brushes

There are three main types of brushes available: hog, which is fairly tough; sable, which is soft and springy (there are soft brushes made from ringcat, ox ear hair, squirrel and mixtures of hairs which are cheaper, but not as springy as sable), and man-made fibres, usually a form of nylon (some of the modern ones are very good and cheap). A good brush wears well and goes back to its original shape quickly. Sables are the most expensive.

Good brushes are essential when you start painting (see p. 73 for how to look after them). I recommend you purchase Round Hog brushes (Rowney series 111), sizes 1, 2, 3, 4, 5 and 7, two of each size. Round Hogs give you a greater choice in the kind of mark you make. (Round brushes are shown at the top of **fig. 1**, starting with the smallest.) Also buy two fine sables (Rowney series 134), sizes 4 and 5 (shown immediately below the Round Hogs). The next brush illustrated is a wide brush which is used to varnish finished paintings. There is a number of other shapes, from long filbert to short square brushes, which you will find useful later. They are all nice to use and you should try them, but they restrict the kind of mark you can make. For example, a square brush makes a square brush stroke, which can be tedious if repeated in all your pictures. The shape of brush you enjoy using is a personal matter about which you should slowly make up your mind.

Painting surfaces

You can paint on a variety of surfaces, which range from very cheap paper to expensive canvas. The crucial thing to remember is that you want the oil paint to become one with the surface, but not sink in so all the vehicle (oil in the paint) is sucked out, leaving behind an unstable pigment which will brush off. For example, if you paint on ordinary cartridge paper the oil is rapidly sucked out and forms a halo round the paint – it dries almost immediately and is a very difficult surface on which to work.

In **fig. 1** there are some painting surfaces, including specially prepared paper for sketching, an oil painting board, a canvas panel, a stretched canvas, a piece of unprimed canvas and three different kinds of primed canvas. Oil sketching paper is the cheapest but is not easy to use because it is too smooth; you need to put a wash of paint on it first (this gives you a surface onto which your paint can join). Canvas can be made of cotton or linen and can be very smooth or very coarse (the best is linen). With a coarse canvas you will have to paint more thickly and leave touches of paint alone. I have painted on almost everything, from wood to canvas to paper. For large works I use canvas, for smaller works, boards. I recommend you use canvas panels at first because they have a 'tooth' which holds the paint and helps you apply it.

Fig. 2

Palette and painting knives

There is a double dipper shown in **fig. 2**; one half is used for cleaning your brushes, the other for holding your painting medium. The best to get is a 38mm (1½in) double dipper. Sometimes I use a single dipper – for example, when I am doing an underpainting in one colour. Palette knives, which have straight blades, are for mixing up your paint and cleaning your palette. Painting knives are more flexible and are cranked to facilitate putting paint onto canvas. There is a wide variety available. I have found the shapes illustrated the most useful – these are the knives which I used for the palette knife paintings discussed later.

Fig. 3

Easels

An easel should be rigid and capable of taking the size of canvas or board on which you want to paint. It is useful if you can vary the height, you can then work more easily on different parts of the picture. In the studio you want an easel which can take a larger picture than you would normally work on outdoors. The studio easel illustrated at the left of **fig. 3** will take a maximum canvas size of 195.6cm (77in). I do not know who designed this easel in the first place, it was long ago, but it remains the universally accepted pattern for a studio easel – it is firm, not too heavy and can be folded up. I have painted larger pictures on such an easel with an arrangement of hooks and string to hold it rigid!

When you go out painting you will need a lighter weight easel. The one shown at the right of **fig. 3**, which I have known for many years, is the best available. It has the great advantage that you can sit or stand to paint (many portable easels do not allow you to do this) and will take a maximum canvas size of 127cm (50in). The head which holds your canvas or board at the top is reversible (one side is smaller for boards, the other is wider to hold canvases). In windy weather, a string hanging from the centre, on which I hang my paintbox, ensures that the easel is perfectly rigid. Both these easels tilt so you can have your picture at an angle which does not reflect the sun.

RANGE OF COLOURS

You should skim through this page in the first instance, but refer back to it frequently. I have divided colours into groups denoting different degrees of usefulness. On the whole, it is better to use a small range of colours and explore what you can do with them. Devices such as a colour wheel will show you how you can get a surprising variation of colours with relatively few paints. Use another colour only when it becomes essential: i.e. the only red on your palette is Cadmium Red and you wish to paint a purplish-red object, so add Crimson Alizarin.

The basic colours

Flake White or Titanium White: Flake White has been used since time immemorial; it dries more quickly and has more body. I prefer it, but many of my friends prefer Titanium White. When I refer to White, I mean Flake White.

Yellow Ochre: This is a general purpose yellow. When mixed with White, it will become quite a bright yellow. It is a very useful colour in almost all mixtures.

Cadmium Red: This is a pillar-box type of red, which is necessary not only for red objects but also for warming up things (see pp. 76–77).

Viridian (Monestial Green): This is probably the most difficult colour to handle, but green is essential on your palette. Sometimes you want to make something greener, rather than bluer or blacker. Mixed with yellows, Viridian can make a lovely series of different greens.

French Ultramarine: This is the best general purpose blue.

Ivory Black: This is the blackest black. Think of it as a colour, not a darkening agent. Remember that Impressionist artists like Monet found it essential for most of their lives.

Colours which are sometimes necessary

These are colours which you will often find essential. For example, it is difficult to paint a lemon if the brightest yellow you have is Yellow Ochre.

Lemon Yellow or Cadmium Yellow: These will produce much brighter yellows in mixtures.

Crimson Alizarin: This purplish-red is sometimes essential, but a difficult colour to handle because it is apt to get into everything. Try using it and you will see what I mean.

Burnt Sienna: This is the best universal brown.

Cobalt Blue: It is hard to describe the difference between this and French Ultramarine, but I find Cobalt's gentleness generally more useful.

Cobalt Violet: Though you can make a violet with red and blue, this is sometimes necessary.

Colours which are sometimes useful

Cadmium Orange: This is a real orange colour.

Light Red: This strong brownish-red can be pleasant, but it is difficult to handle.

Coeruleum: Personally, I very seldom use this, but many of my colleagues find it essential.

Raw Umber: This is the fastest-drying colour and is an excellent colour for underpaintings.

Terre Verte: This is a gentle green which many people find useful when painting portraits.

Cobalt Green: A green which is not as harsh as Viridian.

This palette is set out from light to dark, for a right-handed artist. Note how much paint is put out

SETTING OUT YOUR PALETTE

It is important that you develop habits which save you time. The most obvious of these is to set out your palette in exactly the same way and to put each colour in exactly the same place each time. When I paint, I do not have to look to see where French Ultramarine is, my brush automatically goes to the same place. (Imagine a good pianist, his fingers go to the particular note he wants because he knows where it is without thinking.) In this way, I can concentrate on how much of that colour I want to take. Another point – this habit is helpful when you are working outdoors in a bright light or indoors in a dim one. It is very easy to confuse colours in such lights, thus wasting your time.

There are many ways of setting out your palette, but remember these basic rules. Any method you use should work with your kind of painting and should remain unaltered unless you make a major change of style. It should be sensible – do not go in for odd arrangements just because you think they look pretty on the palette; your palette is where the real work takes place. When you put a stroke of paint on your canvas, it should be the colour you intend, you should have worked it out to the best of your ability at that moment. Do not put colours on the bottom edge of your palette (the lowest edge in the illustrations). It is very hard to pick up the exact amount of colour from this area. Try it out for yourself and you will see that you will have to hold your brush in a different way and concentrate on picking up the colour. Even then, if your brush is splayed out, you will discover it is impossible to be accurate.

At the bottom of these two pages you can see two useful layouts which are the most helpful for you. On p. 60 you will see that the colours are set out in order from white to black (light to dark). In the corner is green, the warmer colours are on the top edge, the cooler colours (green, blue and black) are on the left. This is a useful layout if you are a tonal painter, i.e. tone holds your paintings together. I was shown this way when I first became a student and I have used it ever since. Note that the palette below is set out for a left-handed painter. I am left-handed and many artists I have encountered are left-handed. The big difference in layout is that white comes in the middle and this layout is more useful if your main interest is in colour rather than tonal relationships. At the top are the warm colours (the lightest nearest to white) and at the side are the cool colours (again, the lightest nearest to white). If you favour this system, are more interested in colour and are right-handed, just reverse the whole thing and put the white where the green is in the photograph on p. 60.

This is an alternative method of setting out a palette, this time as a left-handed artist would do it. White is in the middle, warm colours are at the top and cool colours are down the side

CHOOSING YOUR SUBJECTS

Still Life with Mirror, 63.5 × 76.2cm (25 × 30in). Collection of Vera Taylor

Brown Field, 20.3 × 25.4cm (8 × 10in)

In the first instance, choose a subject at which you like to look but, broadly speaking, there are four main areas of subject from which you can pick: still life, landscape, people and imagination. I have added palette knife painting as a fifth 'subject' because some beginners find they are a little timid or mean with paint when working with brushes. Whatever the subject, make sure it has a number of different coloured objects in it and it is not too simple. Paint the objects large; if they are too small you will have difficulty in manipulating the paint and the correct placing of each touch of paint becomes too important (see the two drawings at the bottom of the page).

Still Life with Mirror: Try painting objects you have just left on the table at the end of breakfast. Do not set up special still life arrangements. In this painting I wanted to explore tone – everything in the mirror is a little darker than it is in nature. I did not spend a long time setting it up but rather let the reflections in the mirror dictate the design. Note the size of the objects in relation to the canvas – they are quite big.

Brown Field: Try painting the view from a window of your home, *whatever it is like*. You will not have the problem of flies on a hot day or rain on a dull day. Even a brick wall can be interesting to paint. In *Brown Field* I did not bother at all about the design, but I was bothered by flies! I drew in a few lines to indicate the edges of the fields or clumps of trees and then started to paint. I worked out the relation of each colour to the one next to it in the landscape.

The subject as shown below on the left would be fun to paint, but unless your board or canvas is very large the details of the town would be too difficult for a first painting (each object would be too small). I suggest that, given this subject, you paint the area within the dotted lines. The diagram on the right shows the scale of the objects as they could be on your board

Miko Russell: If you want to paint people, get a friend to sit for you, but make sure he will not mind whether or not the resulting painting bears any resemblance to him. However much you may think a good likeness is essential, it is a problem to tackle later, when you have done a few paintings. Paint either a head or a figure in a setting. For the former you can work out the head in some detail, but in the latter keep the head and hands very simple. Miko Russell is a well-known musician and singer. I painted this in an Irish singing pub between bouts of tin whistle playing by Miko. This was one of the best exercises in concentration I have ever had! Note that I bothered a lot about the character of the head, but not at all about the painting of the jersey and the background, except to establish the colours.

Adam and Eve: Almost all the teaching in these pages is concerned with observation and developing your visual imaginative responses – with painting from nature. Some of you will want to work from imagination. It is best to work from some sketches, however slight these may be, in which you think out the design you wish to paint. If this can be done from nature, so much the better. Try to think of variations on your theme and, better still, paint on several versions at once. *Adam and Eve* is a remarkable painting for an amateur artist. It is very well thought out in terms of design and took a long while to paint. It is large, and even if you think it is ambitious for a beginner, it is a good model for you to study.

Provençal Landscape: With a palette knife it is essential to ensure the scale of the objects is not too small. You must not fiddle and you will find it difficult to do so with a knife. A detailed description of painting with a knife is on pp. 98–101. Here, I want to get across the idea of it being a useful but different way of approaching your subject, rather than discuss how it is done. Painting with a knife lends itself to certain subjects more than others. This you must find out for yourself; I have some friends who paint every subject with a knife. It is useful to the beginner who gets bogged down or finds all his colours are rather muddy.

Your first painting: It is much better to 'have a go', to put down some paint and not bother whether you are doing it the wrong or right way. Gradually try to pick up good habits because they enable you to concentrate upon the ideas you want to express, but do not make a fetish of them. They are a means to an end, not the end itself. Draw your picture on your board with one colour (not black or white) and then paint.

Miko Russell, 45.7 × 35.6cm (18 × 14in)

Adam and Eve, by A. E. Webb, 91.4 × 121.9cm (36 × 48in). Collection of *The Artist* magazine

Provençal Landscape, 25.4 × 35.6cm (10 × 14in)

LET'S START PAINTING

Fig. 4

Fig. 5

These are the sort of diagrams you will find useful. Do not fuss about them, do not show them to anyone, but regard them as private notes

DRAWING WHEN YOU PAINT

I believe that it is important not to worry about learning drawing skills before you paint. I am so insistent about this because more beginners worry about this than about any other subject when I meet them for the first time. I believe it is much more useful to develop skills as you go along because they become necessary. In other words, when you cannot improve any more until you do something about your drawing; then take time off from painting and make careful drawing studies. However, there are ways of using drawings to save you time which I want to discuss here.

Before you start painting you need to decide upon the extent of the subject you want to depict, and the shape and size of your support. Vary the size that you paint unless you have to produce a picture of a particular size (i.e. for a friend or an exhibition). Ideally, you should paint a small picture and then a large one. You will learn from both.

Make a diagram, rather than a drawing, on any old scrap of paper. **Fig. 4** shows a diagram I have made to sort out some points on the back of an old envelope. I drew the subject very roughly, looked at this diagram and decided I would concentrate as much as I could on the three objects. I drew in the lines of the shape of the painting board I had in mind and began to look more carefully at the shapes of the objects. You can see where I have 'looked' by the slightly heavier lines. Sometimes make several diagrams, thinking of different shapes; for example, whether you will paint an upright or horizontal painting.

On occasions you will find your subject seems to dictate a particular shape immediately. Even when this is so, have a look at it in other shapes. For example, a square painting is unusual but sometimes just what you want. At other times you will find you just do not know – then choose a shape arbitrarily and see what happens. In painting nothing is as useful as your own experience, but remember that a shape you find most unattractive on one occasion will on another prove to be the perfect answer – experience must always be tempered by experiment.

Both the diagrams on this page are slight. I am trying to use them as aids to thinking, not bothering about how good they may or may not be. Perhaps the marks made in the still life with a jug (**fig. 5**) show more clearly how I have changed my mind. Note how I have altered the upright lines, gradually bringing them in much closer. By the time I had finished this diagram I was clear on what I wanted to do and was able to move on to the painting. Both drawings led on to paintings illustrated later.

Once you have used your diagrams to decide the extent and shape of what you want to paint and the size of the

Fig. 6

board you are going to use it is time to move on. Of course, you will gain something if you make your diagram into a careful drawing, but it is better, having solved the problems you set yourself, to start on the painting. A lot of nonsense is talked about how to draw on your board before you paint. In **fig. 6** you can see that I have run the whole gamut. On the left I have drawn in pencil, gone on to charcoal in the middle and then used one colour, French Ultramarine, and turpentine on the right.

Charcoal drawing like this is not a good way of proceeding. First, on a board with any grain or 'tooth' it is inaccurate. Does the thickness of the tree trunks I have drawn in charcoal extend to the edge of the charcoal mark, or is the tree described by the inside of the mark? Secondly, when you paint over such marks the charcoal is picked up by your paint, which immediately becomes grey. If there is a lot of charcoal the change of colour can be very marked. Some people try to 'fix' their charcoal drawing with fixative or by drawing over the charcoal lines with a sable brush dampened with a little colour and turpentine. Using fixative in this way is technically a bad method, whilst the latter is most laborious.

Drawing with a pencil, as in the left of **fig. 6**, is possible but not a good practice because the strong pencil lines will strike through the painting in the course of time. By far the most useful way of proceeding is as I have done in the right of the drawing, using one colour and turpentine.

Many beginners seem reluctant to draw in this way on their board, but with practice it can be fun as well as efficient. When I am painting outdoors or when I am concerned most about colour, I find it helpful to draw with French Ultramarine or Cobalt Blue. You can vary the colour you use as long as you do not use Ivory Black because it dries too slowly and White or Yellow Ochre because they are difficult to see. A nice alternative is to mix blue with red, which will give you a cool or warm grey.

When painting indoors, or when I am working on a picture in which the design is particularly important, I use Raw Umber because it dries more quickly than any other colour and does not interrupt the subsequent layers of paint applied on top.

The secret is to paint with a thin sable, using lots of turpentine, to put the lines down firmly and, if they are incorrect, to alter them with a rag moistened with turpentine. You can learn to draw by taking things out or pushing them around with a rag.

Do not mix White with your colour for your preliminary drawing. Use the colour and turpentine only.

PAINTING IN TONE WITH ONE COLOUR AND WHITE

Tone is the difference between the light and dark of objects when compared with each other. It is one of the qualities which you have to take into account when you mix up each colour. The others are the hue (red, green, blue or black) and the temperature (the relative warmth or coolness of objects compared with each other – this is discussed in some detail on pp. 76–77. When you mix up your colours on your palette it is a good plan to ask yourself three questions: What is the hue of the object? What is the tone of it compared with the surrounding objects? What is its relative warmth or 'coolth'?

Sometimes it is helpful to do exercises in which you deal with just one of these qualities; such as painting everything in three tones: light, half-tone and dark. The still life above has been painted in this way – compare it with the illustrations on pp. 68–69. I used Raw Umber, Flake White and turpentine. I put out on my palette large quantities of White and Raw Umber. I mixed some of each to produce as near a half-way house between the two as I could (**fig. 7**). Using these three tones, I painted the still life. It is a little stark but it is a useful way to sort out the main changes in what you paint.

A progressive exercise from this is to mix up five equal tones (White, a new half-way house, the half-tone, a new half-way house, Raw Umber). The most difficult exercise of all is to construct a scale of nine tones, the difference

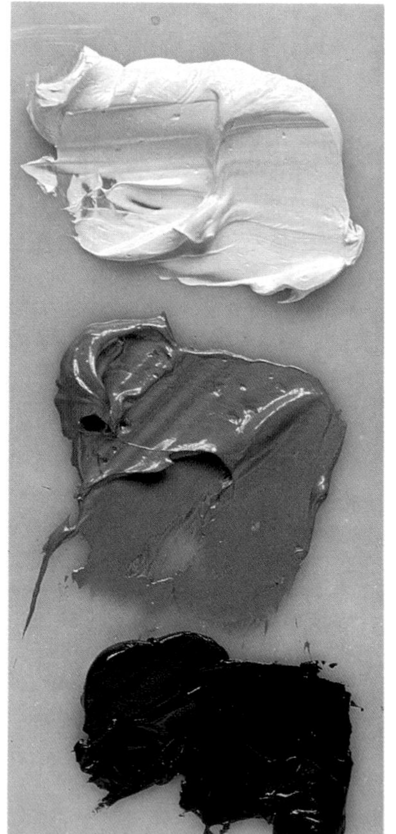

Fig. 7

Devon Landscape, 25.4 × 35.6cm (10 × 14in)

between any two being the same as the difference between any other two. It is worthwhile doing this.

To return to the present exercise, you will find it makes you very aware of shapes. Some of you will discover that you rather like shapes, others may well be aware that the way objects become less distinct in contrast with each other as they move away from you (atmospheric tone) interests them much more.

If you examine *Devon Landscape* you will notice that I have varied the tones considerably – there are many more than nine tones and I have paid particular attention to small changes between one object and another. I used French Ultramarine and Flake White in this painting to emphasize that tone is *not* the difference between the colours black and white, but is the difference between dark and light. Get used to thinking of black and white as colours. You can darken or lighten most hues, but it is obviously difficult to lighten pure Flake White and darken pure Ivory Black. I am not indulging in semantics but trying to explain what is meant by tone.

Going back to the basic colours I have described on p. 60, there are some general rules about lightening and darkening colours. You can darken Flake White with every other colour; darken Yellow Ochre with Cadmium Red, and lighten Ivory Black with everything except French Ultramarine (you would notice scarcely any difference if you mixed these together). For some of you, this will appear to be unnecessary theory but I would like you to grasp the importance of it when painting. For example, when you look at a landscape trees which are the same colour appear paler as they go away from you. There is a difference between the light and dark side of the trees in the foreground of *Brown Field* on p. 62; note how some of the distant hills are lighter in tone.

An awareness of tonal differences and an ability to paint in tone can be one of the most interesting aspects of painting. A judicious placing of tones can hold your picture together.

If you compare the tonal patterns of *Devon Landscape* and *Still Life with Blue Mug*, you can see the great difference in subtlety. If you place a dark on a light the contrast is stark, but if you place a dark accent in a half-tone area and make some gentle changes around it, the effect is more interesting. Suddenly you can emphasize a point by making a harsh contrast, such as the dark tree against the light wall on the left.

Tone is the difference between the light and dark of objects when compared with each other.

STILL LIFE STUDIES

Fig. 8

Every touch of paint has been considered. The final painting has been done on top of this

Fig. 9

Only the general mid-tone of each colour has been considered

A SIMPLE STILL LIFE

Not everyone likes to work in the same way. Here are two ways of starting a still life, both of which you have met before. What you have learnt on the previous two pages should be of help now. Remember, both methods are equally good and the one you use will be dictated by personal feelings rather than anything else.

In the painting in **fig. 8**, first I did a light tonal drawing in Raw Umber and turpentine. Then I mixed up my colours on my palette. I used a different brush for every change of every colour and mixed everything I was going to use. In each case I mixed a small quantity, not enough for use, but enough so I could see clearly what each colour looked like against the others. The purpose of this was to compare the colours I was mixing away from the objects and distractions such as drawing – was I on the right lines or should everything be slightly changed? At this point, it is very easy to start again, but later this is not so.

Then I began to paint, starting in the middle where a number of objects were adjacent to each other. I put down a small touch of the dark blue edge of the jug and placed against it a touch of the white of the cloth. Against that, the yellow of the cloth, then I placed a brown stroke – the edge of the plate. Quickly I moved over to the dark edge of the saucer and on to the lighter bit of the saucer, until I reached the dark shadow at the back of the cup. On this I placed the lighter brown of the cup. I built the painting up in this way (the finished painting opposite was done on top of **fig. 8**). Every touch I put down was important and I tried to make it the right colour in the right place.

The beginning in **fig. 9** has been done slightly differently. Very lightly, with a sable and Raw Umber, I drew the outline of the shapes of every object (these have been covered up by the paint). As carefully as I could, I mixed the general colour (the mid-tone) of each object. Finally, I painted these in quite swiftly. Every artist uses this method of painting from time to time, including myself. The only difficulty is that it presupposes you can judge the exact mid-tone – a feat that most beginners would find hard, but it is a good way of working which some of you will like. The next step is to paint the darker and lighter colours on to this mid-tone.

Opposite is the completed still life. I have worked deliberately and carefully and have tried to paint as close to nature as I could – putting touch upon touch, slightly modifying each area.

I used the basic palette – Flake White, Yellow Ochre, Cadmium Red, Viridian, French Ultramarine and Ivory Black – with the addition of Lemon Yellow so I could

Still Life with Blue Mug, 17.8 × 25.4 cm (7 × 10in)

make a brighter yellow. Please note that I have not used any brown and the Raw Umber has been used only in the underpainting or drawing. **Fig. 10** shows how I have obtained some of these colours. In each 'object' illustrated you will see there is a dark and light mixture, and in two cases, three. You will be able to see more than these in the still life. Study the mixtures I have made and practise making up colours in this way. It is surprising what you can achieve by varying the proportion of colours – often it seems you have made something quite new.

Mix colours on your palette, not your painting.

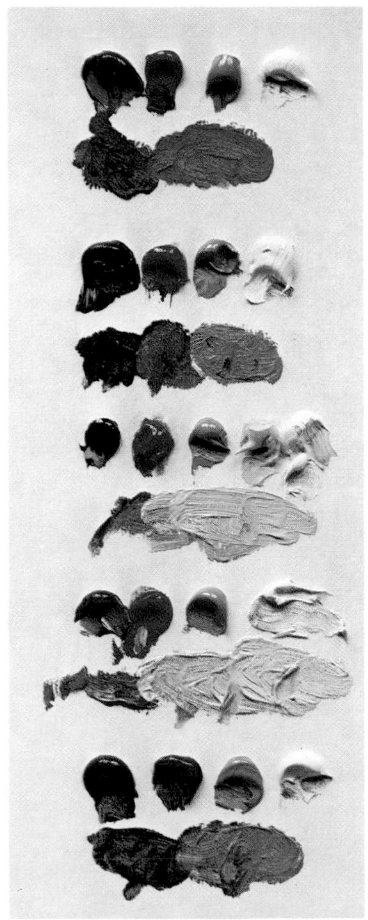

Fig. 10

Fig. 11

A MORE COMPLEX STILL LIFE

Remember the small diagram of a still life on p. 64? I would like to go a little further with that. **Fig. 11** is an underpainting which was done with Raw Umber and turpentine. I started by drawing coarse outlines of the jug, the edge of the cloth and the pot with a hog brush to see if I had got the scale right (I did not copy the diagram directly). When I liked this I began to develop each object a little more carefully. I used a rag dipped in turpentine to help me get the shape of the objects more accurately – you can see this in the apple nearest the front of the picture. I use this type of underpainting to have a good look at the subject – to notice what some objects are like against each other. I painted this in the evening by artificial light; shadows are particularly difficult in such a light and I wanted to think about them in advance.

This is not an accurate tonal painting (the apples are much too light against the cloth, for example), but a development from the diagram on p. 64 observing everything with greater intensity.

Generally, I start with the lightest colours, in this case the cloth, because they are nearest to white. I mixed the colour in the area just above the apple and below the brown bowl. Fix on a specific place and do not make a generalized colour. For the cloth, I used White, Yellow Ochre, Ivory Black and a touch of Cadmium Red. Later I added a little blue.

Then I went on to the apples. Both the warm and cool apples have been made with the same mixture of colours – Yellow Ochre, Cadmium Red, Crimson Alizarin (a touch), Viridian and White, but in different proportions. For the bowl I have used the same colours, with French Ultramarine instead of Viridian. Finally, I painted the jug with Viridian, French Ultramarine, Yellow Ochre, Ivory Black and White.

For each object I have mixed up three or four distinct colours, every time using a different brush; at this stage I was holding 12 brushes. Some of the colours were very similar – for example, two of the greens; and as I went on I used the same brush for more than one object. The purpose of so many brushes at the beginning is to try to analyse each colour clearly. If there are traces of other colours on your brush it is very easy to get muddled when you want to mix up a particular colour again. I added Lemon Yellow and Crimson Alizarin to the basic range of colours, and did not use Raw Umber as a colour. Some people will suggest that it would have been much easier to paint the bowl if I had used Light Red, but it is not an easy colour to handle, it is apt to get into everything in your palette, and we would never have found that such a rich brown could be made from those basic colours and Crimson Alizarin.

On the second evening I started painting from the centre

Fig. 12

Still Life with Green Jug, 27.9 × 25.4cm (11 × 10in)

(the dark at the base of the green jug), gradually working out. In **fig. 12** you can see the point I had reached by the end of the evening. If you compare this with the final version you should note that the yellow cloth in the left foreground is too dark.

The next evening I spent a long time mixing up the same colours I had used before, *even though some were wrong.* You can see these colours in **fig. 13**. Practice in mixing up colours exactly is probably more helpful to the beginner than anything else – not as an abstract exercise but as a way of learning how to judge colours accurately. Then I went on with the painting. The following night I repeated the mixing and finally produced the finished painting you see above.

Think on your palette, put the results of your thoughts on the canvas.

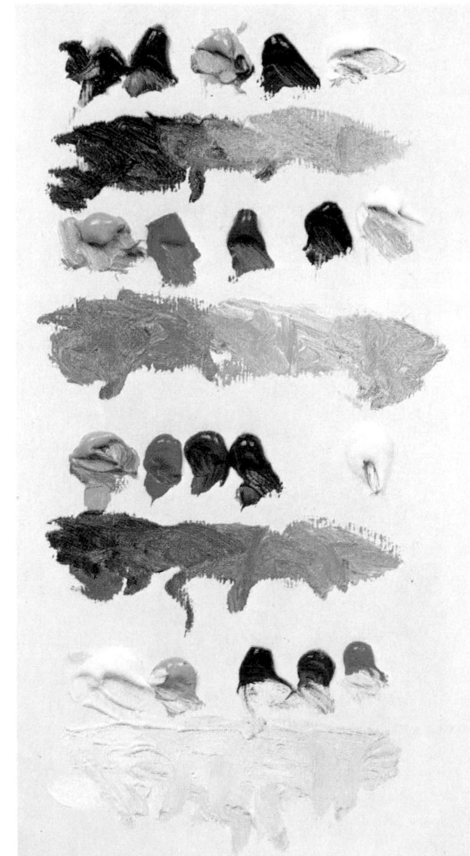

Fig. 13

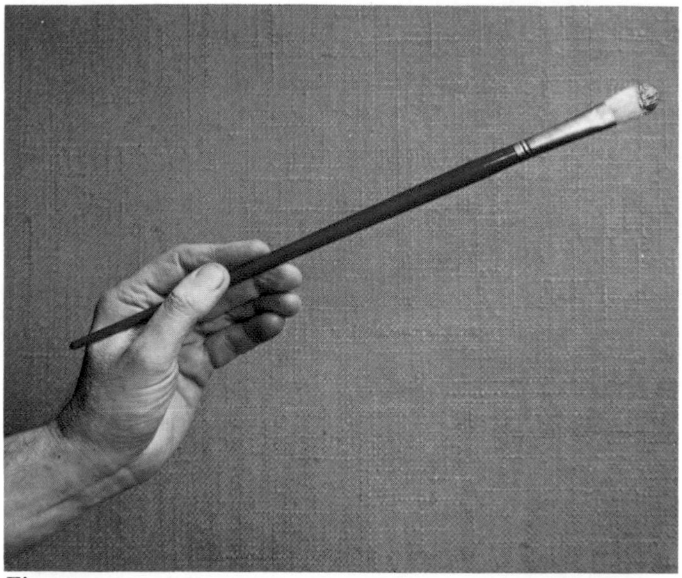

Fig. 14

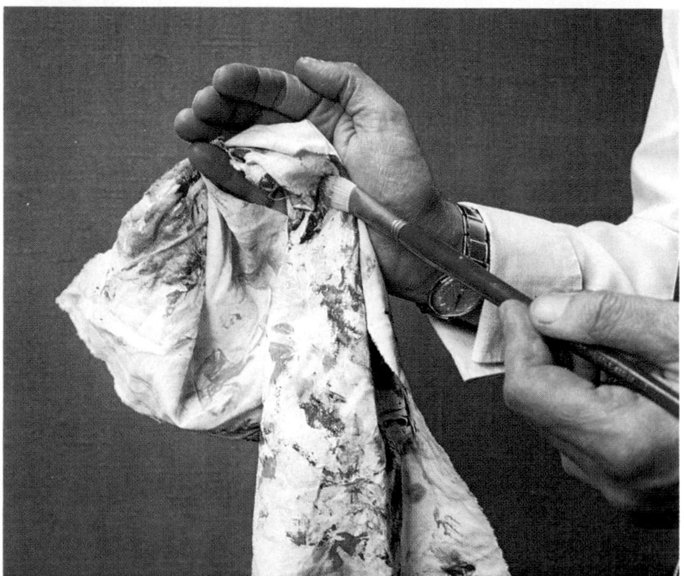
Fig. 15

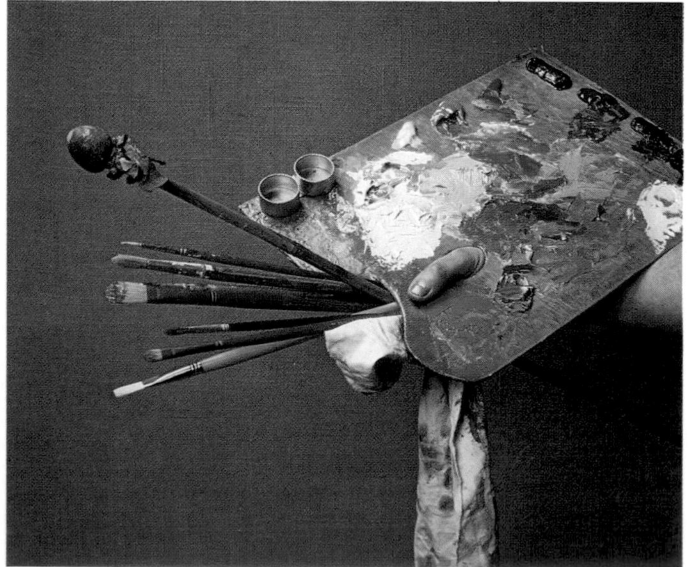
Fig. 16

BASIC TECHNIQUES

On these four pages are a few basic techniques you should master.

How to hold your brush

I like to hold my brush right at the end (see **fig. 14**) because this gives the greatest possible movement. Most of my friends prefer to hold their brush about half-way down the handle. Whatever you do, do not hold it on the ferrule near the bristles; easy movement is restricted and you will find yourself getting so near to your picture you cannot see more than a small portion of it and you will tend to hunch your back, which is bad for posture. Work with your arm extended as much as possible, this ensures you are well away from the picture and you will be able to see it as a whole and judge one part against another. Gainsborough used brushes 1.5 metres (5ft) long; I find it helpful to use 1-metre (3ft) brushes when working on large paintings.

How to use your paint rag

I mind very much about using brushes in good condition, but I have painted with brushes in an appalling state – they were loaned to me! I have never painted without some rag, even if it meant tearing off my shirt sleeve. The rag, which should be of cotton, not man-made fibre, is held looped over the little finger of the hand holding the palette. Use it by picking up part of the rag with a brush, putting it into the palm of your hand, closing your fingers around it and drawing out the brush (see **fig. 15**, but remember that I am left-handed). This has two functions: to clean your brush, in which case your fingers enclose the rag and brush firmly, or to bring paint down to the tip of your brush by pulling the brush through your closed fingers gently.

How to hold your brushes and palette

In **fig. 16**, as well as brushes and palette, I am holding a piece of rag and a mahl stick (this is rested on the edge of your canvas so that your painting hand with a brush in it rests on it; you can then put a tiny dot of paint in the exact place even if your hand trembles). At first when you try to hold your palette and everything else you will find it uncomfortable, but you will soon find it is more practical.

How to look after your brushes

At the left of **fig. 17** are three brushes which have been rinsed in turpentine and then washed with household soap and water. The best way to get brushes thoroughly clean is to put some soap on the bristles and scrub them in the palm of your hand under running cold water (make sure you thoroughly rinse out the soap). The brushes will splay out after some use. To get them back to a decent shape, wrap the bristles with lavatory paper whilst they are still wet (centre brush) – as the paper dries it contracts and pulls the bristles back into shape. The brushes on the right have been subjected to this treatment and you can see how nice they look. Incidentally, the brushes on the left are clean, but have become a little stained with a dye colour. If you take care of your brushes they will last a long time.

Fig. 17

How to stack your canvases

Do bother with your boards and canvases, both when they are new and after you have painted on them. When new, stack them as shown in **fig. 18**; so it is easy to see the sizes. You want to avoid bar marks on your canvas. If the canvas is good quality, you can get out damages by dampening the area of damage on the back; if the canvas is cotton it is impossible to get out such damages. When you have painted on canvases do not stack them face-to-face, but facing the wall at a slightly steeper angle, to avoid spoiling the edges of your picture.

Fig. 18

Palette shapes

Below are the two most sensible palette shapes you can get. The oblong palette (**fig. 19**) comes in a variety of sizes. Very small ones are not useful because there is not enough room on them on which to mix up your colours. The best size is 35.6 × 22.9cm (14 × 9in). The studio shape palette (**fig. 20**) comes in one size, 61cm (24in). It is curved so you do not have to stretch too far to reach your paint and to make it easier to hold. When you first buy a palette rub linseed oil into it for a few days before using it and when you clean it at the end of a day's painting. This stops the paint sinking in and gives you a nice surface on which to work. Flexible plastic palettes and 'tear-off' palette pads are also available, but these are not so good, except that they save you trouble when cleaning up.

Fig. 19

Fig. 20

Fig. 21

Fig. 22

Thick and thin paint

One of the great joys of oil paint is that you can work with it thickly or thinly. From the outset you should try to take advantage of this. Ideally, dark colours should be painted thinly and light colours thickly – they tell more. Every now and again, paint the very light areas as thickly as you can. This will be very obvious in your finished paintings, but you will find that with practice you will be able to make changes in thickness more subtle. If you have painted one area very thickly it is best to scrape it off with a penknife or palette knife if you want to paint over it.

From a technical point of view, you should paint from thin to thick, 'lean to fat' (see **fig. 21**). This is so that the underneath layers of paint dry more quickly than those on top (thick paint dries more slowly). But most people seem to think of thin paint as 'staining the canvas' which can be nice to look at, although it is not a useful way for the beginner to work. It is important that you put enough paint on your board or canvas because this will enable you to see if you are painting the right colour. If you paint too thinly the colour changes because of the drawing underneath.

Applying paint

There are many different ways of applying paint. The most dramatic difference is between using a palette knife and a brush. In **fig. 22** on the left, the brown mark was put on with a knife, all the others were done with a brush. These are your usual tools but you can also use your fingers (when Titian went on with a painting he often used his fingers) or the sharp end of your brush, but not too frequently. There are special fan-shaped brushes for blending edges. If you like using a great deal of paint, house painting brushes are best. There is a whole series of airbrushes, ranging from one that will produce a pencil-thin mark to others which will give a wide band of colour. You could try out some of these tools one day.

Let's return to your more usual implements. Each palette knife will make a different mark because it has a different shape. Broadly, you can apply the paint in thick bands or layers or small, thick touches. When using a brush, remember to keep the paint on the tip, not squeezed half-way down the bristles in an uncontrollable lump. You can put the paint on in very gentle touches when your brush skims the surface and only the paint touches the board. You can scrub it into your canvas with a dry brush; you can cover an area with rapid, thick strokes or slow, deliberate ones. There are only two ways you should not apply paint; as a house painter does, backwards and forwards over the same area, as this tends to make it lifeless and dull; or by mixing colours on your picture, i.e. adding a darker colour to a light one on your canvas and blending them together. Invariably, this will end in an unattractive mud.

Mediums and their uses

There are many mediums you can obtain easily from your local art store. If you look in one of the technical books on painting you will find endless recipes. Please do not use them, they will not help you paint better and most of them demand a complicated procedure which is of little advantage. All the reputable manufacturers make a paint today which is usable as it comes out of the tube. If you need to make the paint thinner (leaner), thin it with turpentine. One word of caution – many people are allergic to turpentine. If you find it irritates your hands or gives you a rash, do not use it. Instead use white spirit, BS 245 (mineral spirit), a petroleum derivative which behaves in a manner similar to turpentine. As you go on with a painting you should use paint with a mixture of linseed oil and turpentine, but never more than 50 per cent linseed oil (linseed oil will make the paint fatter). I tend to use paint with a little turpentine or on its own. Very rarely do I find it necessary to use the linseed oil and turpentine mixture.

When you are working with a dark colour which sinks (seems to go a dull grey colour), it is sometimes useful to revive it with retouching varnish. This brings back the colour you have painted, so you will be able to paint new colour accurately because you can see the old one clearly. Retouching varnish is useful as a temporary varnish for exhibitions. Do not go beyond these simple mediums.

DOES DESIGN MATTER?

On p. 63 I mentioned an excellent imaginative painting, *Adam and Eve*, which is a very good design. Some of you will be attracted to paintings in which the most important attribute is the design. Many European artists have worked in this way and probably the most helpful in this context is Raphael. The artists to whom design was all-important worked from drawings away from the subject. This book is about learning and observing from nature and is written for the beginner. It is easy to say that certain types of design work, and one should teach the principles of these, but all too quickly they develop into stereotypes. My main purpose is to show you ways in which you can advance, ways of criticizing your own work and ways in which you can teach yourself. Such a programme must be based upon *your* personal observations; the trouble with design is that it is based upon taste. It may be taste raised to the highest possible level, a major branch of art, but it is difficult to learn this except from a study of paintings and by reading commentaries or listening to lectures on them. This is helpful but should come a little later in your development. You can learn about design from nature and by criticizing your own paintings.

If you examine the way sea shells seem to go in geometric spirals, the way petals seem to complement each other, and the way one part of a landscape leads you on to another, you will begin to see a certain order; an arrangement of balancing shapes and forms; in short, the design inherent in nature. If you study this you will notice that one group of shapes pleases you whilst another does not and that certain objects make sharp accents that stop the flow of the movement around them. In art it is better to work from what you like than to accept a perfect model. I would like to find that one you happens to like curving shapes that flow into one another, that another you likes sharp, angular forms that jar, whilst yet another you likes variety.

A good design is one which tells the story which you want and makes the spectator understand what you are after. Do not think that I am writing about grand subjects, the rape of Helen and the fall of Troy. I am writing about small things, the silver trunk of that birch tree which shines out from the cool shadows around it, or the warm light which seems to embrace the piece of cloth and the apple on it.

Think of good design as a happy placing of things.

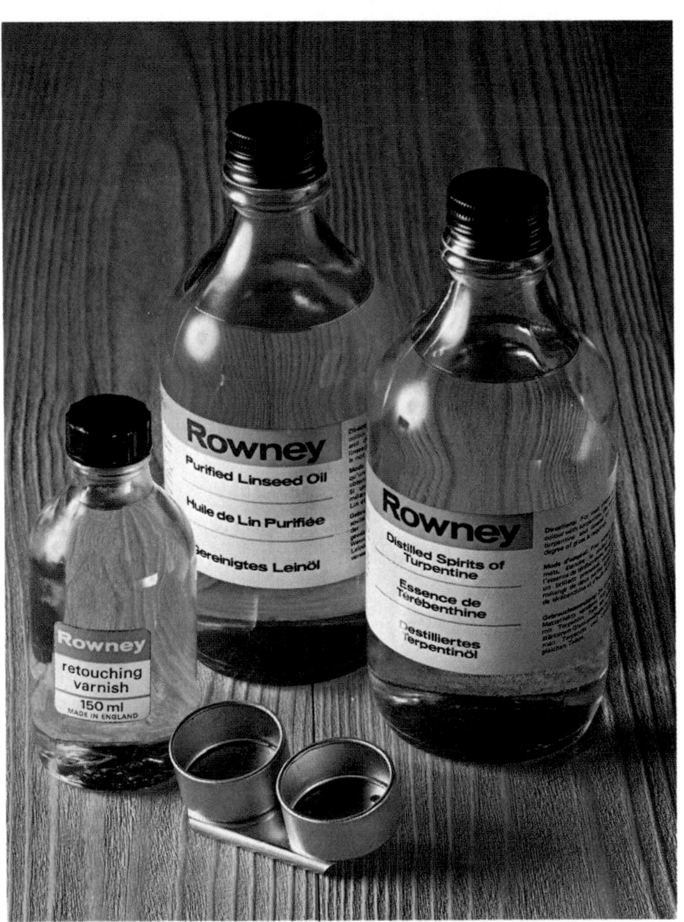

Some simple mediums: linseed oil, which makes the paint fatter; turpentine, which makes the paint thinner, and retouching varnish, which temporarily revives a painting

Fig. 23

Fig. 24

WARM AND COOL COLOURS

On p. 66 I suggested there were three questions you should ask yourself when mixing up a colour on your palette: What is the hue of the object? What is its relative tone? What is its relative temperature? It is an old, well-tried maxim that when painting you should limit your objective, say one thing well and not try to make everything perfect. If you can learn about one thing at a time you have a greater chance of solving that problem than if you try to sort out every aspect. French artists have always accused English artists (I do not think they included the Scots) of endeavouring to paint the perfect picture. Perhaps they were right in the past and you can show them that they are wrong now.

It would not be a bad thing for you to paint the same still life three times, each version devoted to one of the three questions I have suggested you should ask. The term hue is easy and I hope you now understand what I mean by tone. As for the third, the temperature of an object is its warmth and coolness in relation to the surrounding objects.

If you think of warm as going towards red, and cool as going towards blue, you will have made a good start, but do not worry too much if you do not understand the relevance of this. I must confess it confused me greatly as a student. Read through this section and come back to it later. Look at the two illustrations on your left, **fig. 23** is brown, yellow and orange, **fig. 24** is green, blue and grey. The top could be called a warm painting, the bottom a cool one.

In each painting some of the colours are warmer or cooler than others. For example, the yellow jug is not as warm as the orange, but the orange, although it is the most intense colour, is not as warm as the cloth on which it sits – the cloth is much redder. Which would you say is the coolest colour in this painting? It is the right side of the small jug which is a bluish-red. Below, the cloth is not as cool as the blue glass, but is the blue glass cooler than the green bottle? I think it is, because there seems to be a reddish cast in the green. The apple is certainly warmer. The warmest colour is the dirty wall at the back. If you transferred this wall to the top painting it would be the coolest colour there.

I am discussing relative values all the time. It is possible to paint the same subject twice so that each picture looks very accurate but one painting is warm and the other cool. It will depend on the emphasis you place upon certain colours. It is helpful to put up in front of you all the pictures you have painted and try to spot whether they

Lady in Richmond,
55.9 × 45.7cm (22 × 18in)

Irish Landscape,
12.7 × 19.1cm (5 × $7\frac{1}{2}$in)
You can see here how a contrast, the warm roof, sings out against the cool surroundings. Your eye is drawn to that spot immediately

have a tendency to be warm or cool. It is most likely they will be coolish, most painters tend to paint in that direction in the beginning. If this is so in your case, make sure you push the warm colours in your next picture. A good exercise is to set up two still life studies, not too complicated, one predominantly warm and one predominantly cool.

Artists contrast cool and warm colours against each other. I had fun with the quick sketch, *Lady in Richmond*. The red of her jacket, though intense, is not as warm as her cheeks; the blue in the background has a lot of red in it. Even the black hair seems to be a warmish black, but the warmest reds are her cheeks. This makes them much more important. You may think they are too warm for your taste, but I hope the painting gets across the message I want.

The temperature of an object is its warmth or coolness in relation to the surrounding objects.

LANDSCAPES

LANDSCAPE PAINTING ON THE SPOT

This is the first demonstration in which I want to show you a number of stages so you can follow the painting through from beginning to end. I have chosen a landscape because everyone wants to paint the countryside at some time or other, and for many it is the starting off point of their interest in painting. *Distant Hills* is a simple landscape, there are no difficult details to draw and you could handle the painting in many ways. The different stages through which the painting goes were not, in practice, clearly defined, but have been chosen to make a point. The painting, which should be called a sketch, was done on the spot in one sitting which lasted about three hours.

The drawing This has been done with French Ultramarine and turpentine on a white board. When painting landscapes on the spot, I prefer to draw with blue rather than Raw Umber because the colour is sometimes helpful and it does not matter if it grins through. First, I drew in the horizon line and the base of the large central hill. Then I began to work out the lines of the hedges as they came towards me and then the width of the horizontal fields. I put a tonal wash over the distant hill and worked in masses rather than lines. The purpose of this was to establish the main areas of trees and darker tones so that I began to get the sense of the space of the misty landscape onto my board. I wanted to get down the misty light of the sun striking through the clouds. The areas within the light changed so often that it has been more a question of establishing the general 'feel' of the landscape and noting one or two key points, rather than fixing the place of everything. The drawing has been left very loose, as time was pressing and I wanted to mix up my colours.

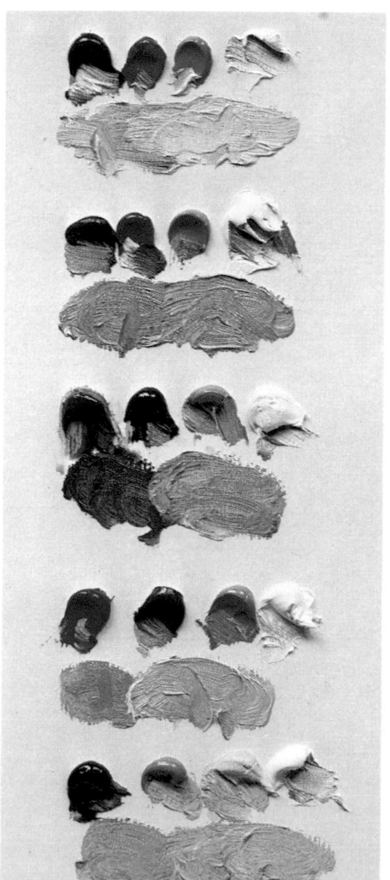

SKY

DISTANT HILLS

NEAR TREES

BROWN FIELDS

GREEN FIELDS

Mixing the colours I cannot emphasize enough that it is on your palette that you mix your colours, it is on your palette that you think and it is on your painting that you put the results of your thoughts. Trouble taken when mixing up your colours is always worthwhile. On the bottom of p. 81 you can see the palette I have used and the order in which I have mixed up the colours. Here I want to discuss the colours rather than the order. On the left you can see some of the mixtures I used. They have not given me all the colours in the painting, but they have given me the range in which I would work. The other colours are variations of these or could be mixed up between these on my palette. At the top of the illustration you can see the colour I mixed for the sky. The mixture for the lighter part in the centre of the sky, at the top, is not illustrated; for that I used White and Yellow Ochre, with touches of French Ultramarine and Cadmium Red. I knew I would start to paint where the sky and distant hills met, carefully relating these together. I mixed up the distant hills next, paying special attention to the differences between the warm and cool colours. All these colours are quite pale, so I turned to the darkest colours, the near trees. Then I made sure I had got the brown fields right, but note that the dark I have mixed up here is too dark. Finally, I did the green fields, but note here that these greens are altered later. I was then ready to paint.

First stage The first colour I put down was the darker part of the distant hill, against which I put the sky. Note that I drew over the hill colour with the sky colour to get the shape right – you can see this on the right. Also note that the blue drawing shows through in several places. Then I began to move towards the front of the painting,

The drawing

First stage

Second stage

putting down blocks of colour against each other, each time endeavouring to put them in the right place. I did not try to finish any one area, but put down a series of 'thoughts' in relation to each other.

Second stage The most obvious difference you will see between the first and second stages is that the sky was taken further and appears much lighter. I painted the areas which I had not touched, and the covering up of the white board makes the previous touches appear lighter, even though they have not been altered. Then I began to develop the sense of distance. For example, if you look beyond the row of green trees in the middle-distance on the right, you will see I have worked a lot at the base of the hill. I have introduced some pinkish blues and modified the dark colours on the hill. Next I worked on the five big fields near you, lightening the greens and changing the colour of the brown field. Notice how many touches of paint are beginning to draw each tree or field a little better.

Final stage Everything has been taken a little further. The clump of trees on the top of the hill were painted and some lighter touches were put into the sky. More paint has been put on the distant hills and all the trees have been modified. I spent most of the time working out the colours and shapes at the base of the large hill because they were very gentle against each other. Also, the subtle changes – a slight change of colour, not tone – were difficult to see in the bright light in which I was painting. (When working outside in a bright light I find a hat with a brim necessary to shade my eyes as I look at the landscape. I hold my palette at an angle so it does not reflect the light.) Small changes such as these can only be worked out in the best place – on your palette.

You can see my palette as it was when I had mixed up all my colours. Remember that I am left-handed; if you are right-handed hold the book up to a mirror and you will see the colours as you ought to set them out. By the time I had finished painting it was not so tidy. Each change of colour or tone I mixed up in the appropriate spot, so there would be various different shades of, for example, sky colour, occupying that space.

At the top of this page there are two details of this painting. The left one shows how the house blends into the surroundings so you do not notice it at first sight. On the right I hope you will see how I have changed an amorphous mass of colours into a group of trees and fields. This is what I mean by drawing – not, you will observe, a linear outline which is filled in.

If you look at the final painting you will see that I have been all over it, slightly changing everything. This is not mere eccentricity but a very useful way of ensuring that you think of each part in relation to the others. You will remember that this picture was painted on the spot in one go, and I cared most about the sense of distance and the misty light. The last few touches, changing the hill and modifying the light below the hill, mattered very much. When you do this kind of sketch always try to give yourself some time at the end so you can make little corrections all over it. Hurry to begin with, paint as if there is no time at all, so you leave yourself time to think of the whole. Do not try to repaint everything; look and see if there is a touch of paint which would help, not so much to complete a detail, but to express the idea more clearly.

Sometimes you need to add red to a green to warm it up.

Final stage

Distant Hills, 22.2 × 30.5cm ($8\frac{3}{4}$ × 12in)

My board was a little too large, so I have put a wash of Raw Umber at the bottom so there was not a glare from the white board. This was cut off with a sharp knife when the painting was dry

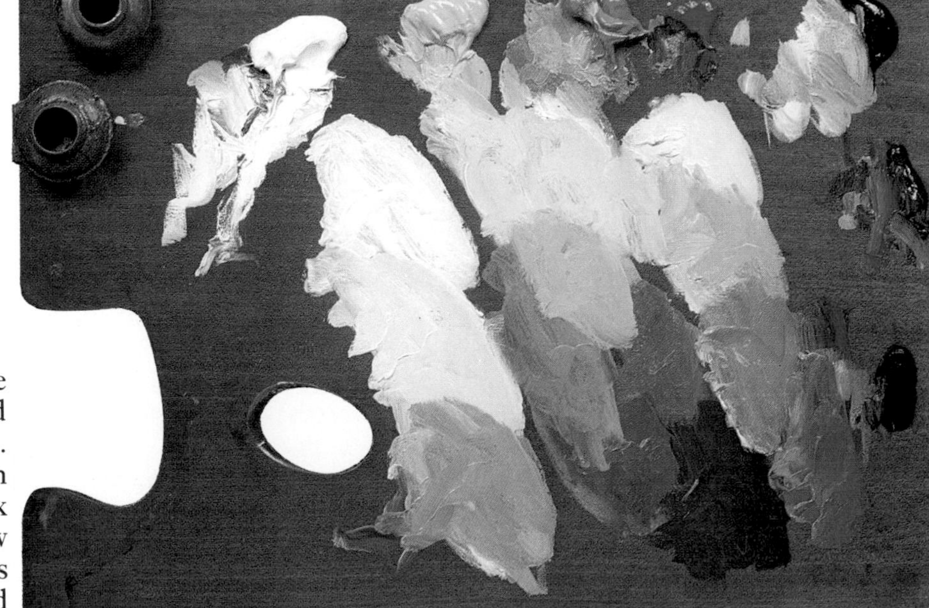

This is what my palette looked like when I had mixed up my colours. Remember that I am left-handed; hold the book up to a mirror to see how you should set out your colours if you are right-handed

A LANDSCAPE TAKEN FURTHER

The previous demonstration was concerned with painting a landscape in one go on the spot. Here I want to discuss taking a landscape painting further, working on it on several occasions. *The Beehive* was painted in four days, starting each day at 3.45 in the afternoon. I also made some corrections when I got the picture back home and I could see it without distractions. Each sitting lasted approximately two and a half hours. It was not possible to photograph the painting whilst it was underway, so I have reconstructed it and painted the stages again. Since I worked on such clearly defined occasions (when the afternoon was waning until it was time for an evening meal) it has been possible to do this accurately.

The drawing The painting was done on a red-brown ground and the drawing on top has been made with French Ultramarine. The main interest of the painting centres on the tree in the left foreground, the field beyond and the hedge on the right. To put this in context I was concerned about what went on behind, for instance, how the movement of the hedges encloses the foreground. Note how I went over the hedges several times in the drawing stage, making a tree on the right follow the shape. I have used a fairly wide brush because I was trying to work out the big shapes rather than paint a lot of details. At the end of the first session I blocked in the sky area quickly with some Flake White.

The drawing stage here was used not only to put the things down in the right place, but also to help me think about the best way to paint the picture. I chose to paint this because I liked what I saw, but it did matter what I put in the painting, i.e. I did not want to include the endless lovely landscape surrounding me but wanted to concentrate on the main subject. This is why there is not more sky. The hills rose up ahead and I was more aware of the landscape than the sky. This may sound a little difficult for you because you may not be as sure as I appear to be about the shape of the painting and what you might want in it. Do not forget that always it is better to make up your mind; to decide one way or another what you would like to have in a picture before you start.

I have heard much talk of 'artistic licence' and that the subject would look much better if you moved a tree or a building just a little way to the left or right. *Please* do not take any notice of this false advice – do not alter what is in front of you. Nature is lovely and it is your business as a painter to understand it – to find the design in what you see, not to think you can improve on it. Also, when you move something you leave a gap which is not easy to fill. It is important that you are able to judge one bit of the painting against another, and it is not a little difficult to do this if you introduce a new feature.

First stage On the second day I spent a long time sorting out the colours. This reconstruction shows the stage I had reached at the end of that day. I do not seem to have pro-

The drawing

First stage

Detail of second stage

gressed very far, but I have been more interested in mixing each colour as I wanted and putting it down very freely. If you compare this with the final painting, it is clear I have been much freer in the early stages than I have been in the final version. Since I was most interested in a special area of the painting and since the way I thought about the hedge demanded working in great detail, the painting inevitably became tighter and tighter.

Do not be afraid of detail or of people who talk about 'knitting'; what they are describing are pictures where every mark and change, every detail can be seen. I would rather say: paint as meticulously as you can – try to look at every blade of grass, every twig and every branch, but always in relation to the scale on which you are working.

The building on the left is, in fact, a grand antique medieval beehive from France. If you compare the first stage with the detail of the second stage and the final painting, you can see that the right side changes tone through the different stages. It is a dull grey in this stage; a brighter yellow in the second stage and brighter still in the final stage. If you paint over a period of four days the light can change – it did very dramatically whilst I worked on this. It is always better to change what you have put down in front of nature because she has changed, unless you believe you have painted an object perfectly. In this case, it was not until the last day I realized how helpful it would be if that building were very light.

The fact that the light changes constantly should be thought of not as a nuisance, but more as a challenge. You should ask yourself: Is the subject I am working on better in a bright light or in a dull glow? In a bright light I could see many details which were hidden; should I have painted them? The distant fields seemed at one moment to be a brilliant brown, and at the next a dull, greyish green; which is correct? All possible permutations of the answer could be right in a picture, but they will not all be correct at the same time (some cancel one another out). It can be fun to choose; painting is not a mechanical exercise in which you follow a set pattern, but an adventure in which you can turn in many different directions, *all* of which are worthwhile.

It would be instructive for you to compare each point in the above stage with the final version. For example, the brown field in the centre background becomes much cooler in the final version, and the field below it becomes more blue and much lighter.

Second stage I have shown a detail of this stage so you can see what I have been doing clearly. Do not forget that it is useful to think of *every* brush stroke as a new idea, requiring you to modify your first mixtures. Has the new brush stroke a little more blue or red (is it warmer or cooler) than your original mixture? Make a decision to go one way or another. The near tree and hedgerow are much too blue, as I went on I noticed that they were much more interesting greens. By now you have probably realized that the correct

Final stage

The Beehive, 35.6 × 45.7cm (14 × 18in). Collection of Chris O'Neill

mixing up of colours is difficult. How often have you said: 'I can see the colour but cannot mix it up.'? Although it is difficult, this is where you should spend the most effort. Always be willing to change anything and always try to put down each colour as correctly as you can.

Final stage This painting aims high in that it forces us to make judgements about detail and subject. It is never useful to aim low; always try to make each picture you paint a little more difficult for yourself – do not fall back on learning how to do it one way. This is very different from *Distant Hills*, but it was painted within a short distance of it. In the detail of this stage (opposite, top) you can see how I have worked hard on the tree, it changes colour many times and the aim has been to sort out the groups of leaves. Carefully I watched where the darker accents in the tree appeared. It is easy to lose your place when you are working unless you fix on a particular spot for each brush stroke. This is even more apparent in the detail of the hedgerow, where you can see I noted the big shapes of the larger bushes and then worked into them (opposite, bottom).

In the left foreground, the muddle of post-and-rail fences caused me much trouble. I found it difficult to see what was happening. I used the tall post between the beehive and the main tree as a key; it caught the light whereas they were in shadow.

I made the large trees in the hedge work as I went along. You can see how I have drawn the branches of the tree by painting the field. In the final painting I have corrected these – do not try to do such details too quickly. It is more helpful to move on from area to area just before you have solved how to deal with each one. Leave the last brush stroke, paint elsewhere and then come back with a fresh eye and see what needs to be done.

You can make lovely greens by mixing black with yellow.

PORTRAITS

The drawing

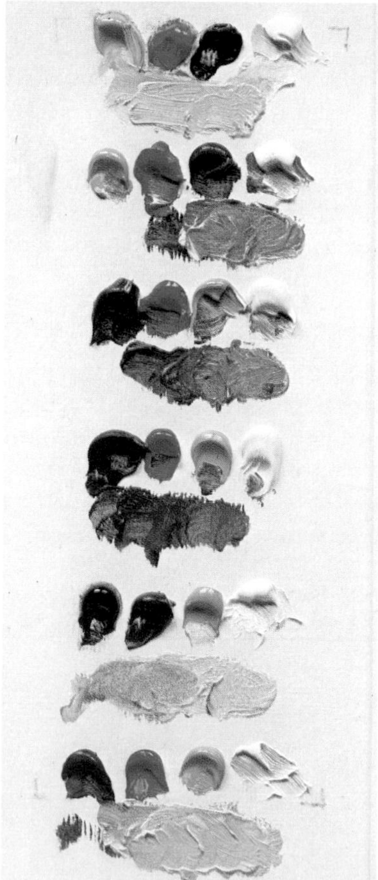

LIGHT FACE

CHEEK

HAIR

CHAIR

WALL BEHIND

T-SHIRT

A PORTRAIT SKETCH

Contrary to popular belief, the way you paint a subject differs only because of your commitment to it, not because it necessitates another way of painting. In other words, you do not approach a landscape any differently than a figure, there is no special way of starting. Because we care more about some subjects than others, we tend to fight shy of those with which we have the least sympathy. I have maintained always that I learn as much about painting portraits when I paint a landscape as I do when I make a special portrait study. Since the kinds of colours in which I am involved are almost complementary (cool reds in portraits and warm greens in landscapes), I find I learn a lot about painting landscapes when engaged in portrait painting. It is true that when I paint landscapes I tend to do it outside, and when I paint portraits I tend to work on them in the studio.

With landscapes, I find it helpful to draw on the canvas in blue, with portraits I use Raw Umber. I have painted many portraits in which I have drawn in blue and landscapes in which I have drawn in Raw Umber, but as a general rule this does not apply because the design of the portrait usually has to be worked out very carefully – more about this later. *Judith* was done in one day – the photographs were taken from time to time when she needed a rest – and is a sketch.

The drawing It can be off-putting to start work on a board or canvas because of its whiteness (here I was working on canvas in the studio). Usually I stain the canvas with Raw Umber diluted with turpentine. I put it on the canvas rather coarsely and very quickly with a large brush. I wipe over it with a rag to make the tone more even and fill in any gaps I have left. Some people prefer to leave this Raw Umber wash more open and varied in tone.

I started the drawing stage by indicating the top of the head with a line, then I went to the edge of the hair on the right. I drew a line down the centre, where her parting would be, to the top of the centre of her forehead. Then I drew a line on the right down the edge of the face on to the chin and up the left side of the face. Quickly I massed in the tone of the hair with a big brush. At this point it is possible to see whether or not you have got the head in the right place on your canvas. If not, wipe it all out with a rag and turpentine and start again. If it appears correct, proceed.

The dark of the eyes (placing these fixed the scale of the head) was done with two coarse brush strokes, followed by the eyebrows, comparing the directions. I put in the line of the shoulders and the edge of the T-shirt around the neck, then came back to the right side of the face and corrected the cheek-bone and edge of the face. I drew in the right side of the nose, then the left, and moved down to the mouth.

Using a large brush, I put in the dark of the chair on the top left and corrected the top of the shoulders. I came back to the mouth, corrected its position and drew the line between the lips. The nose was not right, so I wiped out part of it with a rag and turpentine and then altered the line of the jaw on the left. I moved over to the right side of the face and changed the edge of the cheek-bone.

The purpose of all this was to get the head correctly placed on the canvas, to make the scale in relation to the size of the canvas sensible and to place the features. This is a quick sketch and I wanted to get on with the painting. (The drawing took about 20 minutes.)

First stage

First stage I used a different brush for every tone of every colour. I mixed up all the *basic* colours I was going to use (i.e. I did not bother with the colour of the mouth or the slight redness of the cheek). I put a little touch of each colour on the canvas, starting with the forehead (I have painted this too light), moving to the hair, the eyes and on. Each touch of paint was in the right place (or I should say as far as I could make it so at that stage). Every main colour was put down, sometimes with just one brush stroke. (This took about 20 minutes.)

Mixing the colours You will notice that I have spent as long on the first stage as I did on the drawing, although I have touched the canvas very little. Almost all the time has been spent in mixing up the colours on my palette. I have used the basic palette plus Raw Umber. On my palette, in order, were: Flake White, Yellow Ochre, Cadmium Red, Viridian, Cobalt Blue (instead of French Ultramarine), Raw Umber and Ivory Black. I mixed up the lightest colour of the face with Yellow Ochre, Cadmium Red, Viridian and White. I used the same colours on the cheek but I did try out on my palette the mixture I have shown you, using Cobalt Blue instead of Viridian. The hair was Raw Umber, Cadmium Red, Yellow Ochre and White, and for the chair I used the same series of colours in different proportions. The background used the same mixture as the chair, but without the red and I added Ivory Black to the mixture. I used Cobalt Blue, Cadmium Red, Yellow Ochre and White for the T-shirt.

Second stage

Second stage For the next 30 minutes I worked on everything a bit more. I started to draw the eyes a little better, but did not paint the corners nearest the nose properly. More paint has gone on everywhere. Notes to myself: the drawing of the nose is askew and the corners of the mouth need some attention.

Third stage

Third stage Never work on one area until it is complete at the expense of the rest of the painting. At this stage I was more concerned with getting the surroundings onto the canvas than with improving the face. It is a mistake to think that you can 'fill in the chair' or 'paint the background' whilst the sitter has a rest. You need her there so you can choose the right colours against her face. I sorted out the colours for the hair and began to get the colour of the T-shirt. Always have several tries at an object like a T-shirt; do not mix up the colour and paint it completely. At every stage I worked on the T-shirt a little, slightly modifying the tone or colour until I began to get it to my satisfaction. I corrected the left side of the face and then painted the chair.

It should be clear by now that although I try to put every brush stroke down in the right place, immediately I correct it with another stroke of paint placed beside or on top of it. I cannot emphasize too strongly that you should not use too much medium; you will find you can adjust a brush stroke more easily if you limit the amount of medium you use. (This stage took about 30 minutes.)

Final stage Everything has been taken a stage further, the T-shirt has been completed and the mouth made less disagreeable. Most people worry too much about the likeness; from these few reproductions you can see how the likeness changes and this is achieved by quite small alterations, for example, a touch to the edge of the mouth or the corner of the eye or nose. Try to get the basic structure right and make likeness corrections at the end of the sitting. In this case, Judith, my daughter, was growing tired and somewhat pensive. It would have been possible to make her smile by altering the corners of her mouth (cover them up with your fingers and you will see what I mean). I was more interested in getting her character down than painting her at her prettiest. (This also took me about 30 minutes.)

The sittings lasted just over two hours (she had rests at the end of each stage). It would have been possible to go on further, but if you want to paint a friend do not overdo the time you make her sit on each occasion. When I look back at the final painting there are alterations I would like to make, but what I notice most on the reduced scale you see is that it looks different from the real thing. The final judgement must be upon the painting you have in front of you. Personally, I found it helpful to stop here and leave it alone, but sometimes I like to get the sitter back to make an adjustment at a later date.

You can make orange with yellow and red; and mauve and violet with blue, red and white.

Final stage
Judith, 50.8 × 40.6cm (20 × 16in)

BUILDINGS

I have tried in these pages to write about the sort of subjects that the beginner seems to like painting. Everything is paintable, even a plain brick wall, but you will always like some subjects more than others. Whatever you enjoy painting at the moment, it is quite a good plan to think about buildings, even if your main interest is in landscape – it will be rare if there are not some buildings around. Various details such as the painting of glazing bars, bricks and tiles are of obvious importance when you are painting houses. On this page are two more details you should notice. Chimney pots on the skyline can be a nice accent in a painting. Think of the way they alter the silhouette; even though the large masses of chimney stacks stay the same they vary in shape quite a lot. Although there is not one in the study on the left, may I make a plea for television aerials as they work in a similar fashion. As for telegraph poles, they are even more useful in landscapes because they provide strong perpendicular contrasts against the horizontal countryside, which emphasize the roundness of the trees.

When you are painting chimney pots be careful not to get them too dark in tone against the sky. You see them as dark or light accents and it may be very easy to overdo the strength of this tone or colour. They are small, but you cannot fail to notice them if you get them wrong.

Below the chimney pots is a study of a typical London porch. Both these studies were painted the size they are reproduced because on many occasions they will be this size, or even smaller, in your paintings. Studies of this nature are well worth doing; they do not take long and give you a chance to have a good look. When working on small areas like this I find it much easier to keep the whole thing wet – to paint it all at once. You can see I have corrected the darker strokes of paint by pushing the light colours close up to them. When you paint details make sure the tops of windows and doors are square. Do not let them slope or leave them unfinished. Paint the darks first, then the lights. I work this way with glazing bars and finally correct them with the dark colours. I use a mahl stick and a small brush. I have painted these rather flat without very thick brush strokes. Sometimes it is fun to paint them much more thickly and rather more freely where only parts are indicated, but always make the corners of windows and tops of doors square.

If you look at the detail from *Sussex Landscape* you can see how I have taken trouble to paint the lower window carefully in this way. This is a detail from a larger painting, the rest was trees and bushes and does not concern us here. It was painted on the spot over two evenings. I like painting buildings and trees together this way. In the tree on the left you can see how several touches of the light building were painted on top of the tree – the light correcting the dark, but lower down the bushes were painted over the window and on the right the green leaves were painted on top of the orange building.

This is much more freely painted, with thicker paint than I have used in the two studies opposite. There, I have eliminated almost all the brush strokes. Here I have painted in very definite touches. (I used no medium except to clean my brushes occasionally.) I keep trying to think of useful ways of working which might help you in painting details, but since I try to start painting as if I knew nothing and was seeing the subject for the first time, I can think of none that are useful. Except one overriding idea: Do not try to find an answer which will serve on each occasion, but learn that what is wrong behaviour in one picture can be the only possible answer in another. Every painting must be treated differently, indeed with a detailed subject, if you have worked one way more than once in a painting you *must* find another answer if that problem recurs.

Very often it will be the juxtaposition of a building with a tree which makes a landscape exciting to paint. For example, the particular orange-red I have used for the building on the right works well against the tree. If you saw this painting in tone, in a black and white reproduction, the bush in front would look only a shade darker than the orange-red building. The contrast between bush and building makes sense because of colour, not because of tone.

Red bricks against a green landscape can be difficult to paint because the colours seem to cancel each other out. One distinguished director of the National Gallery was of the opinion that more English landscape paintings were spoilt because of the colour of our bricks than for any other reason. I must agree that I feel most at home when the colour of the building blends into the landscape. But remember from p. 77 that a judicious use of red, a small dot of it, can be useful.

Many people enjoy an urban environment and it is a mistake to feel you must paint only rolling hills and dales. The townscape, buildings around you, are worth looking at. Look at the paintings of Pissarro, Seurat and Lowry; artists as diverse as these have enjoyed such places.

Detail of *Sussex Landscape*, 25.4 × 35.6cm (10 × 14in)

At Home, Looking North was painted out of an upstairs window at the back of my house. It was painted in winter and the view no longer exists; now there is a block of flats and the little bell-tower has been obliterated. I wanted to paint this at that time because I noticed that the fall of snow had changed some aspects of the view – roofs which were dark had suddenly become light. I had always wanted to paint this view, in fact I had looked at it often, but never found a satisfactory way of approaching it, chiefly, I think, because the roofs were too dark. The other point I wanted to make was that I disliked the new building in the foreground. I thought it ridiculous that at the time it was erected it had to have the wooden shed-like structures to house the water tanks, and I wanted to make it look as dull as I felt it to be. Without the little interesting vistas behind the new building I do not think I could have managed the painting.

My point here is to remind you that you can make comments, however tough, however gentle, in painting. Not all of art is about prettiness (think of Goya's horrors of war). For me, the dullness of the front of this painting makes the little details you see further back much more interesting. This is a townscape with a vengeance!

One of the most important things to notice when you are painting on the spot is the design of nature – to take advantage of what is given to you and not try to alter it. For example, the nasty light green bit on the side of the buildings in front happened to be in just the right place to balance the pink curtains in the window of the building behind. The little bell-tower happened to be in the most prominent position it could be and the fact that the roofs were lighter than the sky helped draw attention to the gentle red of the distant buildings.

On your left is a detail of two windows. The curtains were not always drawn the way you see them, but I noticed them like this on one occasion when I was painting. Do alter your painting like this, you should take advantage of a sudden change, not think of it as a nuisance.

Underneath this is a detail of the next street seen through two big walls. On the near side of the street is the snow-laden roof of a black shed. Notice how I have varied the way I have used the paint. The large walls have been painted smoothly and thinly, the shed roof smoothly and thickly, and the houses in the street rather clumsily. When I had first painted them they were carefully done rather like the walls; I wanted much greater contrast and repainted them as you see now. Take advantage of the way you can vary oil paint, you can alter the whole meaning of a passage of paint by the way you put it on your canvas. Incidentally, you can probably see how nasty the paint quality is on the near buildings in the detail opposite.

The spiky, thin shape of the little bell-tower had to be just right. Such details have to be drawn in paint very carefully; a direct contrast to the painting of the street. Beside this and below there is a dark red chimney with a light, pinkish wall above it on the right. The main mass of

At Home, Looking North, 50.8 × 76.2cm (20 × 30in)

houses in the distance is light red. I was trying to have fun looking at all these reds together. I have bothered about the warm colours throughout this painting. All of them have been carefully measured together – a warm, quiet painting which contrasts with a cool green landscape.

I have used the basic set of colours plus Crimson Alizarin, Light Red, Raw Umber and Cobalt Blue, making ten colours in all. This is rather more than I generally use, but I had wanted to make the difference between the reds very clear in this painting. This is an occasion when it is very helpful to use a different brush for every tone of every colour – at one time I found I had 20 in my hand. I took three days over the painting and worked roughly from 10 a.m. until the light went. This is contrary to my usual practice, but as I was looking north on a wintry day the light changed very little.

Do not add black to darken colours. Use black as a colour. There is a difference between a black you make by mixing several colours together and a black pigment.

REFLECTIONS

Over the years I have been fascinated by painting water. At first I enjoyed most the contrast between the actual object and its reflection. I suppose my interest in mirrors is part and parcel of the same thing; I like the slight change of tone. The reflection is a little bit darker in tone, provided the reflection is of the same area as the object in nature – the area that you see. Always be careful if you are painting a reflection of the sky that you paint the reflection and the sky at the same time. It is very easy, particularly in a variable climate, to paint a cloudy sky and find that by the time you reach the reflection the sky is clear, bright blue and the sky and the reflection do not agree.

Since I have been going abroad to hot climates I have found the colours in the reflections of great interest and gradually I have painted less and less of the object and concentrated more and more on the reflection, which has enabled me to keep the colours much brighter. *Collias Reflection* (opposite) is an example of this type of painting. It is a reflection of one of the spans of a large bridge.

I have found it best to do the absolute minimum of drawing because it enables me to keep the colour clear and bright. Below you can see the preliminary drawing for *Gozo Reflections;* the final painting is on p. 97. This drawing was concerned only with placing things approximately. The drawing was made with a large brush, lots of turpentine and French Ultramarine. I have put a wash of colour only where the colours will be darkest. In a hot climate, a drawing will dry very rapidly, and even if you paint with more medium than usual, the paint should not pick up the underneath drawing. The drawing for *Bridge, Moor Park, Surrey* was made with thinner blue lines because the day was cold and I did not think it would dry so quickly. I prefer to do this type of painting on canvases or boards at least 40.6 × 50.8cm (16 × 20in) large. I find I get muddled with the details if I work on a smaller size. On the other hand, I have made studies of the sea and the sky which are smaller, though I have found breaking waves difficult to paint on a small scale.

Painting reflections demands that you get your relative tones right. If you like reflections as much as I do, you will have much enjoyment painting such subjects; if you do not, I recommend you have a try so your appreciation of tone will improve.

Bridge, Moor Park, Surrey is a small painting, the sort

you might well do to see how you get on with reflections. Note how the colour of the bridge becomes much darker and cooler in the reflection whilst the sky does not. It is only a tiny bit darker in tone – I mixed up the sky and reflection together. I used normal size brushes and have not handled it any differently from the paintings we have looked at earlier.

Contrast this with *Collias Reflection*, below, which is larger and more broadly painted. The real secret when painting like this is to sit well back in your chair and paint at arm's length (or stand well back if you prefer). Always use a loaded brush, and whatever you do, do not mix up your brushes. Always paint with the tip of your brush (I know you do this by now; I only remind you because in a moment's aberration you may have forgotten) and you will find you can paint a light colour quite easily over a dark. For example, the touches of yellow have been painted over the green on the left. I had painted this bridge several times and did have the piers in several. If it gives you more confidence, put in a pier at the top.

I find it helpful to paint reflections in one sitting. The time will vary from two and a half to four and a half hours;

Bridge, Moor Park, Surrey,
24.1 × 25.4cm (9½ × 10in)

Collias Reflection,
40.6 × 50.8cm (16 × 20in)

Drawing for *Gozo Reflections*

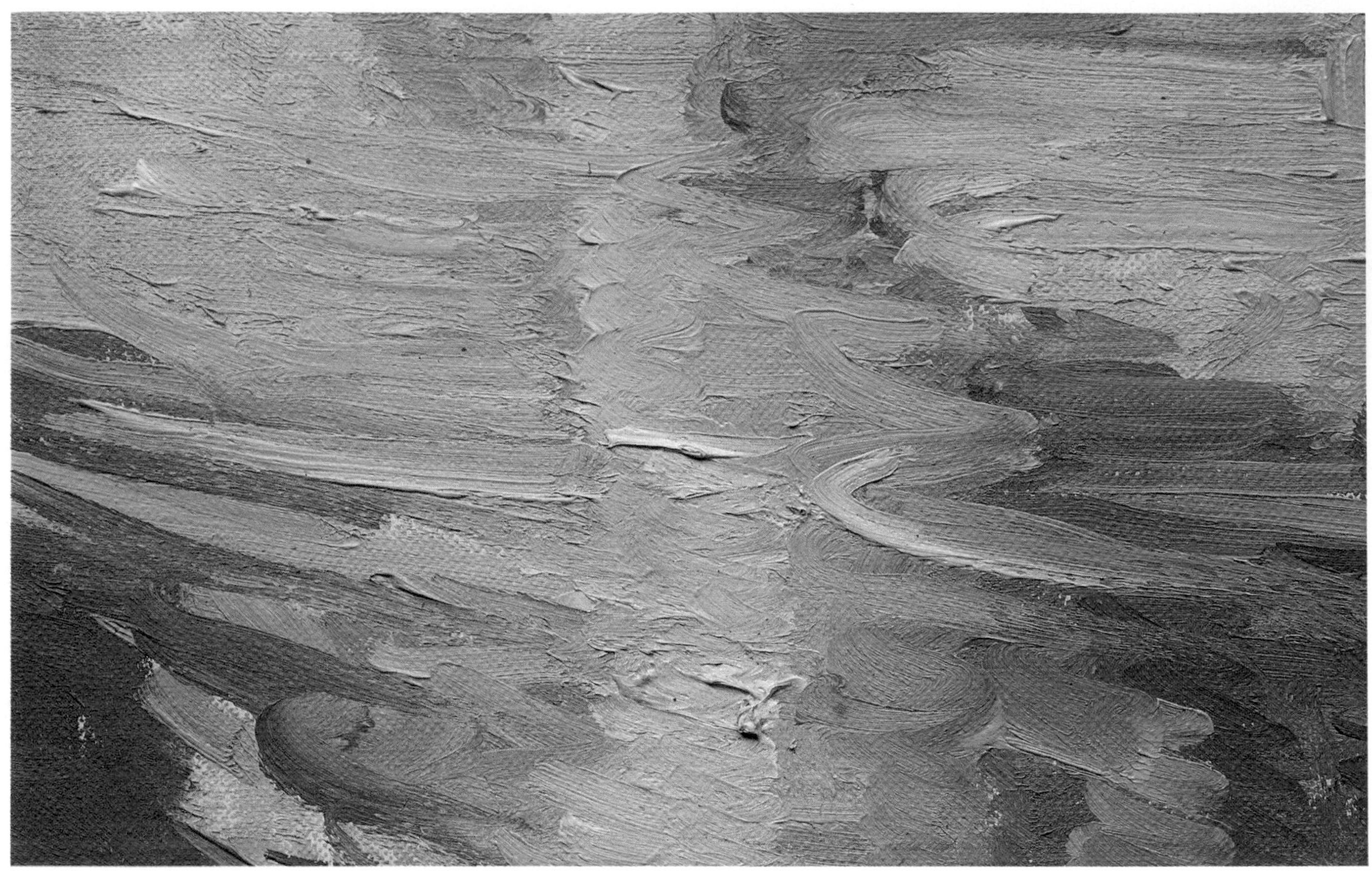

Detail of *Collias Reflection*

I find I cease to concentrate if I work longer than this without a break. Try to have enough paint on your brush so you can work in large, single strokes. Sometimes such a stroke can be a squiggle moving across quite a large area, but you *must not* go over the same stroke. Put your stroke of paint down and leave it alone. If you look at the detail from *Collias Reflection* you can see how I have put down each stroke of paint and left it alone. In the middle of the painting you will see that I have altered the first touches several times, but it is more useful to look at the left side. At the left side of the central area you can see several clear strokes of paint. All of the work has been done like this, some paint had been altered as I went along with subsequent strokes, but the fact remains that this painting has been done by putting down lots of single brush strokes.

I worked at all times with firm brush strokes. I have not filled in areas but have moved across the picture from touch to touch of paint. In the detail you can see that the little dark on the top right corner had been put down first, the light yellow strokes beside this had been put down after and the edges of the dark shape had been arrived at by drawing the lighter colour into them. Of course, the reverse was true sometimes and the dark had been drawn into the light. This is most easily seen in the final painting where the curving lines of light are drawn more firmly by the darks around them. It can also be seen in the left foreground, where the dark greenish colours are drawn into the blue reflection of the sky. I want to emphasize here that drawing and painting become fused, each mark is put down so it explains clearly the statement of some previous touches of paint. They are all cumulative, and the final touch brings it all together.

All this means that painting is a thinking process as well as a feeling one. I do not mean in the short term, tactical sense, but in the long term, strategic sense. You plan your picture and try to sort it out. As you go along you often change your direction, and even change your goal. Unlike the military mind, the original idea has been but dimly felt and as you proceed the aim you originally pursued is changed, not modified. There are painters whose aim does not deviate from the beginning of their sketches, but on the whole this is not the position of the beginner. You, because you are the beginner, should change your original idea often. Not because the idea was wrong, but because the most worthwhile thing you can discover is that there are many ways you could go, not at first, but when you find out what you prefer to do.

Gozo Reflections differs from the other paintings I have shown you in that it is much more brilliant in colour and at first glance appears more freely painted. I have often been asked how can I have such a free attitude to painting

Gozo Reflections, 45.7 × 61cm (18 × 24in)

when I spend so much time advocating great care with every tiny mark? I do not think that what I have done is different in concept; it is different in the way I have worked, not in the way I have thought. The motives in painting *Collias Reflection* and this picture were based upon the ideas I have talked about throughout these pages. Both these paintings depend on an understanding of tone and an ability to put the paint down in the correct place. All the drawing has been done in the act of painting.

I worked very rapidly, this painting was done in two and a half hours, with broad, sweeping brush strokes. This is one of a series I painted looking into the harbour of Gozo, a tiny island off the coast of Malta. Most of the pictures did not have boats in them, they were just about the reflections. Here, I have kept in some parts of the boats because I wanted to paint the rusty iron barrel with the wood on top and it would have been too isolated without the boats.

I started the painting at the top and quickly put in the white boat and the base of the blue boat. A few dark blue strokes took me to the edge of the barrel, where I painted the reflection of it before the barrel itself. Next came the very dark reflection beneath the barrel and the dark 'lines' coming towards the bottom of the painting. These helped establish the flat plane of the water – the contrast between this plane and what you can see through the water is exciting. The dark lines I put down at this point have been altered to what you can see now.

The grey bluish white came next and my first concern was the straight downward part which almost bisects the painting. I was not too worried at this point about the edge of this area against the large blue area, but was more concerned with getting the correct colour. The variations in this were painted as I went along, not afterwards.

The pace at which I worked varied, sometimes I put down a large area, then drew a thin stroke across it. Try to paint like this, do not deal with all the large areas first and then go on to the details. The darker linear patterns have been painted after the lighter areas. Finally, as the light began to fade, I painted the bottom left corner.

Always have a paint rag, especially when you are painting quickly.

PAINTING WITH A KNIFE

I normally paint with brushes and my fingers, but when I work on a large scale it is nice to use a painting knife. I like the mixture of textures, playing one off against another, because you can then make the story you are trying to tell much clearer. Some people, however, prefer to paint with a palette knife all the time. As a beginner there are two times it is useful for you to paint with a knife, apart from the personal enjoyment you may get from playing about with thick wodges of paint.

If you find that you are painting in a muddy manner it is a good idea to paint with a knife – at least it will stop you going over the same stroke several times. Secondly, if you find you are painting too thinly – you are mean with a brush – turn to using a knife. At the very least, try painting with a knife and see how you get on.

There are no special subjects which are more suitable for painting with a knife; with practice and provided you do not paint on too small a scale, you can paint as many details as you like. However, for your first knife painting choose a subject like *The Silk Farm* because there are not too many details and it will give you a chance to get used to using a new tool. The whole painting was done over a period of four days. The stages represent the point at which I stopped each time.

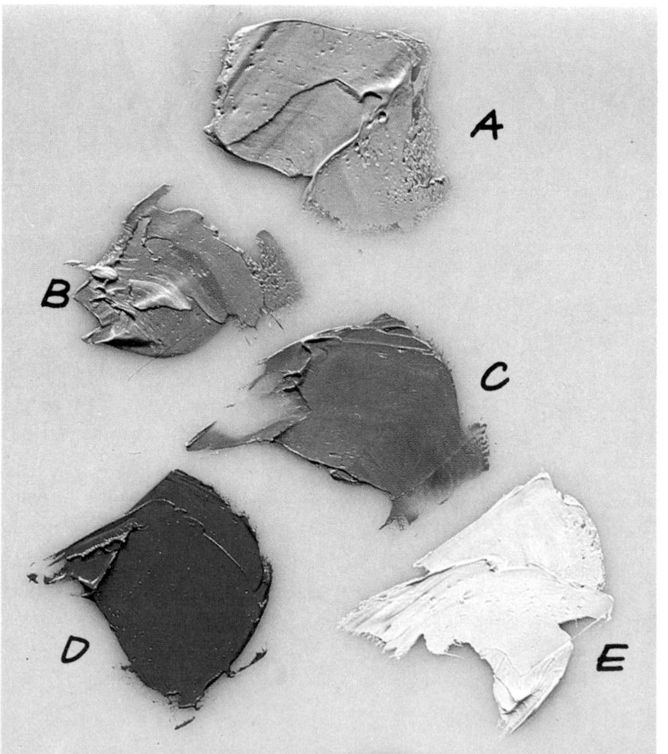

The drawing This is the only time I used a brush in this painting, there would have been no advantage in using a knife. In fact, quite the reverse is true. You want such a drawing to indicate what you are going to paint and to get in the main lines of the composition. You can see as well that I have stated the darker areas fairly simply. I do not think there is any very great advantage in doing this – it could be described as a nervous habit – except that I like drawing in tonal contrasts. Some of you might find such a habit useful because it helps keep you aware of the sense of light. I used French Ultramarine and a lot of turpentine. I used my paint rag often while planning the painting to wipe out incorrect lines.

Mixing the colours Make up quite a large quantity of paint when mixing colours with a knife. It takes me a little longer than it does when I use a brush. It is easier to use the back of the knife and you must take care to mix the colours thoroughly (traces of pure colour can be left in the mixture, with disastrous consequences when you are painting).

You can see the colours I have mixed up (left) in the first stage. Of course, these were not the only colours I had mixed up at this stage – some of the greens were necessary to make sure I had got these colours right. I used the basic range of colours plus Lemon Yellow and Cobalt Blue. I prefer a palette knife to a painting knife for mixing up colours.

First stage I started this painting at the top with the sky. I advise you to do this with your first knife painting – start at the top and work downwards – so you have no difficulty with the handling. You cannot do this throughout the entire painting, but it does stop awkward contortions at first. The sky has been put on with broad, flat strokes

A: *The sky*, White, Cobalt Blue, Cadmium Red and Yellow Ochre plus a touch of Lemon Yellow. B: *The distant hills*, Cobalt Blue, White and Cadmium Red plus touches of Yellow Ochre and Lemon Yellow. C: *The nearer hills*, Cobalt Blue, Cadmium Red, Yellow Ochre and White. D: *The blue-accented hills*, Cobalt Blue, Cadmium Red, French Ultramarine and White plus a touch of Yellow Ochre. E: *The water tower*, White, Lemon Yellow and Red

The drawing

First stage

Second stage

across the canvas. I then put down the top part of the distant hills. Make sure that every time you pick up a new colour your knife is perfectly clean – I get through a lot of paint rag but have found large paper handkerchiefs will do as well when painting with a knife.

The water tower came next. I put it down slightly wider than it was and corrected the shape with the distant hill colours. This has been followed by the nearer hills and then the accented hills. In each case, I brought the colour down further than I wanted and placed the next colour on top of this. (You can see where the paint of the distant hills comes below the accented hills.) You can do this quite easily if you do not mess the paint about – put it down once and leave it alone. With the exception of the water tower, these colours have been put on by holding the knife horizontally and dragging it downwards. Then I added two touches of paint to the accented hills (near the water tower) with the tip of my knife held vertically. The water tower has been painted in the same manner, moving from right to left.

Second stage At this stage I began to get some of the greens onto the canvas and have started on the silk farm itself. This really had been a silk farm – the building was long so that a large piece of silk could be made and laid out. The silk worms lived on the mulberry trees, some of which still lined the roads or were dotted around the fields. The near tree in this painting is a pollarded mulberry tree.

If you compare this stage with the final painting you will see that the dark blue-greens and the colour of the near tree have been altered later. At this point I wanted to begin to establish the trees, and I found it rather easier to overstate these darks, knowing I would modify them. This does have the disadvantage of making the colour and tone in the painting unbalanced. If you find this difficult do not do it; try to make the colours correct, but err on the side of dark rather than light.

I have painted the roof of the house against the trees. I have put the dark on this in a wide stripe under the eaves, and have covered this with the lighter colour of the side of the house. The dark lines below and to the right of the house have been used to mark where I wanted the house or trees to stop and the fields to begin. Again, if you compare the light side of the house with the final version you will see that it has been painted lighter. This was done when the windows and door were added. I have also put down the beginning of the tree trunk and the beginning of the field in front of the house.

Final stage On the fourth day I began to develop the trees a little more. First I modified the near mulberry tree, making it a little lighter by painting over the very dark colours. Then I went on to the big trees in the middle-distance. I have mixed up three different colours for the grass and as I painted I have varied these colours quite a lot. The dark beside the big near tree has been altered and

Final stage

The Silk Farm, 40.6 × 50.8cm (16 × 20in)

I began to repaint the house, making it a little lighter and putting in the windows and door. I have drawn in some details on the grass and put in the fence.

The fence has been painted a dark colour, onto which I have put the light. The last post on the right has been smudged and this shows the darker colour more clearly. This fence had been painted when the green was very wet. Paint details like this with the side of the knife; get a little paint all along the edge and draw it upwards or downwards, depending upon which is the easiest movement to make at that moment.

The windows and door were put down with the end of the knife in the same way as the water tower, a little too large and then corrected with the lighter, modified colour of the house. The darker edge of the far field going up to the house was painted before the fence, but the dark at the base of the fence was painted after I had finished the fence. I painted the half-tone of the trunk of the tree on the left first, then the light tone and finished with the dark touches down the side. The last areas I painted were the dark bush on the right, some darks into the trees beyond and some small touches of light green little trees into the dark paint beside the house.

I varied the way I used the knife, but the most frequent movement was from the top to the bottom of the picture. Sometimes I found it easier to turn the picture on its side (for example, when I corrected the angled end of the house). The paint overall, except for the sky, was fairly thick. Three weeks after I had finished, most of the surface was soft and great care had to be taken when stacking it against other paintings.

Painting with a knife is a much simpler process than painting with a brush, however many variations I make in any colour. Although it takes longer to mix up colours, it is considerably quicker. It is best to paint with dash and bravado, to make up your mind what you intend to do before you approach the canvas. It requires a great deal of thought first, then rapid action. It is more useful not to be too fussy about the manner in which you put the paint onto the canvas. As you paint more pictures in this manner, vary the marks you make more and more.

In general, the darker the colour you are painting, the thinner it should be; the lighter the colour, the thicker it should be.

PASTELS

JOHN BLOCKLEY ARWS

WHY USE PASTELS... AND WHAT ARE THEY?

Ravenglass, Cumbria

Why use pastels?

Pastel painting can be as colourful and vigorous as any method of painting. It is a dry medium, and its powdery surface increases the refraction of light, so pastel paintings emit an intensity of colour unchallenged by any other medium. Because it is dry, there are no frustrations of waiting for the paint or paper to dry. It is dry paint – we pick up the pastel and apply colour directly to the painting surface. It can outlast oil paint because it has no oil or varnish to yellow and crack with age.

In addition to these technical advantages, pastel is an exciting medium. Most people are attracted to the paintings of ballet dancers by Edgar Degas, but probably only a few realize that many of the paintings were made with pastels. Degas, probably more than any other artist, exploited the special properties of pastels. He produced exciting paintings that seem to vibrate with colour. His painting *Dancers in Blue* was painted in 1890 and is typical of his way of handling pastels. It shows a group of dancers dressed in blue and set against a rich tapestry-like background of brilliant splashes of orange and red.

Because pastel is dry, Degas was able to apply colour over previous colour, with short, quick strokes, dashes and dots of pastel, so the colours underneath showed through. He painted racehorses, full of movement, rippling grass and reflecting light. This movement of colour and light is apparent in all his paintings, whether they are figures, interiors, landscapes, beach scenes or big skies. To me, Degas demonstrates more than anyone the possibilities of the pastel medium.

Pastel painting, in its present form, dates back to the eighteenth century, although chalk drawings were made on cave walls in prehistoric times. Pastel paintings more than 200 years old are as bright and fresh today as they were when they were painted. Pastels require no more protective treatment than that given to any other type of painting. The best way is to frame a pastel under glass, with a surrounding mount or narrow fillet between the pastel surface and the glass, which prevents the glass rubbing against the picture.

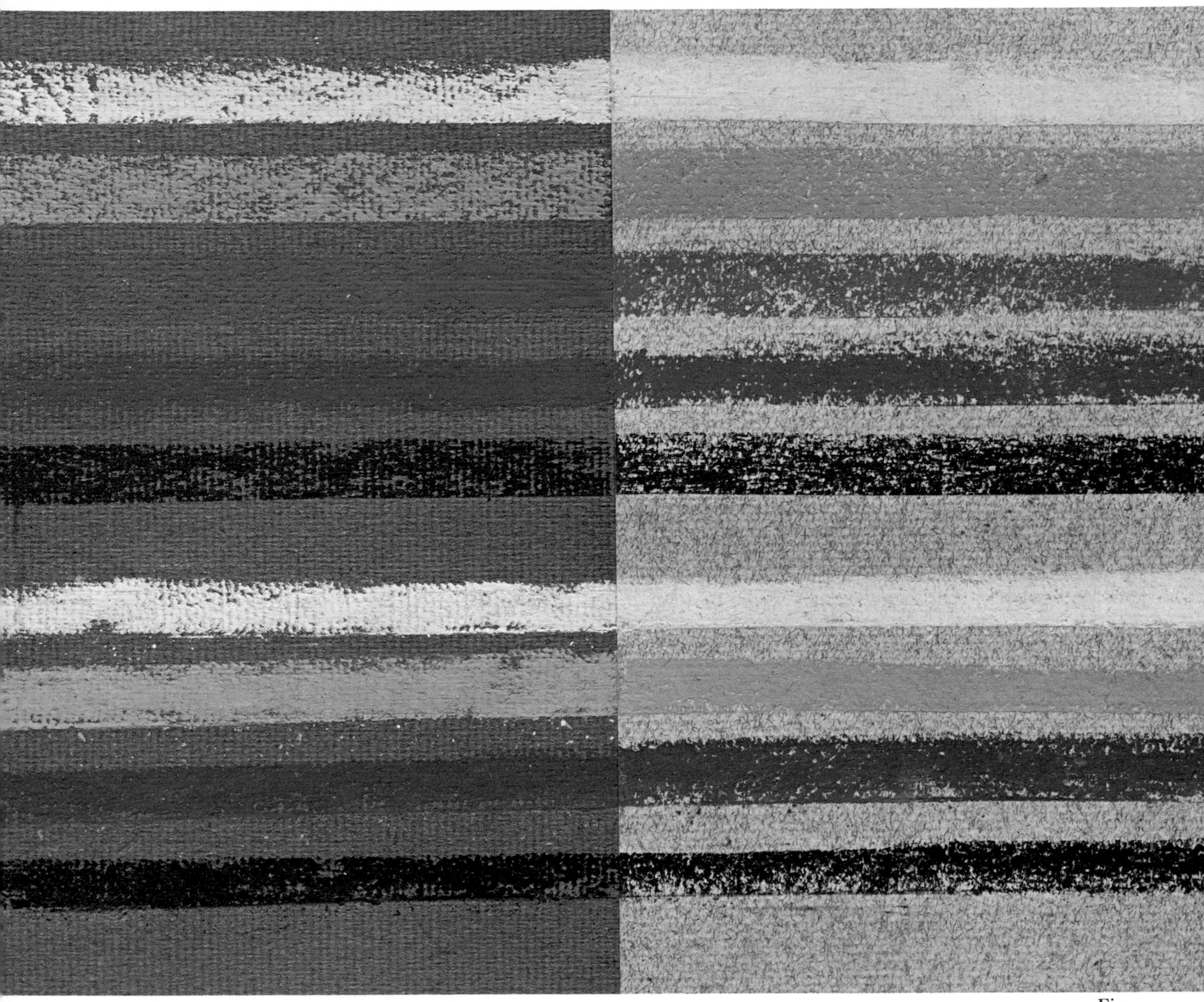

Fig. 1

What are pastels?

Many people do not realize that the pigments in pastels are exactly the same as those used for oil and watercolour paints; the difference lies in the manufacturing process. Oil paints are made by mixing finely-ground pigment with oil, watercolours are made by mixing pigment with gum, and pastels by mixing pigment with chalk and water to make a stiff paste. After checking the colour, and adjusting it if necessary with extra pigment, the paste is pounded to remove air, and formed into long, round strips, which are cut into short lengths of pastels. After drying, the pastels are individually labelled and carefully boxed to avoid damage in transit.

Most manufacturers incorporate a binding material to hold the powder together in short sticks. The quantity of binder in the mixture can affect the strength of the finished product and the quality of the pastel's mark. Rowney are one of the few manufacturers with a process of making pastels without a binder, which accounts for the durability and softness of their pastels.

The strength of the colour in a pastel is determined by the amount of chalk mixed with the pigment. A lot of chalk will produce a pale tint, and a little chalk will give a dark tint, so there is a range of tints within every colour. Rowney pastels are graded from Tint 0 for the palest up to Tint 8 for the darkest. The top range in **fig. 1** is Burnt Sienna, starting with Tint 0 at the top, followed by Tints, 2, 4, 6 and 8. The other range shows Tints 0, 2, 4 and 6 of Purple Grey. I drew these tints across two shades of grey paper to show how different tints appear on different tints of paper.

WHAT EQUIPMENT DO YOU NEED?

I always use Rowney pastels; they are consistently good and I like their velvety texture. Throughout these pages I have referred to Rowney's range of colours and tint numbers. The range consists of up to six tints of 52 colours, making a total of more than 200 pastels.

Pastels

I am often asked how many pastels are necessary to produce satisfactory paintings. I think it is helpful to have a generous assortment because it is very frustrating to find while you are painting that you haven't got quite the right tint. You would have to compromise and use the nearest tint you have, or adjust some of the colours you had already used on the painting. We can mix a required tint to some extent by laying one colour on top of another. For example, we can make a pink tint by covering red with white pastel, but this is likely to turn out to be a crude solution.

Pastels are usually stocked in the shops in two ways – as

A BOX 144 PASTELS – ASSORTED
B BOX 36 PASTELS – LANDSCAPE
C BOX 24 PASTELS – LANDSCAPE
D BOX 12 PASTELS – PORTRAIT
E AEROSOL FIXATIVE – LARGE
F BOTTLE FIXATIVE – LARGE
G AEROSOL FIXATIVE – SMALL
H BOTTLE FIXATIVE – SMALL
I HOG AND SABLE BRUSHES
J SPRAY DIFFUSER
K DRAWING INK
L TUBES OF WATERCOLOUR
M PASTEL PACKAGING CONTAINER
N PUTTY RUBBER
O WILLOW CHARCOAL
P PASTEL PAPERS
Q RANDOM PASTELS ON WORK BENCH
R PENCILS
S PAD OF ASSORTED PASTEL PAPER

rowney pencils
Rowney
sketch book
30 LEAVES OF
ASSORTED (TINTS)
INGRES PAPER
Perfix
AP3
Rowney
fixative
150 ml
Rowney
fixative
2 fl. oz.
MADE IN ENGLAND
Rowney
Waterproof
Rowney
ARTISTS
SOFT
PASTELS
Rowney
ARTISTS
SOFT
PASTELS
Rowney
kneadable
putty
rubber
Rowney
25 STICKS Thin
BURNT UMBER

boxed selections or individual pastels. Boxes come in varying sizes, containing as few as 12 pastels or more than 100. There are also selections available specially for landscape or portrait painting.

Individual pastels are usually displayed in trays, so you can see a large number of tints at a glance. They are a picture in themselves! You should select your pastels from the trays by the appearance of the colours, not by their names. If you should need to order some by post, the names will give you a good idea of colour subtleties, such as Blue Green, Yellow Green, Olive Green, Purple Grey and Purple Brown.

If you are just starting to paint with pastels, you will probably wish to begin with a modest selection. A basic selection should include: Yellow Ochre, Coeruleum, Cadmium Red, Red Grey, Purple Grey, Green Grey, Warm Grey, Sap Green, Burnt Umber and Indigo. You will need a light, middle and dark tint of each colour. Remember that the lightest tint you can get is Tint 0 and the darkest is Tint 8.

When you buy your pastels, each piece will be wrapped in a paper band bearing the colour and tint number. Most of your painting will involve dragging the side of the pastel over the paper, so you need to remove the pastel from its wrapping paper, and break off a piece with which to work. It is a good idea to make a colour reference chart by rubbing each new pastel on to a sheet of paper and writing the colour name and tint alongside it. Otherwise, you will need to replace each piece of pastel in its wrapper so you can identify it when you need to reorder.

Storing pastels

You can buy special boxes which include a plastic corrugated tray to hold the pastels. These are useful for storage purposes and you should form the habit of always returning each pastel to its place after use. You could also mark each corrugation with the details of its colour. Some painters make their own containers by lining a shallow box with corrugated cardboard.

Another method is to have a small tin box for each colour; one for your greens, another for yellows and so on. By keeping all tints of a colour in one box you are able to compare them quickly and select the particular colour and its shade. If you store different colours in a box, it is useful to fill the box with ground rice. This prevents them from rubbing against each other, and the slight abrasive quality of the rice will keep the pastels clean. The rice should be sifted away when you want to use the pastels, and replaced after use to perform its function again.

I must confess that I am untidy in this respect. I just leave my pastels lying on the table while I am working, all colours mixed together, but I am sure it is better to cultivate a more methodical way of working. I think it is a matter of temperament – I am too impatient to be tidy and work in long bursts of feverish activity. If I don't immediately recognize a pastel lying on the table because it has rubbed against others, I rub it on the nearest piece of cloth. This is usually my shirt. I do not recommend this practice. You should work out some way of storing pastels and establish a method of working so you can quickly identify the colours you want.

Handling pastel paintings

There is a lot of exaggerated fear about pastel paintings getting smudged. If they are treated carelessly the pastel will smudge, although the paintings I made for this book were handled many times before they appeared in print. It is sensible to take reasonable care of paintings and not slide one across the surface of another. They can easily be stored in a stack, each one separated by a piece of tissue or sheet of newspaper.

Loose pastel fragments are sometimes dislodged from a finished painting if it is bumped or dropped and I guard against this by spraying my paintings with a colourless fixative for pastels. This comes in both bottles and aerosol canisters. If too much spray is used, and the pastel becomes very wet, it will lose some of its brightness.

If I have used a thick build-up of pastel I often paste the finished work on a piece of mounting board. I place the painting face down on a clean table, brush synthetic wallpaper paste on the back of the paper, and leave it for ten minutes for it to soak in and to stretch the paper. Then I pick up the painting and turn it on to the mounting board so the right side faces up. I then cover it with a piece of newspaper and smooth the paper down with my hand, working out from the centre, taking care not to let the newspaper slip. The paste tends to soak through the paper and helps to fix the pastel. It is necessary to paste a sheet of paper to the back of the mounting board to prevent it from buckling as the painting dries.

I occasionally spray a fixative on the pastel while I am working on it. I can then apply another colour over the fixed pastel without disturbing it too much. I leave some of the first layer uncovered to give a broken, two-colour effect in the painting.

Easels

I stand when I am working because I feel restricted if I try to work sitting down. I like to move about and be able to step back and look at the work instead of always having it under my nose. I walk about and return only half a minute later with a fresh eye and quickly recognize errors. I fasten my paper to a piece of stout hardboard with bulldog clips. It is sensible to put a few sheets of uncreased paper between the pastel paper and the board. This gives a pleasant, cushioned surface on which to work and also prevents imperfections in the board being transmitted to the pastel.

I usually support the board at eye level on an upright studio easel, but a portable sketching easel is equally suitable, and it can also be used for outdoor work. Another advantage of using an easel is that I like to have the painting

upright so I can stand away from it and work at arm's length for rendering broad sweeps of the pastel, and be able to step up close for detailed areas. Should the pastel crumble when I press too firmly on the painting surface, the particles fall and collect in the ledge on the easel, instead of adhering to the painting. An easel also reduces your chances of accidentally rubbing against the painting.

If you are less restless than me, or if you prefer to sit while working, a portable easel can easily be adjusted to a suitable height, or you can use a table easel which can be tilted to various angles, or you can lean the painting against a pile of books.

Supplies

I will discuss later the various papers I use, and I will show how I commence by drawing the subject, sometimes with a pencil, sometimes with ink or charcoal. You should get a bottle of black drawing ink, and some medium-grade sticks of charcoal. The charcoal gives a good black line of a texture and nature which is in sympathy with pastel painting. It is easily erased by using a putty rubber if you make mistakes – and we all do – and when you are satisfied with the drawing you can flick the charcoal with a duster and leave a grey impression on which you can pastel.

The putty rubber is a soft rubber which can be kneaded into quite a fine point. It will erase pastel, cleanly, back to the paper. A painter's stiff hog brush is also useful for removing pastel, so mistakes in a painting can conveniently be erased without affecting the surface of the paper.

WHICH PAPER?

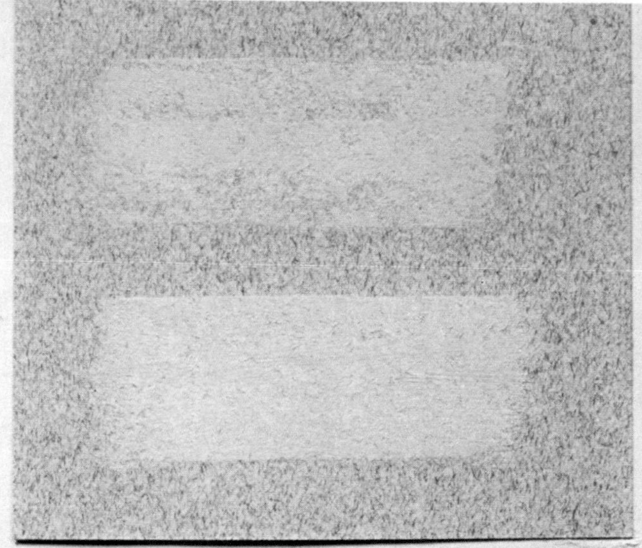

Fig. 2

Some pastel artists paint on hardboard, muslin covered board, canvas or even sandpaper, but most painters work on tinted papers made specially for pastel work. I use Italian Fabriano or Swedish Tumba Ingres papers. I like the subtle texture of these papers which enables me to drag pastel lightly over the surface, so the colour of the paper will show through and give an interesting broken-colour effect, or I can press the pastel firmly into the slight texture to obtain solid patches of colour. I would advise you to work on these Ingres papers, as the rougher surfaces of some papers can break up the layer of pastel too much. This gives a coarse, insensitive finish to a painting, but it may help you achieve a desired effect.

I made some pastel strokes on the sample paper colours in **fig. 2** to indicate that the paper grain can show through lightly applied pastel, or be covered by heavy pastel. Notice the difference in finish between the blue pastel on grey paper and the blue pastel on orange paper. The blue on grey is a subtle combination, whereas the blue on orange is an exciting, vibrant combination.

There are a number of such ways in which the colour of the paper can be chosen to give the required effect. A cool grey paper will give a pleasing background to a painting composed of pink and grey-green colours, and result in a

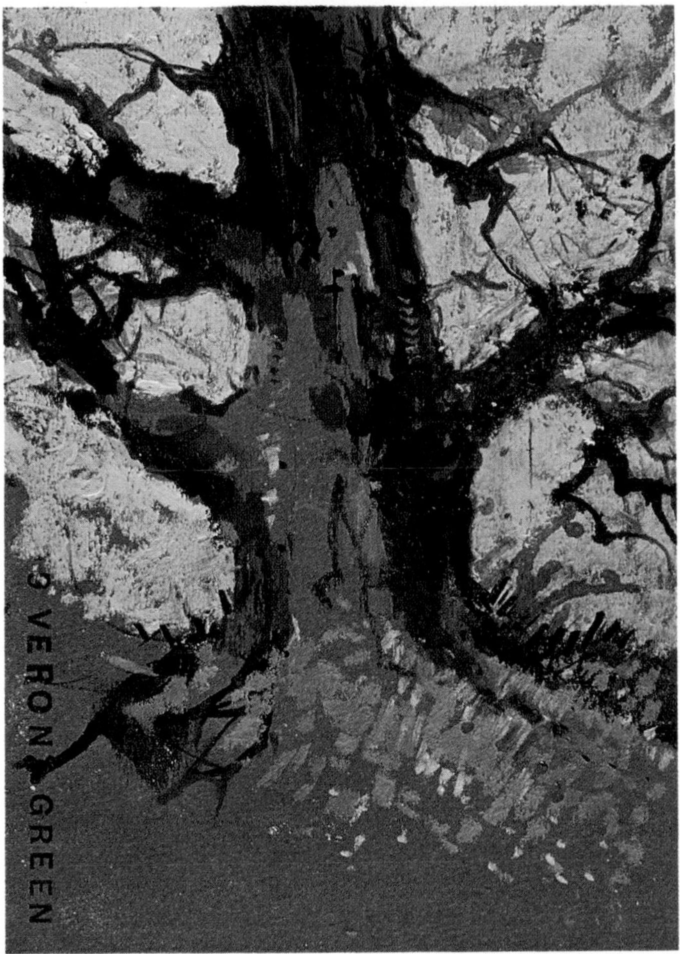

Fig. 3

Fig. 4

restful, easy-to-look-at picture. On the other hand, brilliantly coloured pastels will make a striking picture when painted on brightly coloured or very dark papers.

The tone of the paper has considerable importance. Tone refers to the lightness or darkness of the paper. Dramatic effects, such as a brilliant light in the sky behind a dark mountain, can be obtained by using light pastels on dark paper.

I have discovered over the years that I can work better with a mid-tone paper, one not too light or dark. I use this mid-tone as a starting point against which I can judge the tone of colour I want. I determine if the pastel I am about to place on the paper should be lighter or darker than the paper. I find it easier to judge how light or dark a particular colour should be when working on mid-tone paper than I would working on a light or a dark paper. A mid-tone paper can also reduce the amount of work since a fair-sized part of it can be left uncovered. Although a mid-tone paper is a good starting point, dark paper can help if the subject is generally dark. As we work through these pages we shall be constantly reminded of the part played by the colour and tone of the paper on which we are working.

Paper colour

The range of coloured paper gives us the opportunity of choosing a colour on which to work that will be sympathetic to the subject we are going to paint. For example, if the subject is mainly green we could use a green paper and leave parts of the paper uncovered, letting the paper do a lot of the work for us.

My tree painting (**fig. 3**) was done on Verona Green Fabriano paper and I left the paper uncovered for the foreground and the light parts of the trunk. It is only a small sketch painted on a sample swatch of paper, which I mention in passing to show that the smallest sketches can be effective by making the most of the paper colour with only a little pastel work. I relied mainly on three pastels: Coeruleum Tint 0 for the sky and Sepia Tints 5 and 8 for the dark parts of the tree.

The flower painting (**fig. 4**) was also made on Fabriano, this time Bronze. I used the paper colour for the flowers, with just a few touches of Lemon Yellow Tint 2 on the petals. The colour of the paper is allowed to show, uncovered, in other small parts of the painting. This is also a small sketch, rather stylized with simple, patterned shapes. The pastel medium is ideal for this type of treatment as it can be pressed on to the paper to make patterns of opaque

Fig. 5

colour, as in the blue background, or applied gently, as in the petals.

The simple landscape paintings in **fig. 5** also leave large parts of the paper uncovered; the pastel work is confined almost to the sky and trees and leaves the bottom half of the paper uncovered. I have used the same pastels in both paintings, but on different colours of paper. I used Sienna Brown Fabriano paper for the top painting and Sand Fabriano Ingres paper for the other. The pastels used were Coeruleum Tint 0 and Blue Grey Tint 0 for the skies and Olive Green Tint 2 for the grass. The trees are from Burnt Umber Tint 6.

You should experiment by painting some simple landscapes such as these on various colours of paper. At first use only a few colours. Try the same colours I used and then try a combination of your own choice. You should avoid bright colours for these first experiments. Keep the colours subtle so the colour of the paper is dominant.

Fig. 6

Remember that the purpose of these experiments is to discover how much use you can make of paper colour.

The top estuary painting in **fig. 6** was made on Fabriano Stone Grey paper and the second version on Fabriano Verona Grey. I used Coeruleum Tint 0 and Blue Grey Tints 0 and 2 for the sky and water. I used charcoal for the cottages and allowed the paper to show in both paintings.

Which paper would you have chosen? It really depends on the mood you wish to portray. The Stone Grey is sympathetic to the colour of the pastels and they combine to give a restful mood. Although I used the same pastels in both and applied them in the same way, the green paper is less sympathetic to the pastels, evoking a restless and vibrant mood.

HOW TO APPLY PASTEL

Fig. 10, opposite, shows some basic pastel strokes, made on Bronze Ingres Fabriano paper. The first two horizontal strokes at the top were made with a short piece of Red Grey Tint 2. I pressed the side of the pastel firmly on to the paper and dragged it sideways (see **fig. 7**, right). Notice how the texture of the paper breaks through the pastel. The band below is Red Grey Tint 0, pressed very firmly to fill the grain of the paper.

Alongside these colour bands are short, diagonal strokes of Red Grey Tint 0 pastel, applied openly to allow the colour of the paper to show between the strokes. I overlapped these with similar strokes of Red Grey Tint 2. Where the two pastels cross we get a rubbed combination of the two tints, and in other areas we see the original, unmodified strokes. By this process we can produce broken-colour effects, combined with bits of blended colour. We can extend this process to include additional tints of the same colour, or another colour.

I repeated the exercise using the same pastel tints, but using the end of the pastel to draw lines, rather than bands of colour (**fig. 8**). At the bottom of the paper I superimposed dots of Cobalt Blue Tint 2 over dots of Lizard Green Tint 1 (**fig. 9**). Alongside I combined the three processes; overlapping dots, lines and bands of colour.

You should experiment with these techniques. Use different combinations of colours and tints with various colours of paper. Also, vary the pressure of the pastel, so the colour of the paper sometimes shows through the pastel strokes. You will also discover how heavy pressure on a pastel stroke will affect the layer underneath. For example, heavily cross a line of grey with pink pastel and see how the pink will drag some of the grey with it.

This technique, called cross-hatching, was practised a great deal by Degas. His original paintings show remarkable results from overlaying pastel strokes of varying lengths: short strokes over longer strokes, hatched diagonally, vertically and horizontally, and combined with dots, sometimes crisp and sometimes blended. The flesh colours of his figures positively shimmer with light.

These methods of applying pastel are exciting to do and can produce vibrant effects. Go ahead and see what you can do. Don't paint pictures for this exercise – just draw lines and bands in all directions, overlap them, make big dots with heavy pressure, small dots with rapid stabs of the end of the pastel. Try to discover as many ways as you can of applying pastel.

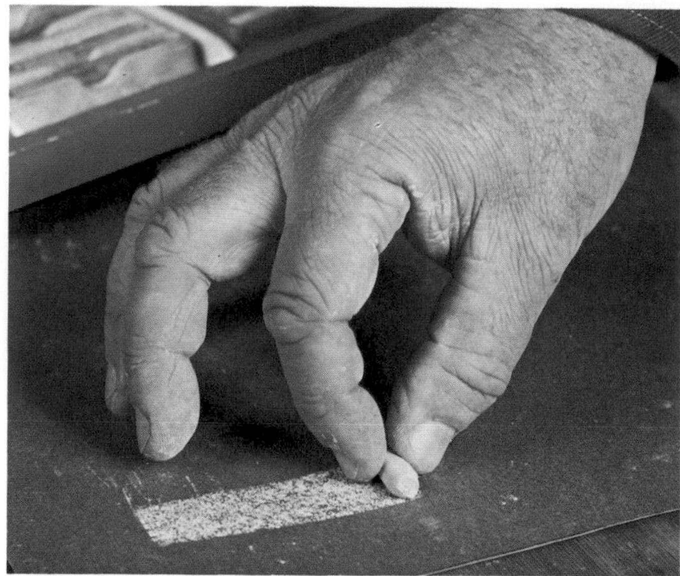

Fig. 7

Fig. 8

Fig. 9

Fig. 10

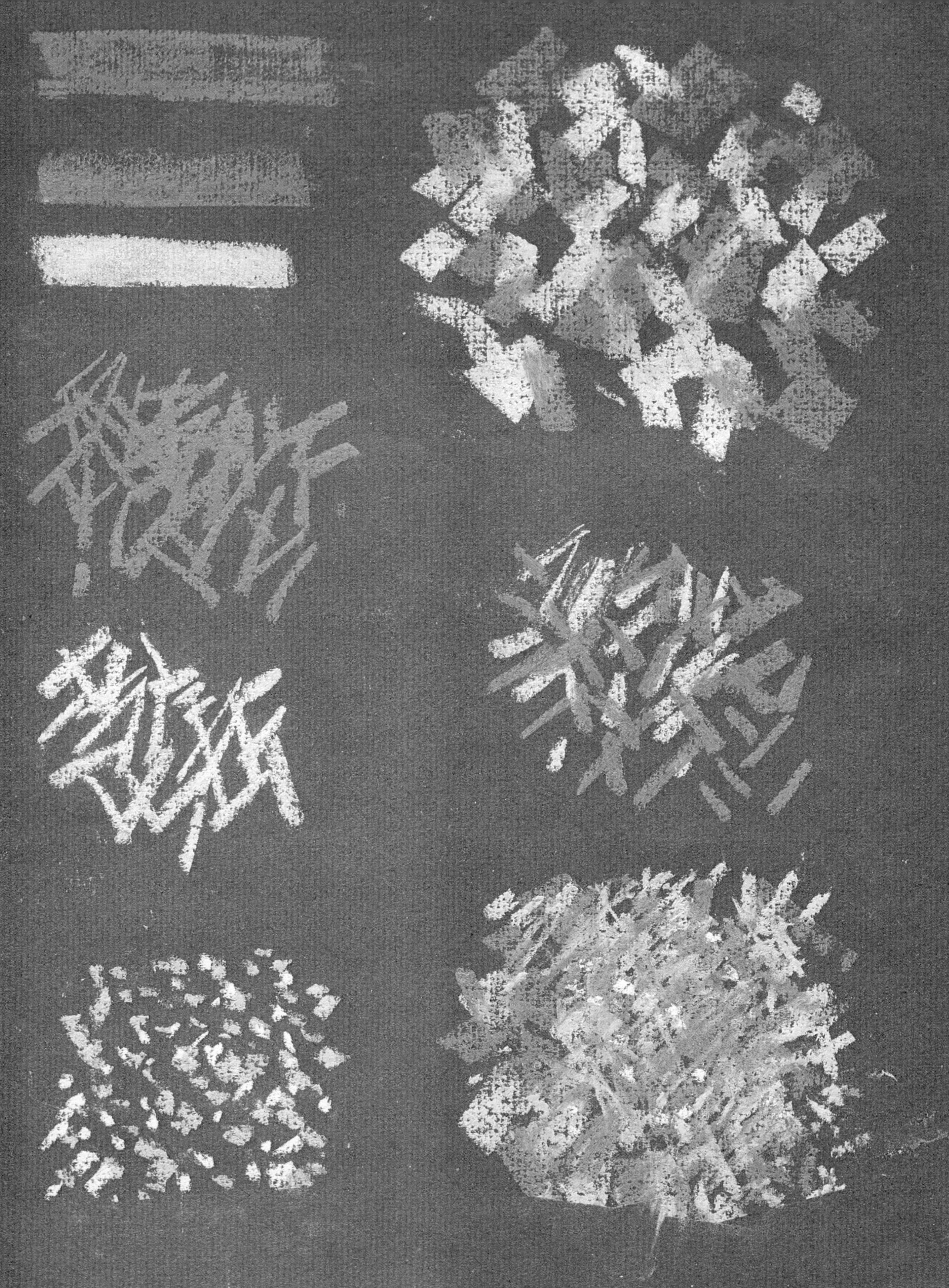

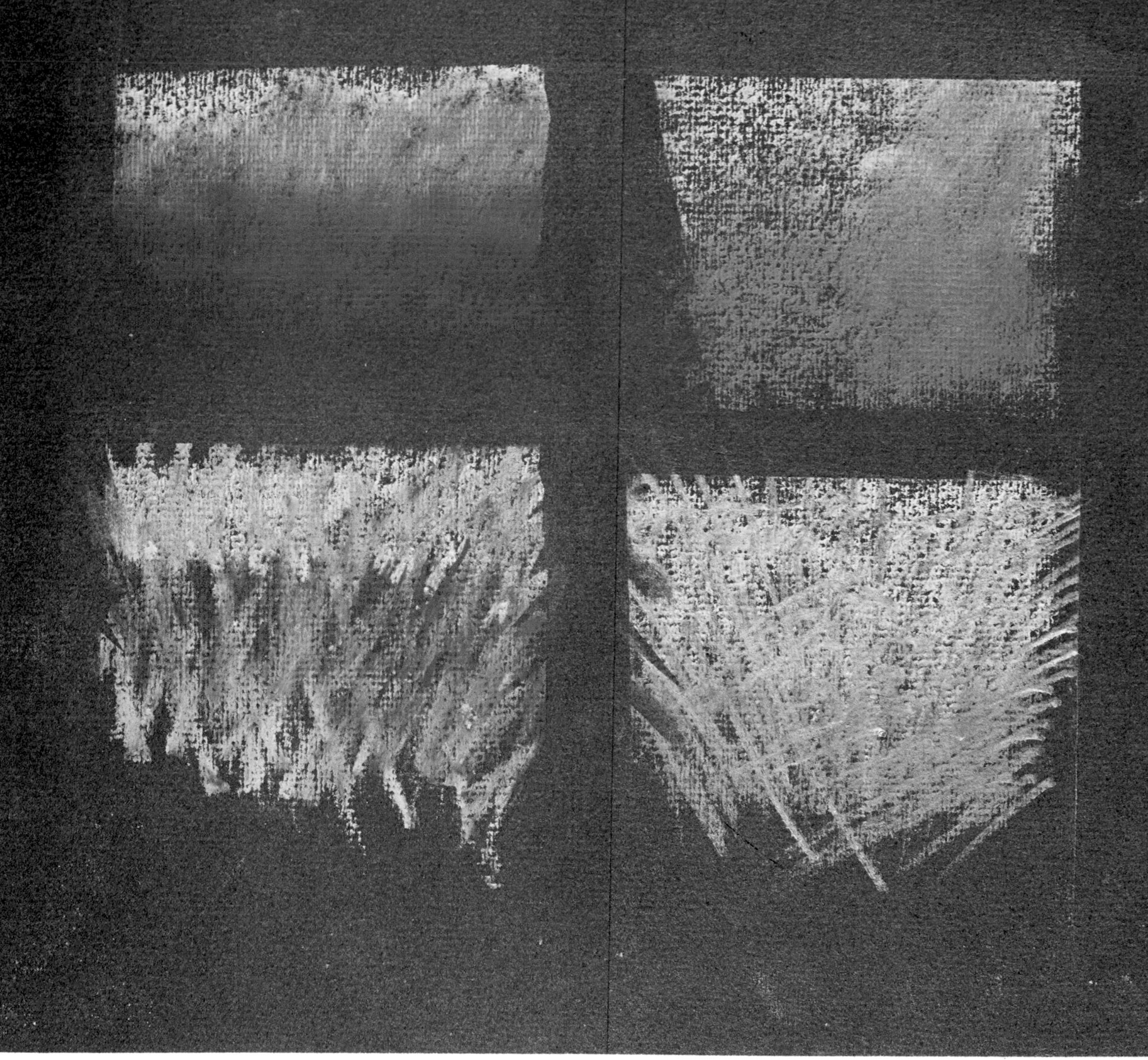

Fig. 11

Rubbing pastel

Highly-finished, smooth pastel work can be produced by rubbing with your finger to blend the colours. This can lead to an overworked, dull painting, where the pastel loses its freshness and bloom. This bloom is unique to the pastel medium and is caused by granules of pigment on the paper reflecting light. It seems a pity to destroy this by rubbing and smoothing the pastel into the paper grain, but this process is used by many painters and you must decide what sort of surface finish you like. I strongly recommend you keep the rubbing to a minimum until you have explored the possibilities of unrubbed pastel. I must emphasize that the sparkle of unrubbed pastel is a unique property of the medium. I want to exploit this, and if I rub the work at all, I do so discreetly to blend colours slightly, and then only as a contrast to textured pastel work.

I have shown examples of rubbed pastels in **fig. 11** above. In the top left corner is a band of Lizard Green touching Cadmium Red and I blended the two together with my finger-tip. Alongside, I repeated the exercise, using bands of Lizard Green and Olive Green. I rubbed the right section to fill the paper grain. I repeated these colour bands below and hatched through them with Blue Grey to blend them together partly, resulting in a more vibrant effect than rubbing produces.

My mountain landscapes on the opposite page are similar in content, but **fig. 12** is rubbed and **fig. 13** is not.

Fig. 12

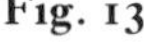

Fig. 13

SKETCHING

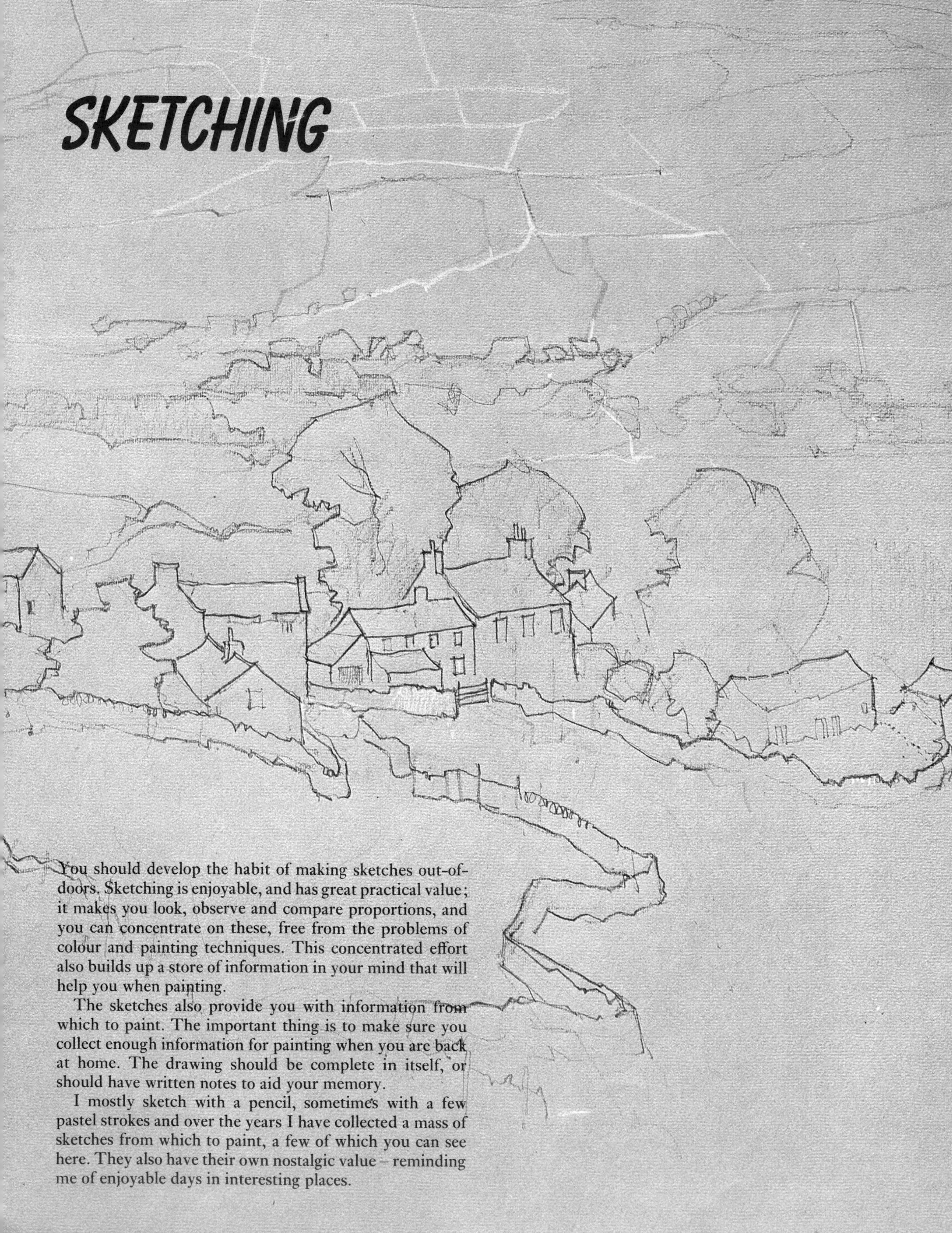

You should develop the habit of making sketches out-of-doors. Sketching is enjoyable, and has great practical value; it makes you look, observe and compare proportions, and you can concentrate on these, free from the problems of colour and painting techniques. This concentrated effort also builds up a store of information in your mind that will help you when painting.

The sketches also provide you with information from which to paint. The important thing is to make sure you collect enough information for painting when you are back at home. The drawing should be complete in itself, or should have written notes to aid your memory.

I mostly sketch with a pencil, sometimes with a few pastel strokes and over the years I have collected a mass of sketches from which to paint, a few of which you can see here. They also have their own nostalgic value – reminding me of enjoyable days in interesting places.

Nant Peris
Potato Fields
Nr St Davids
Pembrokeshire

PAINTING FIGURES

People are fascinating to paint and almost everywhere we see wonderful characters. I love to make pastel studies of people, concentrating on capturing their attitudes, rather than facial likenesses. Tall, thin, drooping figures; short, almost spherical figures, they are all interesting to observe and paint with slight exaggerations, caricatured, but not too obviously. I like to watch people going about their normal activities. It is not always easy, or perhaps wise, to study obviously the people around you, but you can look long enough to record mentally the essential characteristics, possibly aided with a thumb-nail sketch.

The thought of painting figures can be frightening to the inexperienced painter, but some pictures do need a few figures. Imagine a street scene without them. If we remember that the figures for such a painting are usually just incidents within the whole content, and quite a small part of the painting, the fear begins to disappear. I am not saying that serious study of figures is unnecessary; I am talking in the context of fitting figures into a landscape or townscape.

It is often easier to deal with a group of figures. My small, rough sketch in **fig. 14** was quickly done with the end of a brown pastel. I placed one light shape within a darker group, indicated the heads, and flicked downward strokes for the legs to produce a convincing enough group of figures suitable for a street scene.

I chose to do very little drawing for the lower figure – just enough pastel lines to indicate the man with his hands in his pockets. The drawing is not much more than an outline, and I didn't draw the feet, not because feet and hands are difficult to draw, but because I was not interested in them for the overall sense of this drawing. I gave some substance to the drawing by filling in the background with varied pastel strokes.

My painting on the opposite page suggests three figures out shopping. I tried to make the nearer figure more important by making her bigger than the others, contrasting her light, green-yellow coat against a darker coat, and inclining the heads of the other two figures towards her. I didn't indicate facial features because I was not interested in telling you that she had brown eyes – but I did want to indicate to you she is the dominant one and the others won't get a word in edgeways. Try to register the mood and activity of the figures, and the details will look after themselves. I didn't draw their legs very well, did I?

Try drawing a few simple figure groups and see how convincing you can make them with a minimum of drawing. Use a piece of charcoal or pastel so you won't have to worry about registering intricate detail.

Fig. 14

FRESH
TODAY

MOORLAND COTTAGES

This painting summarizes the ground we have covered so far. The illustrations show the painting at an early stage and finished stage. I wanted a dramatic effect of dark stone cottages silhouetted against the light part of the sky and I chose a fairly dark paper, Fabriano Mid Grey. The cottages were placed high on the paper to make them important and leave plenty of space below for the elaborate textures of the foreground. I drew the outline of the cottages with a black pencil and immediately added some sky colour, Yellow Ochre Tint 0. This light pastel leaves the grey paper for the cottages – a good example of effectively using the paper.

I left the sky unfinished and started to develop the foreground. I made pastel strokes of various colours, using short, quick strokes, and longer, lighter strokes and dots. It is impossible to describe every sequence and operation used for this involved foreground, but I developed it with these varied pastel marks. Some areas were painted with Sepia Tint 8, pressed into the paper to make very dark passages to show up the lighter parts. In some areas I twisted the end of a light pastel on to the paper surface to make abstract mottled light shapes, shown at the bottom left of the painting.

I was concerned about maintaining a dramatic sky, so I kept the colours of the foreground fairly muted, but elaborately textured. I had to keep from making too many strong contrasts of light and dark in the foreground because they would have conflicted with the sky. For this reason I avoided the vibrant effects of cross-hatching, but you will notice examples of that technique elsewhere in the book.

The light Yellow Ochre in the sky was applied with enough pressure to fill the paper grain – I wanted an intense area of light so I covered the paper. The light sky is further emphasized by the dark indigo used for the upper sky. I have explained that the Yellow Ochre was applied with pressure to form a flat opaque layer of pastel, and I contrasted this with short, broken cloud drifts of light and medium grey. Employing a different technique in a neighbouring area is a useful ploy to draw attention to part of a painting. This painting, with its textured foreground and dramatic sky, was not an easy subject, but does show interesting applications of pastel.

Early stage

Finished stage

COTTAGE DETAILS

I saw this cottage in South Wales and liked the details of the windows. Then I walked to the back and was interested by this door which opened into the cottage. I made some pencil sketches and painted from them at home. The two men are imagined, although I am quite sure I have seen them somewhere.

The upstairs dormer windows sit comfortably into the slope of the roof and the whitewashed walls on each side of the windows make a good pattern of light, vertical strips against the bulk of the roof. Notice that some of the window panes are dark and some light. The downstairs window is set back in the thick wall, but windows are often incorrectly painted flush with the front of the wall. I took care to show how the upper part of the sash window overlaps the bottom half so that it can slide over it.

The walls of the cottage were whitewashed, but had weathered to reveal underneath layers of previous colours; pink and ochre. I obtained this effect by cross-hatching these colours over each other.

I treated the tree with caution and gave only hints of detail in the branches at the top. An elaborate tree would have competed with the window detail, so I painted enough detail to make the tree look convincing and no more. For the same reason, I understated the gate and wall details.

The door is a very simple subject which I painted to fit this page, but I may extend it sideways to include a window. This sets a little exercise for you to think about – should I extend it, or leave it alone? Is it complete in itself?

The building had been left unpainted. I liked the colours of the stone, warm grey with hints of red and blue, stained from rain and covered with green moss. The textured stone contrasts well with the plain door. The texture was obtained by dragging the side of the pastel over the paper, and by pressing dots of colour into the paper with the end of the pastel. The door is rubbed pastel: lightly applied red, grey and green, smoothly blended with my finger to contrast with the surrounding texture.

The shadow at the top of the door is important. I painted it with sepia, not black, with firm pressure on the paper. Sepia, or any dark brown tint, will give a good, warm dark, more subtle than black.

ANGLESEY COTTAGES

These cottages, with their chunky shapes, were ideal painting subjects, and the whitewashed walls gave excellent tonal contrasts. I enjoyed applying the pastel in a direct manner, unrubbed, to obtain the simplicity of the cottages. The full-size details of my painting show how the white pastel was applied in direct strokes, allowing the paper to break through to suggest the texture of the stone. Notice how the chimney at the far left looks like a solid cube of white stone, without ornamentation. I painted the white side with one broadside stroke. The paper, Fabriano Tan, shows through in the steps and parts of the foreground.

I outlined the cottages, steps and stones at the side of the steps with charcoal. The drawing expressed the positive shapes in the subject, while the rest of the painting is almost abstract, especially in the irregular shapes of the foreground. I didn't explain these because I wanted to concentrate on the steps leading up to the white cottages. I wanted the viewer to walk up those steps, so I emphasized the stones on the left. I also tried to attract the viewer by pressing the pastel hard into the paper to intensify the white on the right end of the left cottage.

Every time I make a pastel stroke, I query its purpose and ask myself if I want to draw attention to it. The stones to the left of the steps are hard-edged and contrast in tone, and I outlined them. By comparison, the stones to the right are subdued, so they don't compete with the left and cause the eye to jump from one side to the other. This sort of thinking becomes instinctive with practice, but you have to work at it by always asking yourself questions.

You can see from this discussion that painting is concerned with not only methods and technique, but also ways of seeing and thinking. Try to choose some aspect of the subject that interests you, and discipline yourself to concentrate on that one message.

First stage

Second stage

STAITHES, YORKSHIRE

We have been talking about working on paper specially made for pastel painting, but I now want to introduce the possibility of tinting paper ourselves. Good quality cartridge or watercolour papers are readily available and can be tinted with watercolours. We can tint the paper one colour all over, or in various colours. For example, the paper could be tinted grey at the top – as an underpainting for a pastel sky, and the lower part could be painted Raw Umber for the ground. Here, I extended this process by painting a misty sort of watercolour to use as a basis for a pastel painting.

First stage I pencilled the outline of the building on a not too rough piece of watercolour paper, very lightly so that it was only just visible. Then I mixed some Raw Sienna watercolour with water in a saucer and brushed it all over the paper. While this was still wet, I brushed a mixture of Cobalt Blue watercolour on the top left corner, and a weaker mix of this on the bottom half of the paper. While the paper was still wet, I added some brush strokes of Burnt Umber, Raw Sienna and Light Red watercolour in the middle. These brush strokes can be seen in the finished painting as soft-edged, shadow-like drifts of colour.

Second stage I mixed Burnt Umber and Cobalt Blue watercolour together, with a little water, and brushed this mixture into the damp paper to form the shape of the houses, leaving the blue sky of the first wash uncovered. This is where the pencil outline was useful. The process of painting a shape such as this into a damp wash requires a good deal of practice, so don't worry if your first efforts are not as successful as you would wish. It is not necessary to produce a perfect watercolour painting – you only need to produce a change of colour, grey-brown for the general area of the buildings, and blue for the sky as a base on which you can pastel.

Finished stage I started to pastel over this misty watercolour impression by slightly emphasizing the distant chimneys with various tints of Warm Grey. I also dragged some of this colour over the general area of the buildings to create some stone texture. I defined the nearer buildings with Purple Grey Tints 4 and 6. While doing this, I left a lot of my watercolour painting still showing and mostly concentrated the pastel on the chimneys. This was enough to clarify the nearer buildings, leaving the distant ones less definitive. Then, with great enjoyment, I registered the bright roofs with Raw Umber Tint 1 and touches of

Finished stage

Madder Brown Tint 2. I continued to liven up the painting by very lightly dragging Hooker's Green Tint 1 over the sky and water. I used tints of Raw Umber for the beach, with Sepia Tint 8 for the dark parts. The water was completed with horizontal strokes of Green Grey Tint 4 and Cobalt Blue Tint 0. Finally, I indicated the boat, added a few varied tints within the buildings, dotted a few highlights, and hung the washing on the line!

LOW WATER

First stage

This subject had strong contrasts of dark and light passages, so I immediately realized that it would be helpful to use a light paper with some dark colour washes added to it. This gave me the best of two worlds: a piece of paper which was both light and dark on which to pastel. Instead of tinting watercolour paper as I did in *Staithes*, I chose a tinted pastel paper, Tumba Purple Grey. The colour of this paper matched the colour I had in mind for the sky and the water.

First stage With a stiff oil painter's brush I made dark sweeps of Cryla acrylic paint across the bottom of the paper and in the area of the boats. I used Burnt Umber, Coeruleum, Olive Green and Burnt Sienna Cryla colours. This process requires little or no skill; the brush strokes are applied quickly and crudely, only to register the general pattern of light and dark. The advantages of Cryla colours are that they dry very quickly and give a good surface on which to work. Designers Gouache colours also give an admirable base for pastel work. The general pattern of the painting was then established and even this crude image

Finished stage

suggested the light passages of water and the dark boats.

Finished stage I then started to apply pastel. I defined the boats quickly by applying light pastel to the surrounding water, leaving hard-edged shapes of the dark underpainting to represent the group of boats. I would like to emphasize that I didn't paint the boats themselves, I explained them by painting the surrounding water. Later, I added a few touches of Burnt Sienna pastel to suggest the paintwork of individual boats. I continued to explain the water by drawing strokes of pastel across the paper, using Blue Grey Tints 0 and 2, Coeruleum Tint 0, and a little White. I left bands of the paper showing. These strokes of pastel were applied decisively from left to right, with a good deal of pressure. I continued this treatment in the foreground to make the dark passages of mud and streaks of reflected light. I used tints of Vandyke Brown ranging from Tint 1, which is almost pink, to the very dark Tint 8. Finally, with the end of the pastel, I made light dots to create sparkle. This has been my aim – to emphasize the intense contrasts of the dark boats and mud against the bright water.

HILL FARMER

First stage

This painting was based partly on imagination and partly on memory. I paint a great deal in mountain and hill country, so I frequently meet farmers looking for sheep on the mountainside, in the wind and pouring rain. I wanted to capture these conditions in my painting.

First stage I drew the figure on Blue Grey Tumba Ingres paper with a blunted wood cocktail stick dipped in black drawing ink. When the stick was first dipped into the ink, it produced a dense black line, but the stick quickly absorbed the ink so the line became grey and broken, giving an interesting change of density.

Second stage While the ink was still wet, I smudged parts of it with my finger-tip to create patches of black. The idea was to have, instead of blue-grey paper all over, paper that was grey in some parts and black in others. You will see the purpose of this in the next stage. When the ink was dry, I started to block in the pastel background with strokes of Grey Green, Indigo and Burnt Umber and added touches of these colours and Raw Sienna to the coat.

Finished stage Then I really started to make use of the ink drawing. I dragged a light pastel, Madder Brown Tint 2, over the dark ink in the face, and a dark pastel, Burnt Umber Tint 8, over the light side of the face. The purpose of this seemingly contradictory process was to intensify the brightness of the light pastel by allowing the black ink to show through. The hands, and other bright accents in the painting, are also emphasized by dragging light pastel over black ink. I was careful to apply the pastel in gentle strokes so the black ink was not obliterated.

As a contrast to the bright highlights, I wanted some dark, hard-edged shapes, so I painted the cap, trousers, boots and parts of the coat by pressing the pastel firmly into the paper. It is important to have solid, blocked-in shapes such as these as a foil to the free pastel strokes elsewhere. As I painted the boot, I carefully shaped the heel, because I think that small, accurate statements such as this give a feeling of conviction within the overall impressionistic style of the painting.

Then came the rain, slicing across the painting. This could not be treated tentatively. I subdued any fear of spoiling the painting and attacked it, slicing lines of pale grey across it. This vigorous drawing action cut across the edges of the figure, breaking up the edges so the form of the figure was partly lost in the rain.

Second stage

Finished stage

PORTRAIT

Portraits are often painted with almost photographic accuracy and pastels are very suitable for this sort of finish. The pastel can be rubbed into the paper to give a smooth surface, and to blend and fuse the colours to give subtle gradations in the flesh tones. This sort of treatment was very much favoured in Victorian times and some painters continue this polished treatment today, with remarkable results. I prefer a less finished surface; I like to see the way the pastel has been applied with open, unblended strokes. The skill here lies in accurate judgement of the colour and tone of neighbouring pastel strokes. If they are correctly chosen, they will sit comfortably alongside each other, but still show the spontaneity of the medium.

The first thing was to decide which tone and colour of paper to use. This is particularly important with portrait painting where the tonal variations of the flesh can be very subtle. There is a danger with a dark or a very light paper that tones can contrast too much. I chose a mid-tone grey, Fabriano Stone Grey Ingres, to help me achieve the tones of the face. I used this mid-tone as a starting point and worked either side of it with slightly paler or slightly darker pastels, gradually building up to the main highlights and the darkest parts. When I painted the darker parts, I dragged the pastel gently over the paper, allowing the cool grey to break through the pastel and suggest cool tints within the dark areas. This process was especially useful in the shadowed parts.

Diagram and first stage My first step was to draw some guiding lines. I did these decisively and crisply. While making the drawing, I related points and lines to each other. I noticed the triangle formed by the points at the base of the nose and the ends of the eyes. I looked for the top of the ear and related it to the level of the eyes. I noticed that the outer slope of the ear was parallel to the slope of the nose, and the slope of the nostril echoed the slope of the eyebrow. I made a separate diagram to show you these relationships. I do not consciously strive for a likeness of the sitter. The likeness will come if I accurately judge the relative spacing, positioning and angularity of these points. Sometimes, I slightly emphasize the angularity of a line to bring out a particular characteristic that interests me.

In drawing the portrait, I used combinations of Blue Grey Tint 4 and Warm Grey Tint 3. I then added tentative slabs of tone, in Green Grey Tint 1 and Blue Grey Tint 4, with sideways strokes of the pastel, just to start feeling my way into the process of painting.

Second stage I first looked for the main structural planes of the face and indicated these lightly, but decisively, with sideways strokes of Green Grey Tint 4. Detail was ignored and I looked for the shape of the eye socket and massed it in with flat slabs of colour. Notice how the eye socket is mostly in shade. This is because the underside of the eyebrow was turned away from the light and cast a shadow which extended below the eye. Within this shadow, a little area of light caught the upper eyelid where it curved over the eyeball. The upper lid also cast a line of shadow on the top of the eyeball, whereas the lower lid melted into the face. Many beginners make the mistake of drawing a line around the whole eye – the only line is under the upper eyelid. I extended the tone of the eyebrow as a continuous shape down the side of the nose, over the cheek and under the nose.

The colours I had used so far were mostly Green Grey and Blue Grey. I then indicated some flesh tints with Burnt Sienna Tints 0 and 2 on the forehead, nose and chin. I also added a little background tone with the Blue Grey to help me define the shape of the face. I indicated the cap and jersey with slabs of Indigo Tints 4 and 6.

Third stage This was a fairly simple stage, where I began to strengthen the colours and tones already on the paper. I added more Blue Grey to the shaded eye socket and the side of the nose, and a little Green Grey under the nose. While doing this I was careful not to cover up and overwork the previously applied pastel; leaving some of this pastel uncovered gave a look of freshness. I dragged a little Indian Red Tint 2 over the cheeks, forehead, nose and chin, and began to place the highlights with Burnt Sienna Tint 0. The eyes were slightly darkened with Warm Grey pastel.

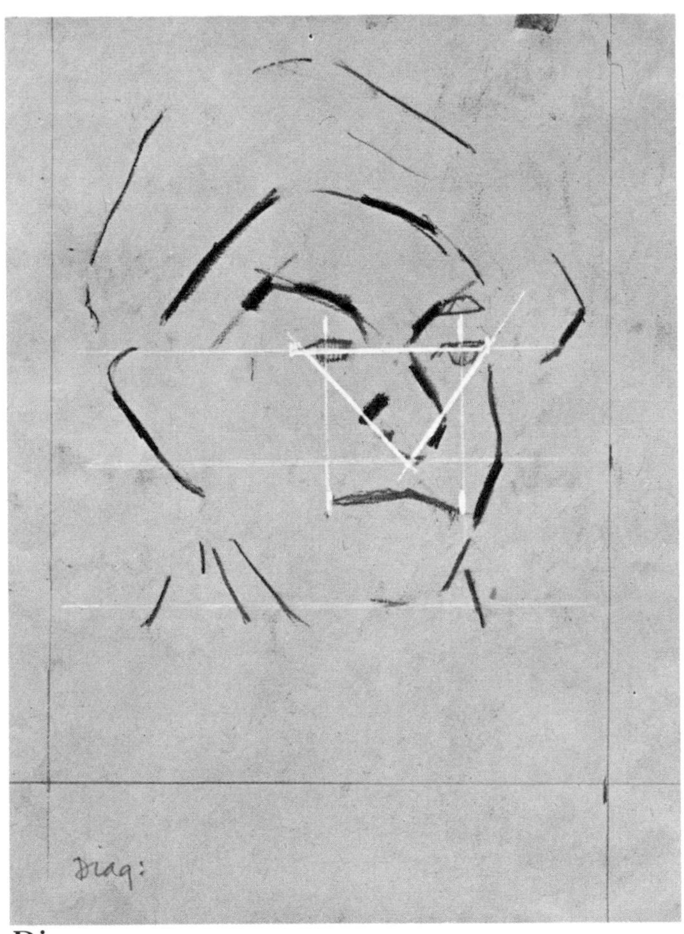

Diagram

First stage

Second stage

Third stage

Finished stage I quickly massed in the background, repeating some of the colours I had used in the face: Warm Grey, Green Grey and traces of Burnt Sienna. The cap was strengthened with Indigo firmly pressed on the paper. I continued to build up colour on the face – repeating the previous colours with greater pressure, always leaving some of the previous applications uncovered. Notice that I didn't paint the white of the eye; I left the original grey, adding just a little more pressure to the dark shadow of the eyelid, to give just the merest hint of highlight. If you ever wish to paint the white of the eye, never use white – use a pale grey such as Cool Grey Tint 1. Also notice that I used hardly any colour for the mouth – I just indicated the upper lid and used a hint of light pastel for the lower lip. The jersey was blocked in with bold strokes of Indigo and touches of Black.

G. John Blockley

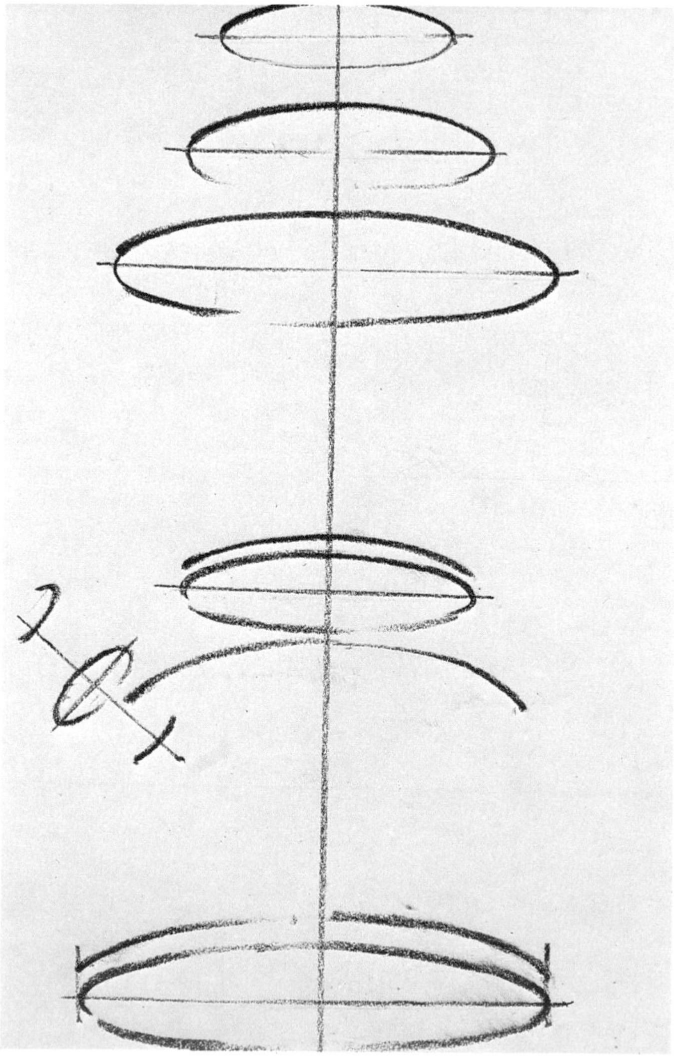

OIL LAMP

I am rarely interested in painting still life groups such as pots and glass jugs carefully arranged in front of a drape. I prefer to paint a group of objects just as they occur. After all, we can't rearrange the landscape and we paint that as it is, with perhaps a few adjustments. So with a still life group I never pose the objects; I wait until my eye is caught by a group of objects lying around just as they were left, preferably in some disorder. When considering such a group don't think that all the objects have to be wholly contained within the picture. There are many paintings by leading artists where objects are cut in half by the edge of the painting. It is much more important that the arrangement is interesting, as a pattern, or in colour relationships, than nice and tidy.

It is useful to make a few simple sketches to try out such compositions. My brass oil lamp normally hangs in a corner of my studio, but the very quick pencil sketch which I made some time ago shows it standing on a bench surrounded by other bits and pieces. I viewed the group from different angles and made a number of little sketches, fitting the objects within a roughly drawn frame. In this sketch I aimed for a satisfactory arrangement of dark and light shapes of varying sizes. I was primarily concerned not with fitting the oil lamp itself into a picture, but with the way its shape related to other items standing on the table.

I did not rearrange any of the items, and was not over-concerned with any one item. Indeed, I was not worried about having cut off the top of the lamp – I was interested in the group as a whole. I looked at the shape of the items and the spaces between them. Negative shapes, as these spaces are called, are often as interesting as the shapes of the objects. It is a good idea to make little sketch motifs with a soft pencil or piece of charcoal, concentrating on the shapes and light and dark tones. Walk round the group, look down on it, view it from below, and don't move anything. See if you can design a satisfactory composition within the existing group.

First stage For this painting I concentrated on the lamp itself, hanging, as it usually is, from a beam in the corner of my studio. The lamp demanded accurate drawing, especially as I decided to make it the only feature in the painting. My diagram shows how I started to construct the lamp by drawing a vertical line through the centre, and then horizontal lines on which I drew the ellipses of the lamp. When I drew this basic construction, I had to judge how far apart the ellipses were. This can be done by mentally comparing the relative distance between them, or measuring each distance with a pencil held vertically, at arm's length. I also had to compare the spacings of the ellipses with their widths. My problem was not only to draw accurately the ellipses, but also to judge the width and depth of each one, and fit them all in their correct spacing relative to the height of the lamp, which in turn had to fit into the height of the paper.

This element of judgement is present in all drawing; we have to judge the width of a window in relation to its height, and the spacing between the windows. This judgement obviously comes from practice, so it is a good idea to make such mental measurements whenever you can, not just when painting, but even when you are walking down the street. Stop, and mentally proportion the windows and doors, and if you have time to stop and draw the proportions, so much the better. It is not easy to fit all the sizes and proportions into a given paper size, so it is good to carry out such exercises whenever you can.

Once I completed the basic drawing construction, I was ready to start the painting. I chose Tan Fabriano Ingres paper, because it roughly corresponded to the dull brass of the lamp and I was able to let some of the paper show in the painting. I drew the outline of the lamp with charcoal. For the purpose of this demonstration, I drew a much stronger line than I normally do, but charcoal is easily removed by flicking it with a cloth, and I did this before applying the pastel.

Second stage I studied the tones and colours of the lamp. Within the brass parts, there were subtle changes of colour and only a few really dark tones. I decided to leave these subtleties for a while, and get on with the easily-identified dark passages. The light came from the left, so the lamp cast a shadow on the timber frame from which it was hanging. This was a positive area with which to start. I used a piece of Madder Brown Tint 8 pastel about 1 inch long and drew a band of colour down the paper, following the contour of the lamp. This one downward stroke of pastel defined the profile of the lamp and cast shadow in one drawing action. The bottom part of the lamp cast a big, rounded shadow, and I used Indigo Tint 4 to extend the Madder Brown shadow to make this interesting shape.

I worked a little Indigo into the shadow near the glass bowl. This change from brown to indigo introduced a little variety into the shadow. The brown and indigo are similar in tone, that is, they are equally dark, so they blend together

First stage

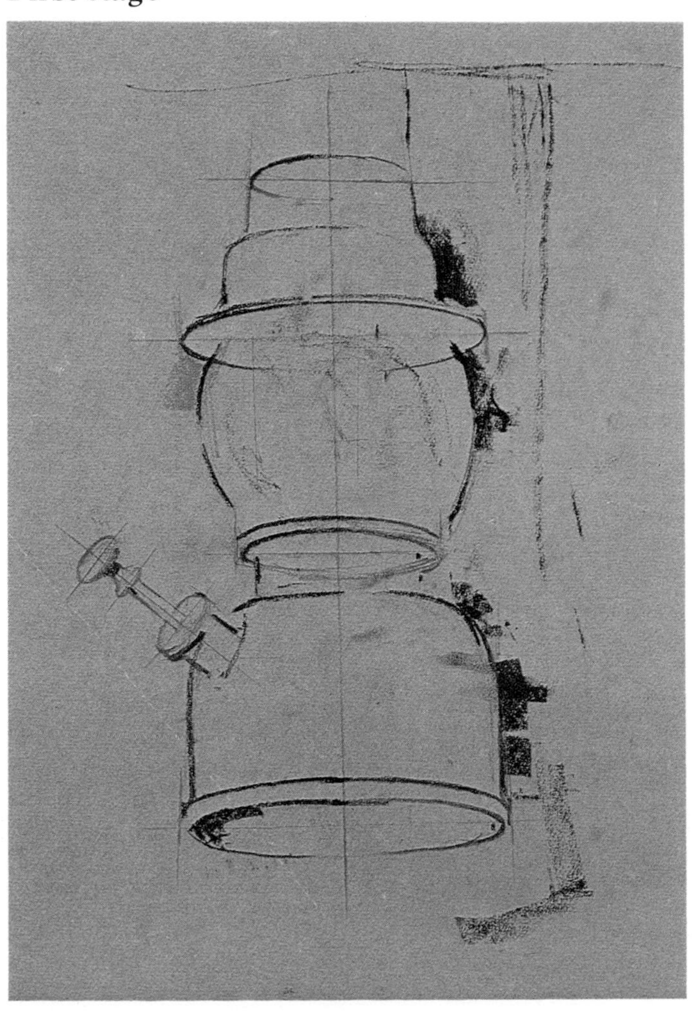

Second stage

Third stage

nicely. With the same tint of Madder Brown, I registered the other darks; under the top rim of the lamp, on the base of the lamp and in the shadow behind the timber frame. These dark passages, on the tan paper, immediately gave volume to my outline drawing and the painting took a rapid step forward.

My painting then consisted of the light charcoal outline and the dark shadows, and I began to consider the lamp itself. I drew bands of Hooker's Green Tints 8 and 5 and a little Warm Grey Tint 3 for the glass bowl. I used bands of Warm Grey Tint 4 and a little of the Hooker's Green for the brass parts. I left quite a lot of the paper uncovered. There is always a great temptation to put in the highlights at this stage, but I like to leave these until the end.

Third stage The painting needed some finishing touches to pull it together, so I strengthened the dark shadow at the bottom and the dark parts of the lamp. I intensified the lighter parts of the lamp by adding more of the original colours with increased pressure on the pastel.

Finished stage I merely repeated the colours to cover more of the paper surrounding the lamp. I added a few accents of green and grey on the lamp, and hinted at the white mantle inside the glass. Finally, I firmly placed the few highlights.

APPLES

Here is another quick pencil sketch to explore the possibilities of a group, this time some apples and a wine bottle. It is a deliberately rough sort of drawing, made with a soft pencil, mostly with the side of the lead held on the paper instead of the point. By holding the pencil this way, I was able to block in the drawing with thick lines and quickly establish the pattern of light and dark. This is a working drawing, a private drawing for my own use. Several such drawings can be made in a short time to decide the best arrangement. We have to concentrate on their pattern making purpose and discipline ourselves not to get concerned with a 'nice' drawing or with the technique of the pencil work.

The pencil can be rubbed, smudged and worked over to discover an arrangement that pleases. I chose pencil for this drawing, but I sometimes use a flat-ended oil painter's brush dipped in gouache or watercolour, charcoal or, of course, pastel. Anything that makes a mark will do. Some painters rub charcoal all over the paper and rub away the light parts with a putty rubber. Whichever medium you use, it is great fun to make these rough exploratory drawings. The process should be uninhibited, without fear of spoiling the work.

First stage

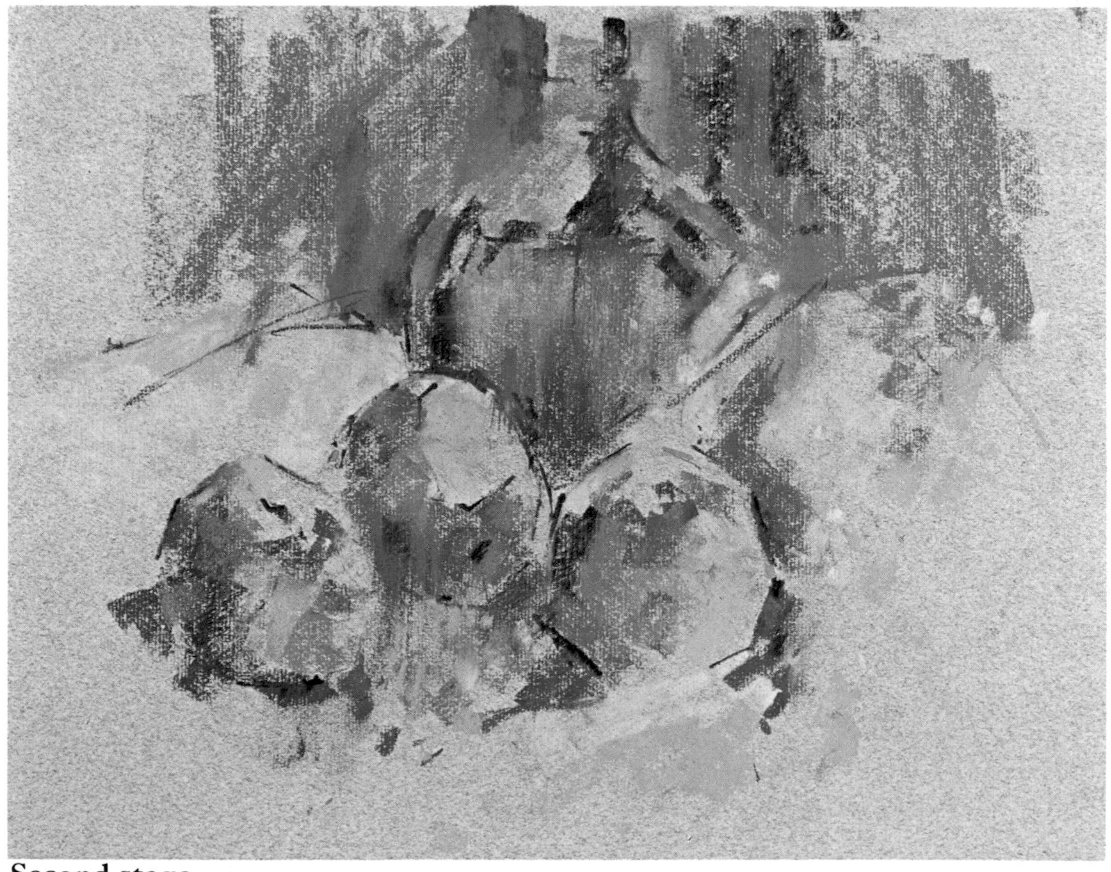

Second stage

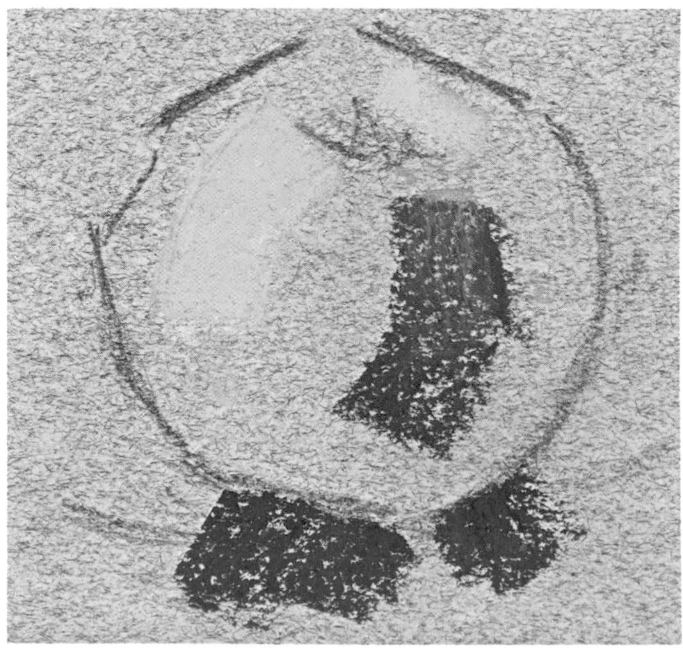

In the later stages of the painting, you will see that I applied the pastel with the same positive strokes but I used the side of the pastel lightly, so I did not fill the grain of the paper. I wanted the paper to break through to give a luminosity to the pastelled surface. I thought of the curved surface of the apples as being built up with a number of almost flat planes – like the facets of a cut diamond – so I made short, rectangular slabs of colour. The directions of the pastel strokes are important – they follow the general curve of the apple, but with short, angular changes of direction. This treatment is one in which the quality of the pastel application is of great importance. I wanted to involve the viewer and invite him to examine the way the paint was applied.

I had a growing feeling that I wanted to keep the painting light and sparkling with some space around the group of apples. I think this feeling came from the light reflecting from the apples. They are fresh, green and bright, with small flashes of highlights on their smooth surfaces, which echo the glints of light in the folds of the

Finished stage

pale blue cloth. I decided to paint a horizontal picture, to give a sense of space around the group, and I chose a fairly light paper, Tumba Ingres Purple Grey, a lot of which I left showing in the final painting – sometimes in large, uncovered areas, or breaking through lightly applied pastel.

First stage Apart from this change to a horizontal format, I kept the positioning of the apples and bottles generally the same as in the sketch. My first step was to draw some guiding lines for the shapes of the apples and the bottle with charcoal. I drew these lines with positive, firm strokes. Although we might think of the apples and bottle as spherical shapes, notice that I made the lines short, straight and angular because of my feeling for the subject and the medium I chose. I felt the angularity of the drawing gave character to the apples and was in keeping with the direct strokes of the pastel. I started to make a few trial pastel strokes. I used Green Grey Tint 4 for the background, Sap Green Tints 1 and 5 for the apples and Indigo Tints 1 and 3 for the cloth.

Second stage I continued to apply these colours, progressively pressing them more firmly into the painting, always working in short, angular directions. I was careful to keep the pale Sap Green clean and unsmudged, because I wanted it to sparkle as reflected light. I sharpened the edges of the dark tones on the bottle and added Raw Umber Tint 1 and Madder Brown Tint 6 to the label. I blended a few pastel strokes together, by gently rubbing with my finger.

Finished stage I continued to build up the features with the same colours and intensified some of the shadows under the apples and the bright highlights on the apples. I then added a few important finishing touches. I suggested a feeling of dazzling light reflecting from the apple surfaces by flicking bright strokes of pale Sap Green in vertical strokes over the apples. These strokes broke up the surface and the edges of the apples to create crisp flickers of light.

TREES

Trees are a fascinating subject for a painting. These three were part of a row standing along the top of a grassy bank. I liked the pattern they made with the sky showing between them, and was intrigued by the mottled surfaces everywhere. The tree trunks were blotched with black, grey and tints of bronze and the pattern seemed to continue into the bank, with its patches of grass growing between stones and eroded soil. The painting is about the decorative surfaces and I thought in terms of a mosaic of echoing shapes and colours.

This sort of thinking plays a great part in my own painting and you should consider similar ideas yourself. Look for an interesting characteristic of a subject and influence your painting towards it. In this painting the interest was obvious; even the sky spaces between the branches were roughly similar in shape to the patterns in the tree trunks and ground.

I sketched the outline of the trees with charcoal on Stone Grey Fabriano Ingres paper and immediately cross-hatched the sky, temporarily leaving the paper to represent the tree trunks and branches. For the sky, I used Coeruleum Tint 0, with hints of Indian Red Tint 0. I hatched the lines close together so the sky was almost unbroken colour, as I wanted to confine texture to the trees and ground.

I then had a piece of grey paper with the light shapes of the sky on it and I started to register the general pattern of the mid-tones. With the side of Warm Grey Tint 3 I drew bands of colour, in various directions, over the foreground. This pastel was slightly warmer and a little darker than the grey paper and by dragging it lightly over the paper I was gradually able to indicate a pattern all over the foreground. I then added firmer strokes of the same pastel and some darker tints of it. Occasionally, I softened an edge with my finger and left round and oval shapes of the paper uncovered. I outlined a few of the rounded shapes with the end of a Sepia pastel. I continued this process, adding tints of Autumn Brown pastel as I worked the pattern into the trees.

Finally, I pressed strokes of Sepia Tint 8 into the paper to arrive at the very dark passages. Don't be frightened about painting such strong darks. They are important in this painting to emphasize the pattern. I also used the end of this pastel to draw the finer branches.

I followed the same procedure to paint the single tree study. I enjoy picking out a single motif such as this, and painting a small, intimate picture.

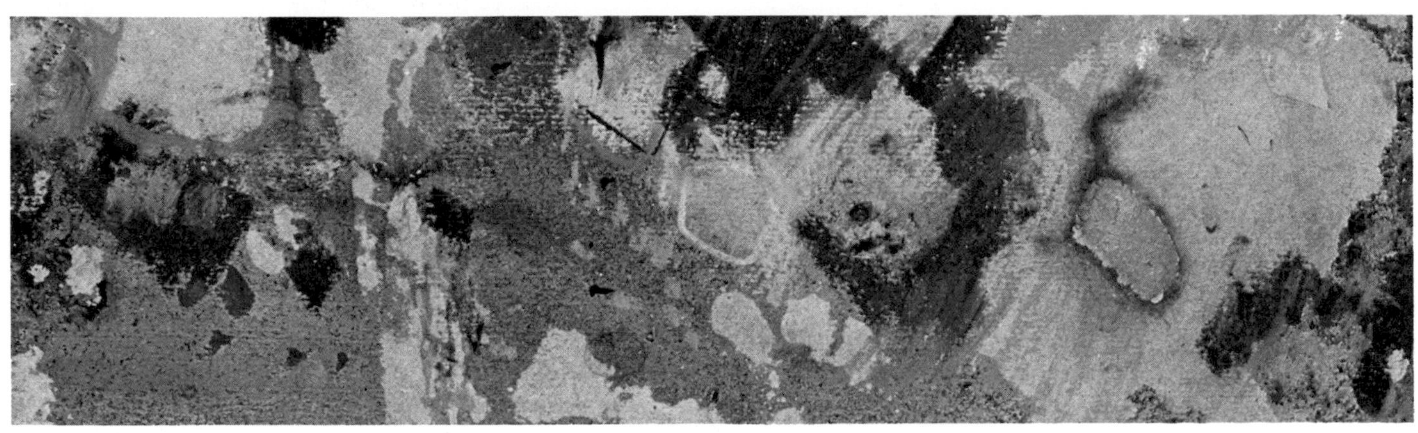

COTSWOLD LANDSCAPE

This landscape is typical of the upland countryside surrounding my studio; big and open with wonderful skies. I love to go up there, especially in the early morning or evening when the quality of light seems to bring out the colours of the landscape. In this painting, I wanted to record the storm clouds building up, and even as I looked, local rain slanted down to break the distant skyline. The sky was dark indigo at the top and lightened towards the skyline with broken paler blue, almost green, with a hint of pale cream here and there. The lighter clouds seemed to glint with light against the sombre indigo, and I immediately felt the effect could best be described with short, staccato strokes of pastel, applied crisply and unrubbed.

The colours of the dark clouds were echoed in the long sweeps of the distant hills, and in other parts the normally brown soil of the landscape was modified by the grey clouds to bands of dark purple-brown. These low-toned sweeps of colour were relieved by hard-edged slices of brighter colour, almost pink. I asked myself what pastel colour I should use for this, and thought of a lighter tint of Purple Brown. When you have experience of looking at the landscape and painting it, you will find yourself thinking in terms of pastel colours at all times, not only when you are painting.

First stage I chose Deep Stone Ingres Fabriano paper, because it seemed to match the middle tones of the landscape, and I drew a few lines with charcoal to register the main shapes and contours of the landscape. These are the black lines in the illustration. I did not draw the precise shape of each field because there was a danger of painting in a detailed way, filling each individual shape, as if I were 'painting by number'. I wanted to apply the pastel in sweeping motions to suggest the long undulations of the landscape, so I drew only a few guiding lines. The profile of the tree was drawn with straight, angular lines.

For this demonstration I pressed the charcoal on to the paper much stronger than I normally do; I only need the faintest guiding line. I had to remember to dust the line drawing down by flicking it with a rag before going on to the next stage because I didn't want the black outline to show in the final painting. I lightly indicated the outline of the clouds with white pastel to establish the cloud pattern. Clouds will constantly change, but it is impossible to keep changing the painting, so we have to register an interesting pattern and stick to it.

The work so far had consisted of drawing lines with the end of a piece of charcoal or pastel. I then started to use the side of the pastel to drag bands of colour on to the paper. I registered the light tones of the sky with Silver White and a few mid-tones with Blue Grey Tint 2. I indicated the lighter green of the tree with Olive Green Tint 4 and the darker green with Tint 7. The brief bands of light across the landscape were made with Raw Sienna Tint 1. At this stage, I was just beginning to feel my way into the painting, so I kept the pastel strokes simple, tending to stroke them all in the same direction. I was careful not to concentrate on any particular part of the painting, and instead I aimed at covering most of the paper with open pastel strokes. As the painting proceeded, I filled in the spaces and built up the layers of pastel.

Second stage The pastel had been applied with positive strokes, but only light pressure. I continued to expand these colour strokes, using firmer pressure on the pastel, to cover more of the paper. I kept checking in my mind that the colours looked right. Gradually building up to the final intensity of pastel is a good way to work; although mistakes can be removed with a brush I think it is good discipline not to rely on correction.

I pastelled long strokes of Purple Brown Tints 1 and 6 and Green Grey Tint 1 across the foreground.

Third stage I stopped and had a good look at the painting and even walked away from it for a few minutes. This little break is enough for the eye to look at the painting again, with a fresh appraisal, and errors not previously noticed often become obvious. I asked myself if I was satisfied with the pattern of shapes and relationship of colours that were firming up on the paper. My interest was mainly with the sky, so I checked that I was sticking to this in the painting. Were there any bright parts in the landscape that attracted attention away from the sky? Yes! The pink to the right of the tree was too bright and must be subdued. How could I have done this? I could have smudged it into the grey paper with my finger, but that would have led to an indecisive quality in the painting. I could have dusted it down with a stiff brush and applied new pastel of a slightly darker tone. I decided that as the pastel had been put on the paper fairly gently I could safely apply another quick layer of a darker tone without making it smudged and overworked. I thought that when I did this the colours in the landscape would be sufficiently subdued in relation to the sky.

Then I took a hard look at the sky. I decided the pattern of the clouds was sufficiently interesting, with each light cloud almost echoing the shape of its neighbour, and all of them sloping in one direction. Notice my pastel strokes in the clouds; although the clouds themselves slope down to the right, the pastel strokes within them slope down to

First stage

Second stage

Third stage

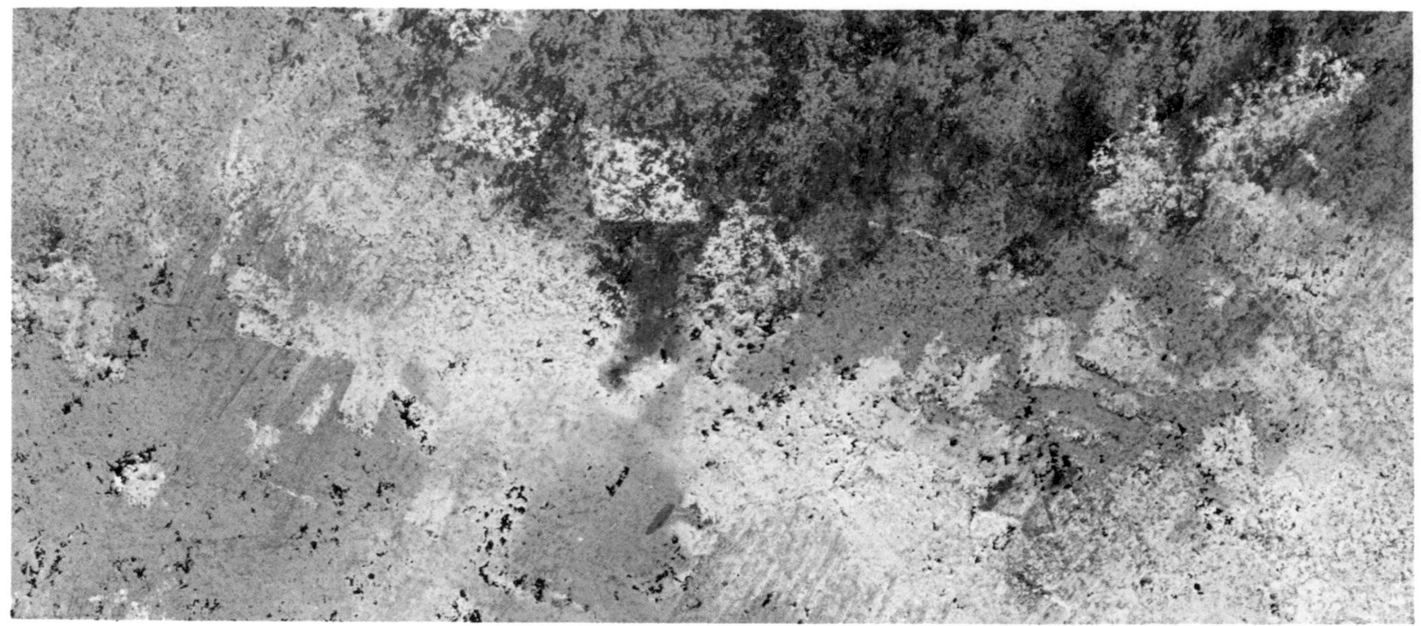

the left. This was a deliberate ploy to counteract the movement of the clouds, sliding out of the picture. The opposition of movement also created some agitation in the sky which helped my wish to draw attention to the sky. I would also like you to notice that the shape of the pastel strokes contributed to the general liveliness of the sky. They are short, quickly-applied slabs of colour; almost jerky and abrupt. I quietened this feeling of movement here and there by overlapping some of the pastel strokes so their edges blended, but did not rub them with my finger.

This was an important stage of the painting, where I looked critically at its progress. As I decided each part was satisfactory, I built up the pastel with firmer strokes.

Finished stage I completed the sky by adding Indigo Tint 3 along the top and pressing in short strokes of Coeruleum Tint 0 to create the greenish-blue pale lights in the white clouds. I strengthened the darks of the landscape with further strokes of Purple Brown and Green Grey. I made some strokes crisp and edgy and allowed others to blend together and soften.

Throughout the painting, I kept in mind my original interest in the sky. I registered the glints of light with crisp flicks of pale pastel and contrasted these with darker greys and blues, sometimes smoothed into atmospheric qualities by gently rubbing with my finger. Having decided at the beginning this was the best treatment for the sky, I stuck to this decision, and limited this treatment to the sky. The landscape was painted entirely with long strokes of pastel, which accentuated the short slabs of pastel in the sky, and also explained the gentle undulations of the landscape.

Finished stage

Here and there, I allowed some light passages across the landscape, but mainly kept the colours fairly sombre so the light was concentrated in the sky.

I also employed smoother strokes in the ground by occasionally rubbing with very slight finger pressure. In contrast, I left the sky unrubbed, in thick layers so the pastel granules clung to the paper surface and reflected the light. I really meant that I wanted the sky to have layers of pastel, so I helped this by fixing each pastel application by spraying it with fixative and pastelling over it. I repeated this at various stages of the sky and left only the final layer unfixed, which gave a shimmering quality to the light parts of the sky.

When painting, I always ask myself questions before each stroke. 'Is this pastel colour light enough, or dark enough; is it the correct tint; is it correct in terms of my main interest, will it support my interest in the sky or will it compete with it?'

You should always try to decide what particular aspect of the subject interests you before starting to paint, and keep this in mind as I do by asking yourself questions throughout the painting.

ACRYLICS

ALWYN CRAWSHAW FRSA

WHY USE ACRYLIC COLOURS... AND WHAT ARE THEY?

Why use acrylic colours? I am constantly asked this question. The quick answer is that I *like* using them and they suit my personality. I will explain that in more detail and then finish this chapter with a brief technical description of this medium. Acrylic colours first arrived on the market in Britain in 1962, in a form called Standard Formula. As you can see from the photograph above, this formula, in the smaller tube, is very thick and has a buttery consistency similar to oil colour. Because of its consistency it was used mainly for palette knife work. The painting could be built up to achieve a tremendous amount of relief work (impasto). The immediate advantage of acrylic over oil colours used in this way was that oils would take months to dry but acrylics would take only hours, even when put on really thickly. Besides artists working with palette knives, there were also artists like myself using brushes with this new medium.

Then, along came the ultimate for the brush man – Standard Formula's stable mate, Flow Formula. Look again at the illustration above and you can see the difference in consistency. Flow Formula, in the large tube, flows; it is better to use with the brush and takes a little longer to dry than Standard Formula. Since then, there has come on to the market a retarder one can add to the paint to slow down the drying time; and a paste called Texture Paste for building up heavy impasto. There are also high-quality nylon

Fig. 1

See the results given by the various kinds of acrylic colour: at the top the colour is mixed with Texture Paste for maximum relief. Below, Standard Formula colour is liberally applied. Stage three shows Flow Formula colour painted flat and stage four shows how a watercolour technique can be achieved

brushes, which I use all the time and find best for acrylic painting, apart from small detail work. More recently, a Staywet palette, which keeps the paint wet on the palette almost indefinitely, was introduced and proved a tremendous breakthrough since it saves a lot of paint that was once wasted through drying too soon.

Why do acrylic colours suit my personality? I believe that a painting comes from the inner self, this gives it the mood – the atmosphere – the invisible quality that makes a painting look alive. If we make a ridiculous assumption and say you have a tremendous urge to paint a particular landscape from one of your sketches and you could paint it in three minutes while that urge was there, then that painting would express your true, uninterrupted feelings on the canvas. Now, three minutes to paint a picture is ridiculous. However, because acrylic colours dry so quickly, a certain speed is possible. As one stage of the painting is done, you can overpaint immediately without picking up the paint from underneath; consequently, you can keep working while the inspiration is there. If circumstances permit, you can start a painting in the morning and finish it in the afternoon as each stage will be dry enough for you to follow on with the next. If you like to put detail in a picture, you can do so as and when you feel it necessary, because the paint will dry quickly enough to allow you to work on top of the previous layer. Being able to paint in this manner is the nearest thing to being able to maintain that feeling for the painting. Even if the whole picture can't be finished at one sitting (which is usually the case), at least certain passages can be worked up to your requirements without being dictated by the long drying time of the paint. It is a direct way of painting and this is one of the reasons why it suits me. You can decide what you want to paint, then go ahead – and you can keep going.

Naturally, as with all painting whether it be oil, gouache, watercolour or whatever, there are techniques to be learned and certain disciplines to be acquired before you can master the medium. These techniques are described in later chapters; by that time, if you have been a good student and have not skipped a few pages, you will have learned quite a lot about the handling of the paint. An interesting exercise is illustrated in **fig. 1** to show the versatility of acrylic colours. Starting from the bottom, we have a canvas, then a delicate watercolour treatment, followed by Flow Formula painted flat, then plenty of Standard Formula giving texture to the surface, and finally acrylic colour added to Texture Paste to get the ultimate in relief work.

We will now look at the basic working methods. The colours come in tubes; always remember to put the cap back on or the colour will start to dry in the tube. You mix

Fig. 2

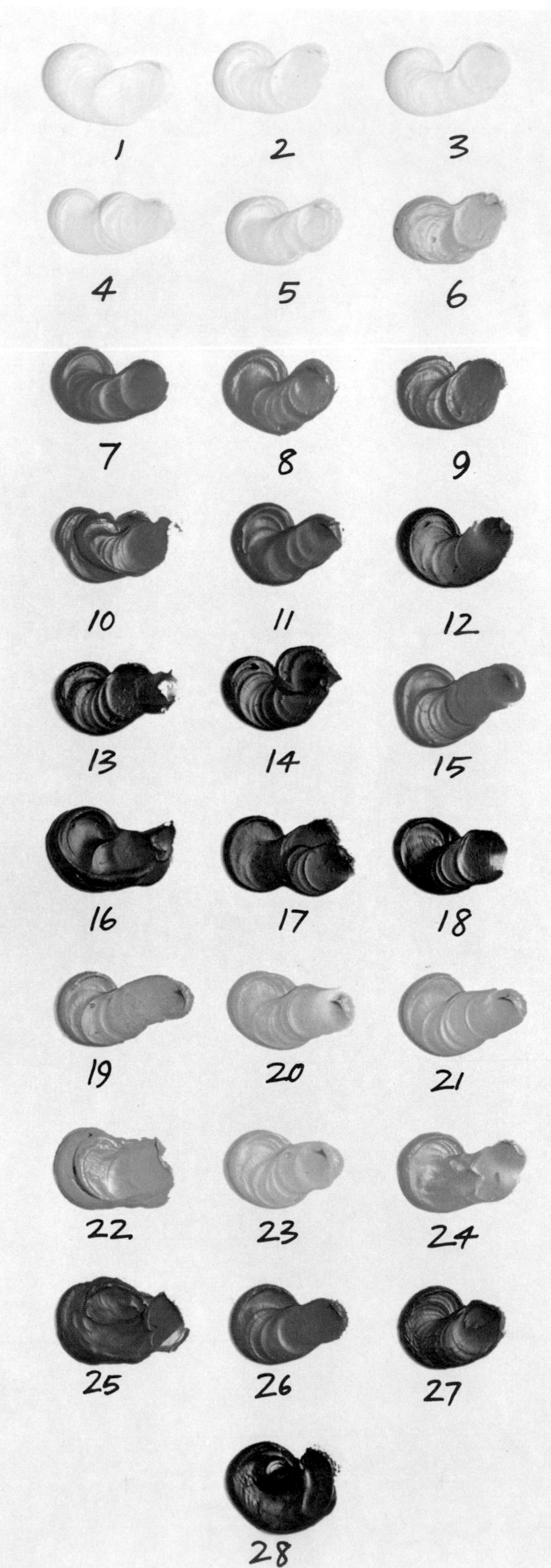

the colour with water – not white spirit or turpentine – and wash your brushes out in water; there is no smell given off when using acrylic colours.

It is advisable to keep your nylon brushes in water all the time – twenty-four hours a day. I have brushes that have lived in water now for seven years. No harm has come to them and since I have been using this method, none has gone hard because of paint drying on it. If by accident you let a brush get hard, soak it overnight in methylated spirit, then work it between the fingers and wash it out in soap and water. When you finish using a brush, even if you know you will need it again in a few minutes, *put it back* in your brush dish; make this one of your first disciplines. When you take it out of the brush dish to use it again, dry it out well on rag. Keep some clean rag handy at all times for this purpose. Only use a *damp brush* when working normally as the acrylic's own consistency is all you need. If you use sable brushes, however, never leave them in water – wash them out immediately after use.

When you squeeze your paint out on to the palette, *always* put the colours in the same *position*; this is another important discipline. The reason is simple: the way you pick up colours from your palette must become second nature as you will have enough to worry about without searching for a particular colour. You will see that in **fig. 3** I have laid out the colours I use in the order I have them

1. Primrose
2. Cadmium Yellow Pale
3. Lemon Yellow
4. Permanent Yellow
5. Cadmium Yellow Deep
6. Cadmium Orange
7. Vermilion (Hue)
8. Cadmium Scarlet
9. Cadmium Red Deep
10. Permanent Rose
11. Red Violet
12. Deep Violet
13. Permanent Violet
14. Indanthrene Blue
15. Cobalt Blue
16. Monestial Blue
17. Monestial Green
18. Hooker's Green
19. Opaque Oxide of Chromium
20. Pale Olive Green
21. Rowney Emerald
22. Turquoise
23. Yellow Ochre
24. Golden Ochre
25. Burnt Sienna
26. Venetian Red
27. Transparent Brown
28. Black

on my palette. There is no magic about the way these are placed; I started this way at art school and I have stuck with it ever since. Because this colour layout works well I suggest you adopt it. I use these ten colours normally but illustrated on the left, in **fig. 2**, is the range of additional colours that you can get in both Flow and Standard Formula.

If you are *not* using a Staywet palette, then use either a glass or plastic surface, or even a dinner plate upon which to mix your colours. Remember that the paint will start to dry while you are working. Do not put out more paint than you will be able to use at one sitting *unless you are using a Staywet palette*.

I think that's enough to absorb for the time being but, for the technically minded, here is the make-up of acrylics. Artists' acrylic colours are made with the same organic and natural pigments used in the manufacture of oil colours. Instead of being bound in a drying oil as in the case of oil colours, or a water-soluble gum as in the case of water-colours, these semi-permanent pigments are bound and dispersed in a transparent, water emulsion of acrylic polymer resin.

Acrylic polymer resins are the product of modern chemistry and are familiar to most people in the form of transparent plastics such as Perspex. The term polymer means the joining together of small mólecules, called monomers, into long chemical chains forming plastic materials. These resins are converted into milky white, water emulsions which will dry as a crystal clear film once the water has evaporated. These emulsions are versatile adhesives in their own right. Combine these resin emulsions with permanent, artists' quality pigments and you have the near ideal situation of a permanent-pigment particle encased in an inert, transparent coating which is not subject to deterioration, yellowing or embrittlement.

Acrylic colours allow a versatility of technique far greater than that of any other medium. The use of additional mediums is covered in the section Basic Techniques. The films of paint formed are tough and flexible and not subject to yellowing. Acrylic paintings can be cleaned by gentle sponging with soap and water.

Acrylic colour is today's modern, instant, permanent and multi-purpose artists' medium.

Fig. 3

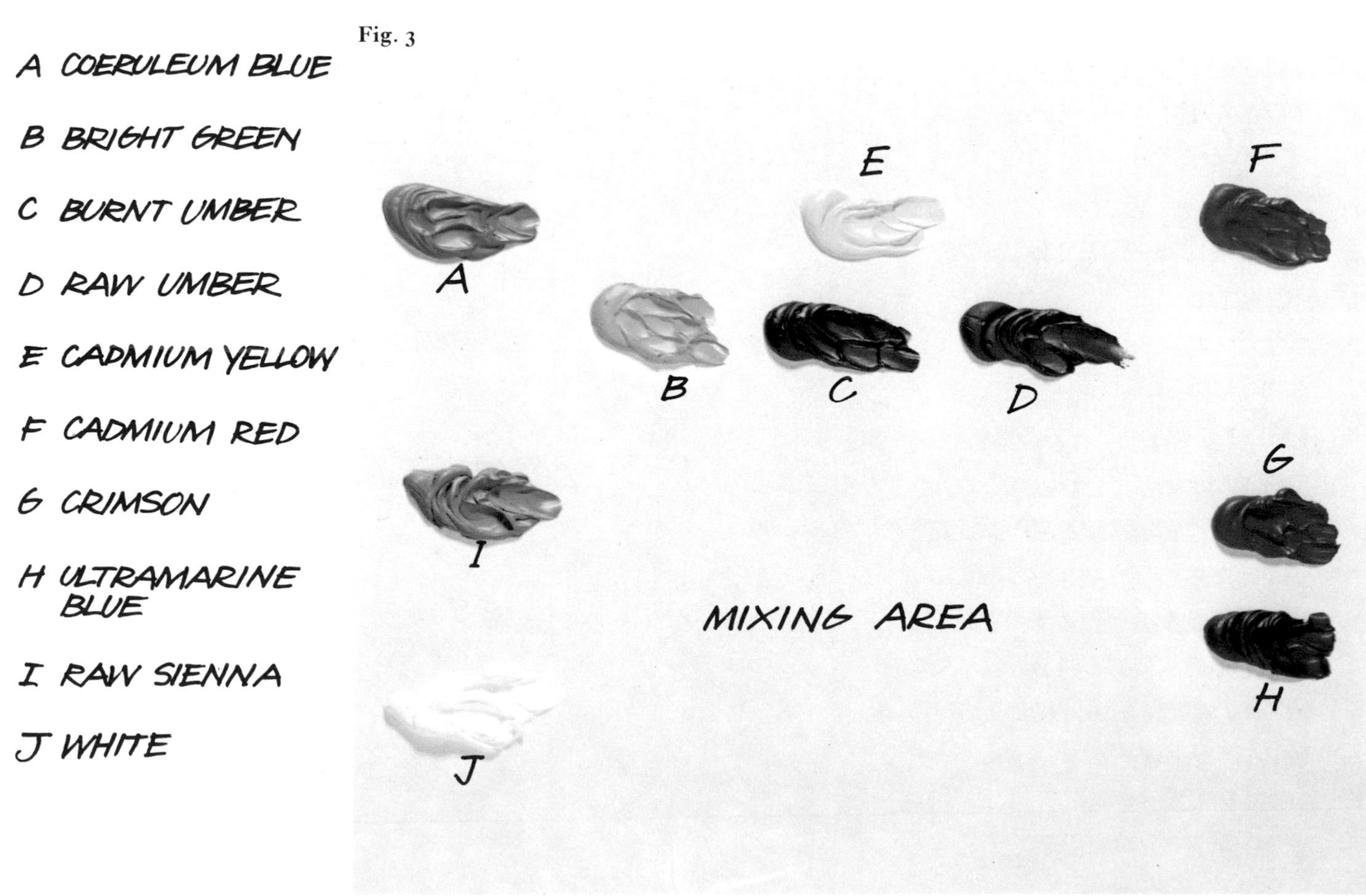

WHAT EQUIPMENT DO YOU NEED?

Equipment can vary from the basic essentials to a roomful of easels, boards, canvases, a wealth of brushes and so on. Some people collect brushes like some anglers collect fishing floats. There's nothing wrong in this at all – in fact, I tend to collect brushes; I have far more than I will ever use but I enjoy the feeling that somewhere I have a brush for the job. Anything beyond the basic equipment, I think, must be left to the individual. I will now guide you through the list of basic essentials, bearing in mind that I will recap at the end of this section.

On the facing page is a photograph of my working table in my studio. It is slightly overcrowded intentionally, so as to show art materials in a working environment and to illustrate how to set up your equipment: the key is below.

Having discussed acrylics earlier, we will now consider the brushes you will need. These are the tools of the trade, they are the instruments with which you will create shapes and forms on your canvas and are by far the most important working equipment you will ever buy. I am asked time and time again: What brushes do I need? My answer always is: The best quality; remember, it is the brush that allows your skills to be expressed and seen. Never treat a brush as a show piece when you are working with it. The brush has to perform different movements and accomplish many different shapes and patterns. If it means that you have to push the brush against the flow of the bristles – then do it. This way, your brushes will gradually become adaptable for certain types of work; you will get to know them and thus

A CANVAS
B EASEL
C WOODEN LAY FIGURE
D WATER CONTAINER
E BRUSH TRAY
F BRUSHES & BRUSH HOLDER
G PENCILS
H VARNISH BRUSH
I TEXTURE PASTE/VARNISH
J PRIMER
K PALETTE KNIVES
L ERASERS
M MEDIUM NO.1 – GLOSS
MEDIUM NO.2 – MATT
WATER TENSION BREAKER
N GEL RETARDER
MEDIUM NO.3 – GLAZE
O FLOW FORMULA COLOURS
P STANDARD FORMULA COLOURS
Q PAINT RAG
R DRAWING BOARD & PAPER
S STAYWET PALETTE
T SABLE BRUSHES

Rowney R
PENCILS
Pencils
PENCILS
colour
formula acrylic
colour
formula acrylic
rowney
rowney
cryla
medium
No. 2 MATT
rowney
cryla
water
tension
breaker

will be able to get the best out of your painting. As one says of the colours on the palette, know your palette, so one should say, know your brushes.

Illustrated here are three different series of nylon brushes and two watercolour series which I use. The Series 201 nylon brush holds less paint than the Series 220 and it is this brush that I use the most. I use Series 260 in place of sable brushes when I want to be more rough with them. As for sable brushes, I use sizes Nos. 1, 2 and 3 of Series 56 for fine line work, and sizes Nos. 3, 4 and 5 of Series 43 for larger, delicate work.

Some artists prefer to use a palette knife instead of a brush. But don't be too rough with the palette knife or you will put a knick in it or catch it in the canvas and flick paint everywhere. Three knives are illustrated and these could be used as a set to start with.

I have already mentioned palettes and a Staywet palette is illustrated on page 159. This is also the best palette for painting out-of-doors. You will also need the materials upon which to apply the paint. Canvas, wood, cartridge paper, brown paper, all these can be used as surfaces for acrylic painting. When we start on our first lessons we will be using some of these surfaces. You will need a drawing board upon which to rest your paper, to give you a firm support while painting.

Three easels are illustrated. Easels are not essential for small work if you are working on paper pinned to a drawing board, but the small table easel is ideal if you want your board at an angle on the table. The large, radial, studio easel is essential for large work as the support you are using must be held firm. The last easel illustrated is a portable one for use out-of-doors; it also folds down and turns into a carrying box for your paints and a canvas up to 69cm (27in) deep. It can also be used inside as your permanent one.

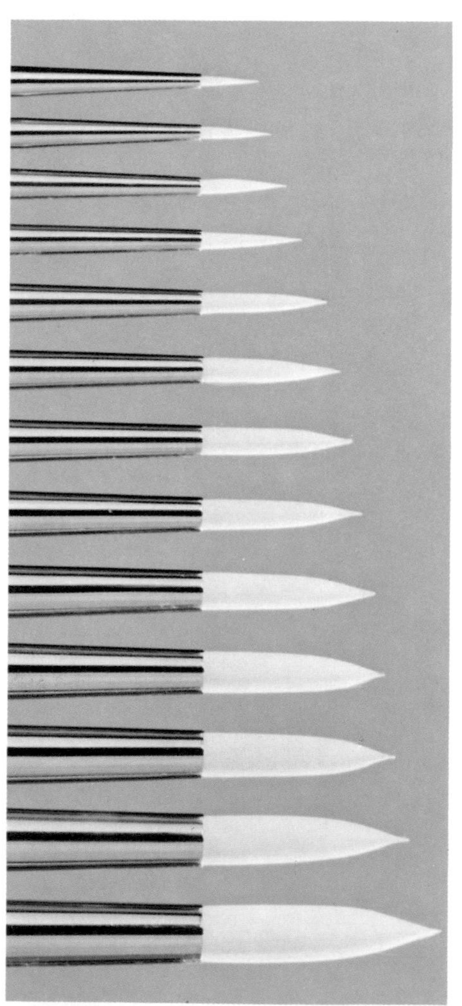

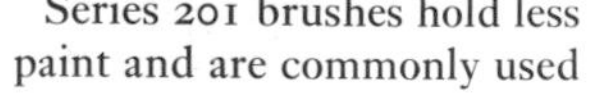

Series 201 brushes hold less paint and are commonly used

This is Series 220

Series 260 brushes are often used in place of sable brushes as they stand up to tougher treatment

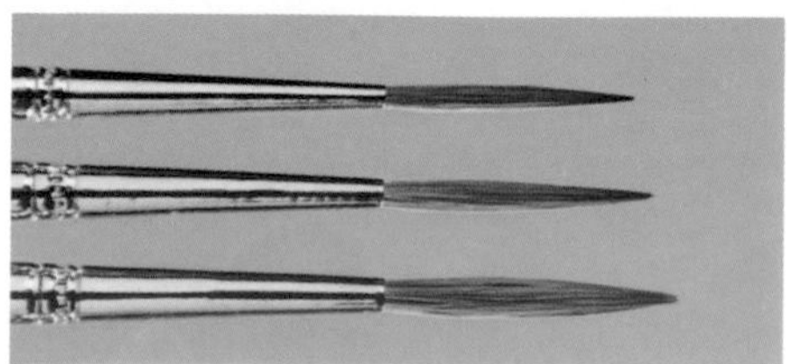

Series 56 sable brushes are used for fine line work

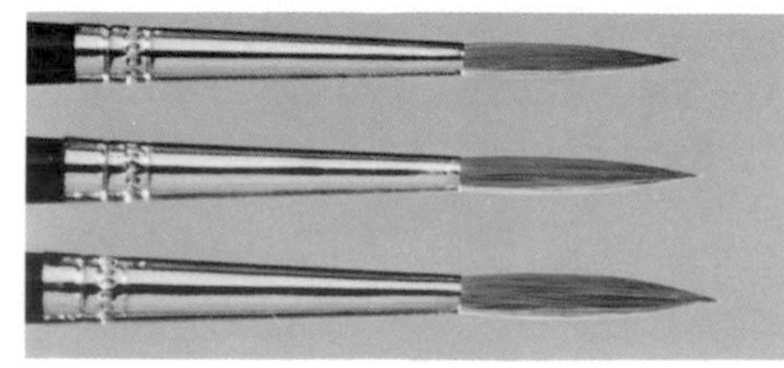

Series 43 sable brushes are used for larger, delicate work

The tray in which I keep my brushes is an old ice box from the fridge; it is long and flat and has been the permanent home for my brushes for the past seven years. When I go about demonstrating I use a tin-foil container, which is just as efficient. Finally, there are special containers on the market for holding brushes in water.

Gel Retarder is very useful to have as it is used for large areas of painting wet on wet. We will come to this in the section Basic Techniques. You will need some acrylic primer for surfaces that are porous and Texture Paste for the Basic Techniques exercises. You will need a water jar for washing out your brushes; this can be anything from a jam jar to a Ming vase. Finally, you need HB and 2B pencils and an eraser.

And so, your basic equipment list will be as follows: a set of ten acrylic Flow Formula colours – colours as on p. 157; brushes, Flat 'curved-in' Nylon size No. 2, Flat Nylon sizes Nos. 4, 8, 12, Round Poster Writing size No. 1, Long hair Sable – Designers Brush size No. 5; Staywet palette, drawing board, brown paper, white cartridge paper, brush tray, acrylic primer, water jar, HB and 2B pencils, and an eraser. This basic equipment will see you through the first exercises and, as you gain more confidence, you can add to your range.

Below is a range of palette knives suitable to start painting: be careful how you use them! On the right are the three most useful easels: a small table type, a large radial studio easel, and a portable, folding one which converts to a carrying box for paints and canvas

LET'S START PAINTING

PLAYING WITH PAINT

Well, the time has come to start painting. If you have not painted before, you must be feeling very excited, but also very apprehensive. Never mind, you will soon be on your way to painting masterpieces. I find that the most difficult part of painting for a complete beginner is actually to put paint on to paper. I think the reason for this is that a beginner expects to see something take shape on the paper, when in fact all that materializes is a funny-shaped area of paint. This is very natural as he or she has not yet learned to control the brush and, more important, has no idea what will happen when paint meets paper. It is at this time that well-meaning friends or relatives tend to make thoughtless remarks like, 'What's that?' Naturally these comments are meant in good humour, but they can be devastating to beginners and even put some sensitive students off painting for good. So we must get over this first hurdle. If we try to take short cuts and run before we can walk, then we have problems. The secret is to start at the very beginning and work through each stage steadily.

To begin with, we will consider colours. If you look around you even as you read this book, wherever you are, there are hundreds of colours. To the beginner the very thought of re-creating those colours in paint can be daunting. But in fact there are only three basic colours – red, yellow and blue. These are called primary colours (see **fig. 4** on the right) and from a combination of these three colours all other colours and shades of colour are made. In painting there are a number of different reds, yellows and blues to help the artist re-create nature's colours. **Fig. 4** shows two of each primary colour and a further three colours and white to make mixing easier. As illustrated earlier, I use these colours

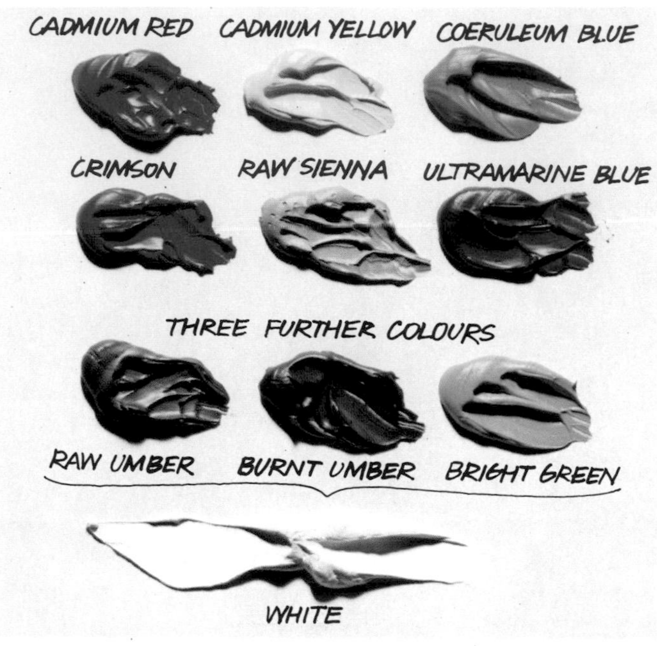

Fig. 4

for all my acrylic painting.

Now to break the barrier of putting paint on to paper (before you start mixing colours). Find a piece of brown paper and play around with the paint on it. The object of this exercise is to see what the paint feels like – you are not trying to paint a picture. You can even use your fingers if you like; try a brush, a palette knife, anything; add more water, less water, mix colours together. You will end up with a funny-looking piece of brown paper, like mine in **fig. 5**, but you will also have experienced the feel of acrylic colour and become more familiar with it.

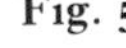

Fig. 5

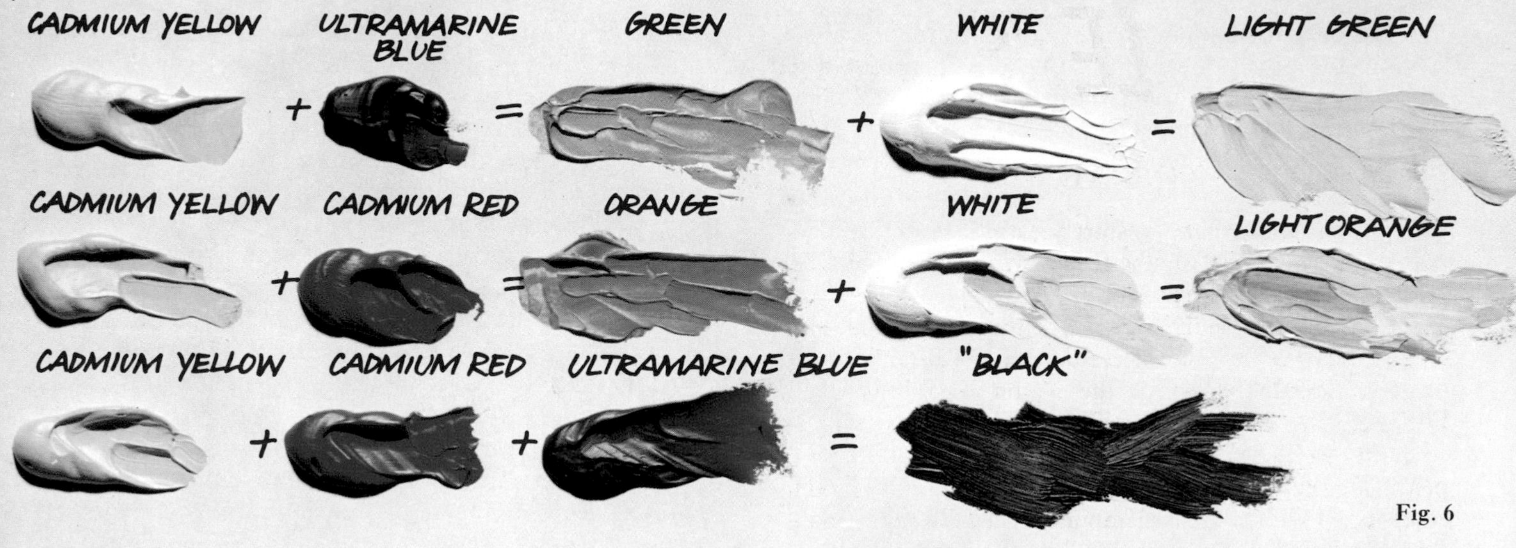

Fig. 6

MIXING COLOURS

Before you start the exercises, you must first practise mixing colours. Take your time and enjoy it. In **fig. 6** I have taken the primary colours and mixed them to show you the results. In the first row, Cadmium Yellow mixed with Ultramarine makes green. If you then add White, you finish up with a light green. In the second row, Cadmium Yellow is mixed with Cadmium Red and this makes orange. To make orange look more yellow, add more yellow than red, and to make it more red, add more red than yellow. Add White to make the orange paler.

As I explained in the section on watercolours, I do not use black when I work in that medium; well, the same applies to acrylic colour and for the same reasons. I was brought up at art school not to use it because it is a dead colour with no life in it. Naturally some artists use it, so by all means try it if you want; but use it sparingly or your colours will become muddy and dull. I mix my 'black' from primary colours. On the whole, if you want a colour to be cooler, add blue, and if you want it warmer, then add red.

Using white cartridge paper, practise mixing different colours. Mix these on your palette with a brush and paint daubs on to your white paper; don't be concerned about shapes – concentrate on the colours. Keep working at this exercise; the more you do, the sooner you will be mixing the colours you want. Whenever you are sitting or standing doing nothing, look at the colours around you and try to imagine how you would mix them with your primary colours.

Remember that as there are only three basic colours, it is the *amount* of each colour that plays the biggest part. You can easily mix a green as in the first line in **fig. 6** but you must experiment on your palette, varying the proportions of yellow and blue, until you achieve the exact shade of green you require. Mixing colours is one of the most important lessons you have to learn. With some people it is more natural than others, but we can all learn through practice.

PAINTING WITHIN GIVEN SHAPES

While you have been mixing colours you have not been concerned with painting particular shapes or lines. Now the time has come to do this and to learn to control your brush. We can start by painting edges of areas that have to be filled in with paint, like the circle in **fig. 7**. Take a two-pence piece or something similar and draw round it with an HB pencil on either cartridge paper or brown paper. Use your small sable brush with plenty of water. Remember, with nylon brushes you should dampen the bristles, but with sable brushes you should just dampen the bristles, but with sable latter to run out of the brush. Try it now, before you start filling in your circle, and get used to the right mix.

When filling in the circle, start at the top and work down

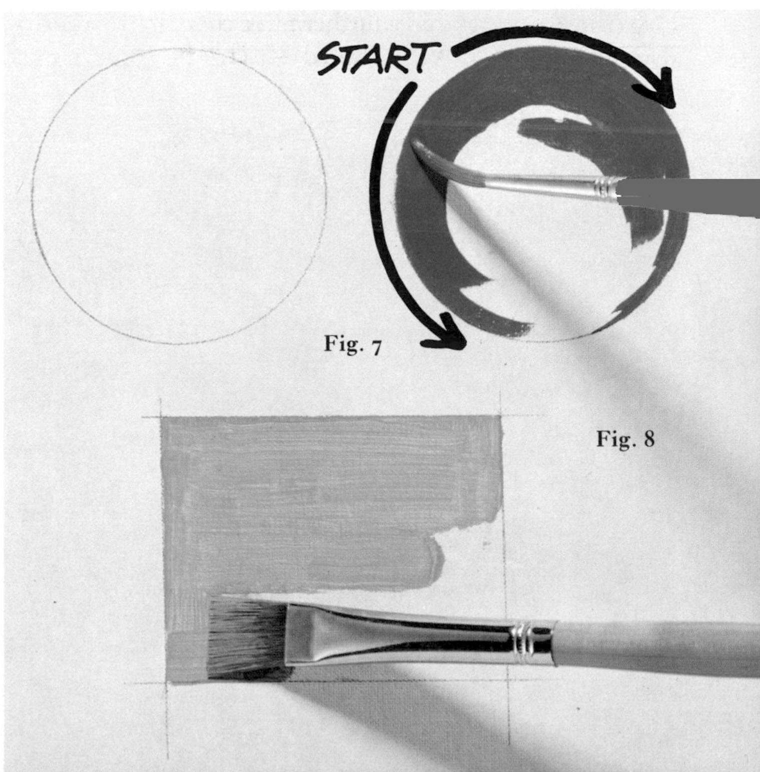

Fig. 7

Fig. 8

the left side to the bottom. Let the bristles follow the brush, i.e. pull the brush down. Try to do this in two or three movements. While painting the left side you will notice that you can follow the pencil line, but as you start at the top again and paint the right-hand side, your brush will cover some of the pencil line and you will feel slightly awkward. You may have found the answer already: turn the paper round and paint the second half like the first! Well, full marks for initiative, but there is a problem – what happens if you are painting a very large canvas or a mural? You can't turn *that* round to suit your brush strokes. The answer is to accept that it feels a bit awkward but that the more you practise the more natural it will become.

Next, let's move on to drawing straight lines. Try drawing a square, like the side of a box, but do not draw round anything – do it freehand. It is important to remember that whenever you are drawing straight lines (other than very short ones), you must move your whole arm and wrist, not your fingers. If you try to draw a straight line downwards moving only your fingers, you will discover that the line will quickly start to bend. By moving only your hand and bending your arm at the elbow, you can achieve a straight line.

The edges of the box can be painted with a small sable brush again, or a small, flat, nylon brush as in **fig. 8**. Experiment with this flat brush, trying out various ways of holding it, and use it to fill in the square.

Now let us take this exercise a stage further. Draw your own shapes and mix your own colours to work with; after all, that is what a painting is – a number of painted shapes. Look around you for colours to mix, and try drawing and painting a 'real shape' – something very simple, like an apple or a box perhaps. If that is too advanced at this stage, don't worry – keep trying and practise as much as you can.

It is helpful to have a knowledge of drawing before you start painting. Some basic guidelines concerning elementary perspective and drawing are given on page 21 in the section on watercolours and these, of course, apply to all media. You do not have to be a perfect draughtsman to be able to paint, however, and if you want to enjoy painting you must not be discouraged if you are not particularly capable at drawing in detail. If you go round an exhibition by a number of artists, you will see a tremendous range of different types of painting. Some are very detailed, some are almost flat areas of colour.

It is important, however, to be aware of light against dark whenever you are painting. Next time you are in the country, look at a scene and half close your eyes: you will see definite shapes that you can easily draw; you will see the light areas against the dark ones and you will find that painting that particular scene is much easier than you had thought. In **fig. 9** I considerably simplified the original drawing of this scene when I painted it. This is what you have to aim for at this stage.

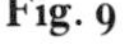

Fig. 9

SIMPLE EXERCISES

We are now ready to paint some simple and familiar objects. If you have practised with your colour mixing and drawing, you will not have much difficulty in copying what I have drawn or in finding your own objects to paint from life.

The best way to start is to copy my illustrations. This will save your worrying about the drawing problems inherent in copying a real object. However, when you have copied from the book, then get the object, set it up in front of you and have a go from the real thing. You will thus feel more familiar with the object itself, having painted it first from the book.

These simple objects must be treated in the broad sense without worrying about detail. Remember: when painting from the real thing, half close your eyes to see the forms and light and dark areas which simplify the shapes where the object is too complicated. Try to paint direct, in these exercises; in other words, go for the colour you see and try to get it first time on to the paper. These exercises are not meant to try your skill at details but to give you experience in painting a whole picture, observing shapes and tones, and applying what you see to paper. In this lesson we will use different supports (surfaces) on which to paint. Let's use cartridge paper first.

Our first simple object is a brick; I am sure you can find one somewhere. Paint the brick in the same way as the box but this time, try to paint each side separately with its own colour (the background was painted beforehand), i.e. the top of the brick was painted first, using the colours shown in **fig. 10**, then the light side and finally, the very light side. The recess in the top of the brick was done last by adding shadow to its left-hand side (**fig. 11**).

We will now use newspaper. On page 166 is a newspaper with a banana painted directly on to it. The banana was drawn on the newspaper with a 3B pencil and then the

Fig. 10 Fig. 11

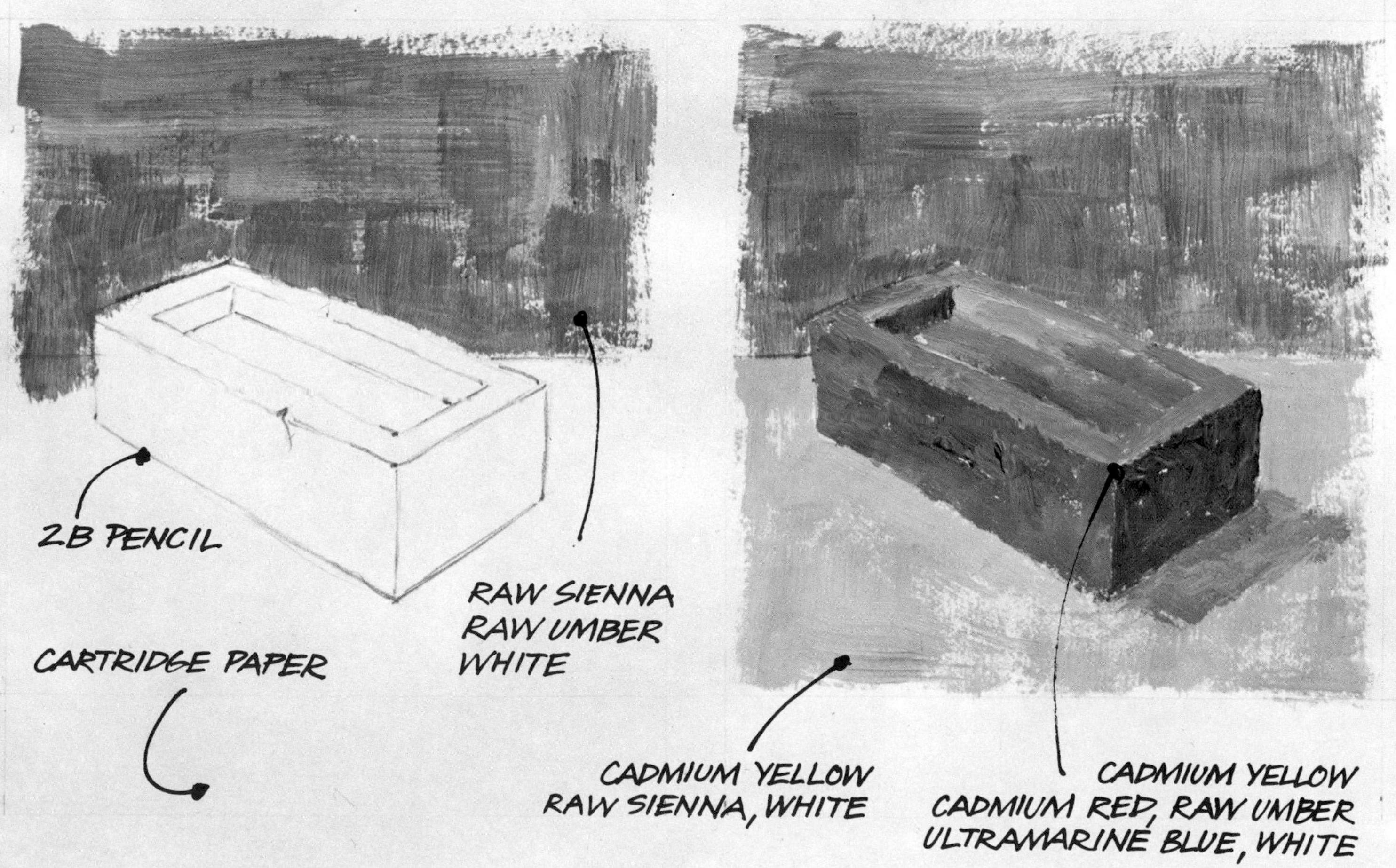

Matched teams in melee

A STRUGGLE TO DRAW

BEXLEY 1, CHOBHAM 1
(Spartan League)

ALTHOUGH Chobham held the lead for most of the game, they were very lucky to get a point as Bexley posed a very real threat from start to finish. Certainly during the first half a goal to Bexley seemed inevitable as they won the majority of the high balls.

Their attacking moves called for many good saves from an improved Steve Osgood and goal-mouth clearances by Mickey Elliott, Pat Folan and Phil Marlow.

LGO benefit
n transfusion

TABLE TENNIS

CKETERS
NDOORS

Field still out of luck

MALDEN TOWN 1, WESTFIELD 0
(Home Counties League)

FIELD must be wondering what they must do to change their luck. Playing against an experienced Malden side, they completely outclassed them for long periods of the match.

Town started with a strong wind in their favour, but the dash and control of Channon, Stillwell, and Jones had their defence in a shambles.

WESTFIELD RES. 3
VIRGINIA WATER 1

Home team in vain bid

RICHMOND VILLA 4,
MONUMENT RANGERS 2

Cards loose grip

WOKING RESERVES 0, STAINES RESERVES 4

Rese... out

FRIMLEY GREEN RES. 1, SHEERWATER
(Surrey Intermediate Cup)

SHEERWATER travelled to Spartan Leaguers Frimley Green and were unlucky to come away empty handed.

The visitors dominated the first half and as early as the first minute a Dave Steel shot was cleared off the line by a defender.

After 20 minutes Frimley took the lead against the run of play, when a long throw-in was headed in by Hickman.

Sheerwater continued to attack and were unfortunate not to equalise before half-time.

After the interval Sheerwater continued to pressurise for the goal they deserved, but to no avail.

Manager Tony Bristow made two substitutions which almost paid off when one of them, Dave Watts, broke through the defence and shot inches wide in the last minute.

Replay will decide issue

BISLEY 3, HORSELL 3

Flying sta...

Netball

Rugby

(Saturday, October 14)

A XV: Chobham v. Guildford and Godalming; Ex A XV: Chobham v. Haslemere; B XV: Chobham v. Haslemere; BAe 1st XV v. Wimbledon II (away); BAe 2nd XV v. Wimbledon II (home).

ext Home Match

ALDERSHOT v. ARTLEPOOL UNITED
Saturday, October 14
League Division Four

Admission to Ground
Adults £1

Woking takes command

HAMBLE OB II 5, WOKING II 2

THE teams were well matched. The score could easily have been Hamble 8, Woking 8, but it was not to be, and Hamble ended up winners on the day.

background was painted. Don't try to keep to the pencil line as if it were a magnet. If you go over, it doesn't matter because the colour will cover it up. Now paint the banana using a size No. 4 nylon brush and a mix of Cadmium Yellow, Raw Sienna and White, and Burnt Umber for the spots. Use Burnt Umber and Ultramarine for the background. Keep the paint thick rather than wet, as the newspaper is porous and water will make it mushy. Once the paint is dry, it will strengthen the paper because you have put a thin layer of plastic (paint) on the surface.

The next banana (bottom left) was painted on top of primer. The paper was primed first with acrylic primer to counteract the absorbency of the newspaper. When it was dry, I drew the banana with a 3B pencil and painted it using the same colours as before.

The orange (bottom right) was painted direct on to the newspaper without priming. Mix Cadmium Red, Cadmium Yellow, Burnt Umber and White for the fruit, Bright Green and Burnt Umber for the background. This time, try using the paint very thick; use Standard Formula colours to create texture. You will also gain experience in using paint that is not quite so easy to handle as Flow Formula.

Now let's turn to brown paper; find some, and we will use that for our next exercise. I have chosen a pan for this one, for a very good reason: you will have to draw a round object instead of a square one. Here the only problem is the ellipse; that is the oval shape you see when you look at the pan. When you draw the ellipse, never give it pointed ends, the line must be continuous as if bent out of a piece of piano wire. An ellipse is a circle that gradually flattens according to your eye level. Take a two-pence coin and hold it upright in front of you: it is now a circle. Now turn it round, closing one eye; as you turn, the circle flattens and becomes an ellipse. If you look closely, you will see there are no sharp corners but just one continuous line all the way round. Instead of the clean, crisp edges of the box, you now have rounded forms which will enable you to practise moulding and graduating your colour to show a curved surface. On the pan side, you can do this by either working the paint from light to dark or by starting with the dark side and adding lighter colour as you go to the light edge of the pan. You may need to work at this pan more than once to get used to round surfaces.

And now back to cartridge paper. Find yourself a book,

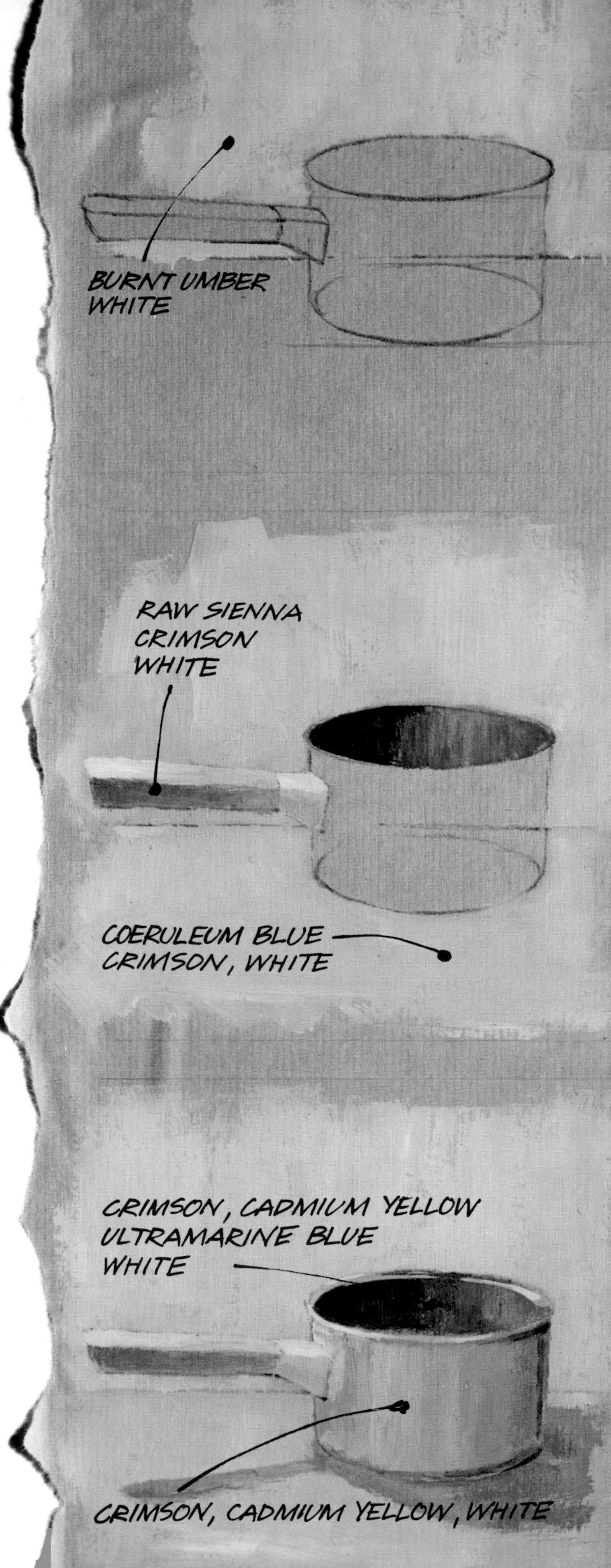

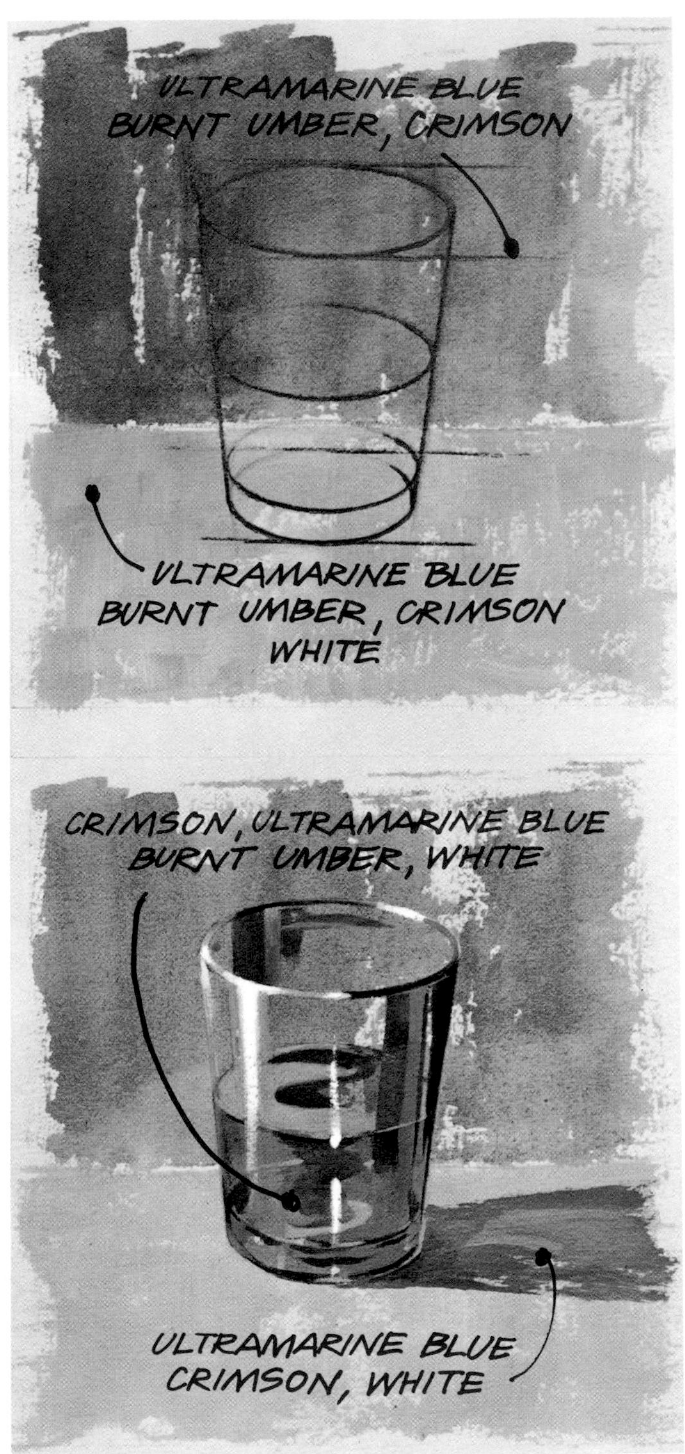

A book and a piece of glass – two more objects to experiment with, each presenting its own particular problems: white pages are not really white and do you honestly think that water is colourless?

preferably a plain-coloured one, and try this on white cartridge paper. We are back to the shape of our box again but this subject demands the extra skill that you should have now acquired.

Paint as usual but where you come to the pages, half close your eyes to see how dark the white pages are on the shadow side. I think you will be quite surprised to find how dark they are. Use a Series 201 brush and take it along the pages; you will find that some of the brush strokes look like the edge of the pages.

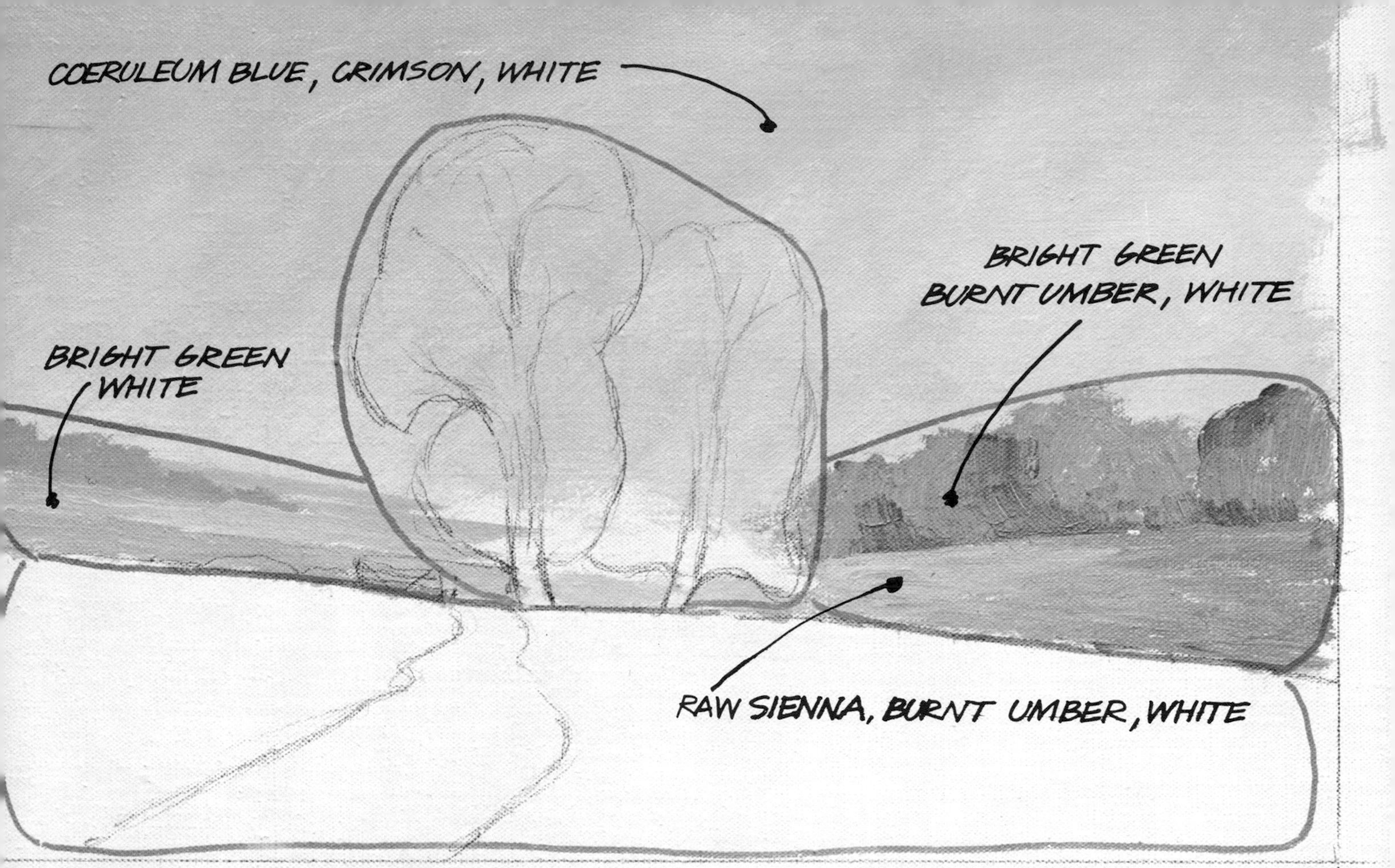
COERULEUM BLUE, CRIMSON, WHITE
BRIGHT GREEN
BURNT UMBER, WHITE
BRIGHT GREEN
WHITE
RAW SIENNA, BURNT UMBER, WHITE

BRIGHT GREEN, CADMIUM YELLOW
RAW UMBER, WHITE

Coloured Paper. Here is the trickiest so far, a glass. Use one that is plain and simple in shape; the secret lies in what you leave out, not what you put in. Paint the background thinly, to let the drawing show through. Then, working from top to bottom, put a dark tone on the shadow side of the glass. Remember the ellipse; now draw that on the top and bottom of the glass with a small sable brush. Working again from top to bottom, put in the highlight on the left.

Now try a canvas. In this exercise I have sketched on canvas a simple landscape with a tree. This is the last exercise you will do before you learn some of the different techniques of acrylic painting. It may be somewhat advanced at the moment but it will add a little spice to the exercises you have been doing. I want you to use the same methods you have been using up to now, avoiding detail and going for the shapes, colours and tones.

Draw the picture with an HB pencil and paint a clear, blue sky, using the colours shown. At a second stage, when the sky is dry, paint the middle distance. Next, using a broad treatment, paint the large tree and foreground. For the lighter greens and for the foreground try using Standard Formula; it will add texture and will help to bring the foreground near to us, pushing the background further away. Don't try to put detail in this picture, that will come at a later stage.

BRIGHT GREEN, RAW UMBER, WHITE
RAW UMBER
WHITE

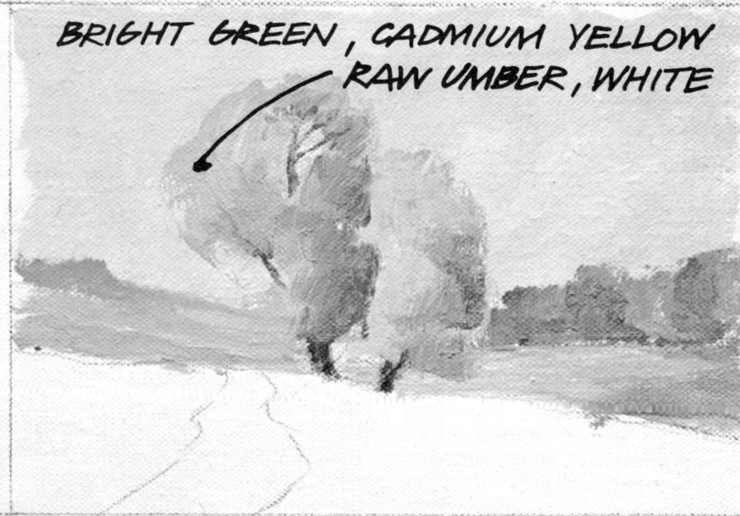

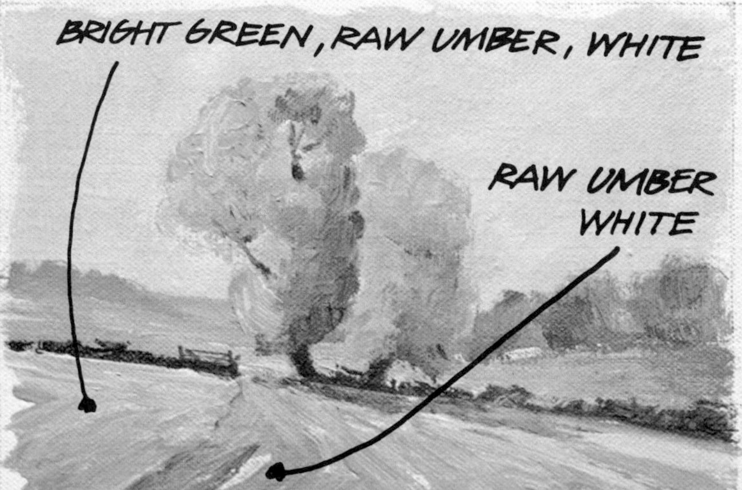

SOME BASIC TECHNIQUES

By now you should be used to handling acrylic colour and know the feel and texture of it. While working on the previous lessons, you will have found different techniques for using the paint. This you could have done consciously or subconsciously. If you have found a way of painting a thin line with a thick brush for instance, don't think this is wrong. Generally speaking, any way you find to achieve a desired result is fine. In this section I will explain some of the techniques I use for acrylic painting.

In all the illustrations I have marked the movement of the *brush strokes* with black arrows. To indicate the movement of the brush in relation to the canvas, i.e. working from top to bottom or bottom to top, I have marked the direction with an outline arrow. For instance, if you look at the first illustration, you'll see that the brush is being moved left to right, from top to bottom.

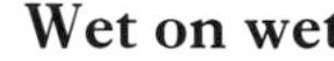

Wet on wet

This is a name given to the method of brushing wet paint on to and into more wet paint on a canvas. This helps to mould colours into one another and graduate them evenly from, say, dark to light. On small areas, this can be done quite easily with acrylic colour, but if a larger area, say 51 × 41cm (20 × 16in), is to be painted wet on wet, use acrylic Gel Retarder, which will slow the drying process and allow wet on wet painting. Try using one brush of Gel Retarder to one of paint. You will find from experience how much you need for your own requirements. Move the brush from side to side, moulding the colours together, getting soft edges; and work from the light of the cloud, down the canvas to the darker tones.

Painting thin

Painting thin is a way of painting transparently and can be done at any required time. If you paint thinly, it means that the surface will show through your paint. The surface could be the clean canvas or areas of colour. Painting thin is a way of glazing. In this example the painting thin technique is being used to paint the sky over the drawing of buildings while still retaining the drawing. To achieve this, brush the colour in more than usual and it will spread, thin out and become less opaque.

Dry brush

This is a technique applied to most forms of painting: watercolour, oil etc. It is used to achieve a hit-and-miss effect, thus giving sparkle and life to the brush stroke. Although it can be applied to many subjects in order to express certain feelings, one of its most natural areas of application is water. Dry brush can give ripples, sparkles, highlights and movement to water. The illustration shows water reflections and the dry brush is adding sparkle and movement.

Dry your brush out more than usual, load it with paint, work out the excess paint on to your palette, then drag the brush from left to right in straight *horizontal* strokes across the water. The paint will hit and miss, leaving some background showing through. For some effects you can work thick paint in a dry brush technique over the same area time and time again. This will give you depth in the area you are painting. With acrylic colour this can be done quickly as the paint is quick-drying.

Misty effect

A misty effect in a landscape or seascape can give it a lot of atmosphere. Using acrylic colour, I have found that I can add the mist to the painting at any time, rather than having to work it in as the painting is being progressed. Since the paint dries quickly, there is usually no waiting time for this effect to take place.

Dry the brush out and add a small amount of paint, rubbing it backwards and forwards on the palette until it is very dry. It is really a very, very dry brush technique. Scrub the area to be painted with the brush and you will cover areas in mist; by continuous scrubbing you will find that, as the brush uses up most of its paint, the areas of mist now being applied will be more transparent, showing some background through. This, of course, is part of the effect. The mist on the right was painted in this way.

NB: try not to have too much thick paint left by earlier brush strokes on the surface where you intend to have your mist patches.

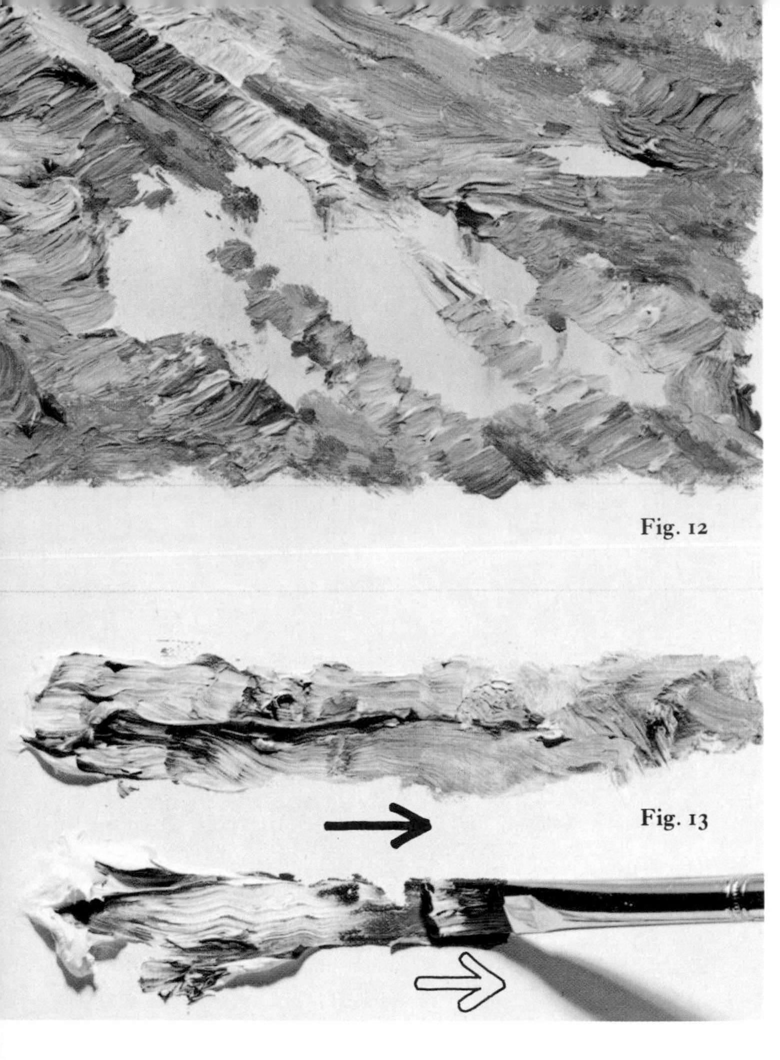

Fig. 12

Texture paste

Texture Paste is an acrylic polymer extender for building up heavy impasto textures. That is the technical phraseology! It looks and feels like a very thick, white paint. It can be put on canvas or any painting surface very thickly, two centimetres thick if required. When it sets, it is hard and can be painted over. It is extremely adhesive and an ideal medium for collage work. I use Texture Paste for foreground work where impasto effects help with moulding (see **fig. 12**).

Put some Texture Paste on your palette as you would do with paint. Lift some off with your brush and put two or three lumps on the painting. Then load your brush with paint, push the brush into the Texture Paste, press and pull away (**fig. 13**).

The ways of moulding the Texture Paste on the canvas are endless. You will find that the colour of the paint will be weaker where it was mixed with the white of the Texture Paste. If you want darker areas, paint those when the paste is dry.

Fig. 13

Fig. 14

Palette knife

Standard Formula colours are unsurpassed for thick impasto work. The colour can be used undiluted, with a painting knife, to create many textures and forms. The paint retains its sharp edges and will not crack, even when put on very thickly. **Figs. 14, 15** and **16** show a variety of shapes and forms that can be produced by different painting knives. In **fig. 14**, the small, pear-shaped knife is shown producing first positive and then negative shapes. The flexibility of the blade allows sensitive control. **Fig. 15** shows a medium, pear-shaped knife being used to mould forms and create surface-texture patterns. **Fig. 16** shows a narrow, trowel-shaped knife being used to cover an area with paint. Always clean painting knives after use.

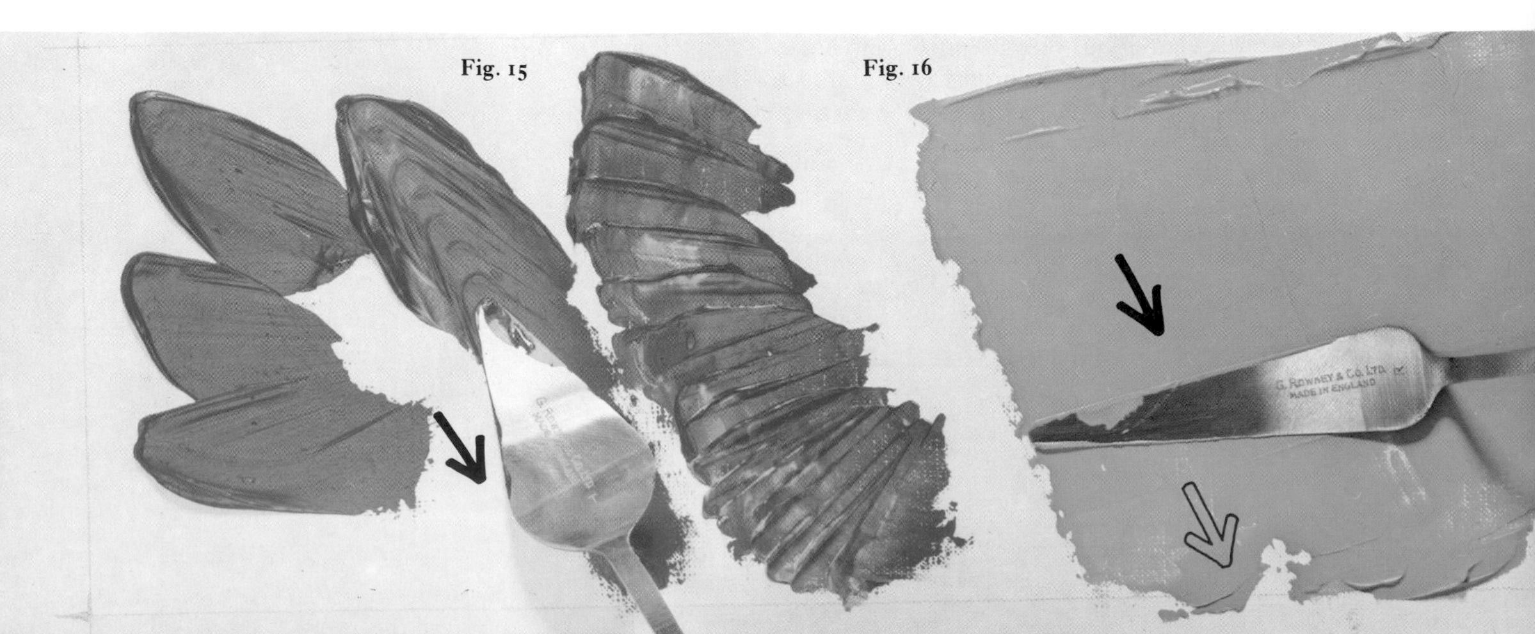

Fig. 15

Fig. 16

Fig. 17

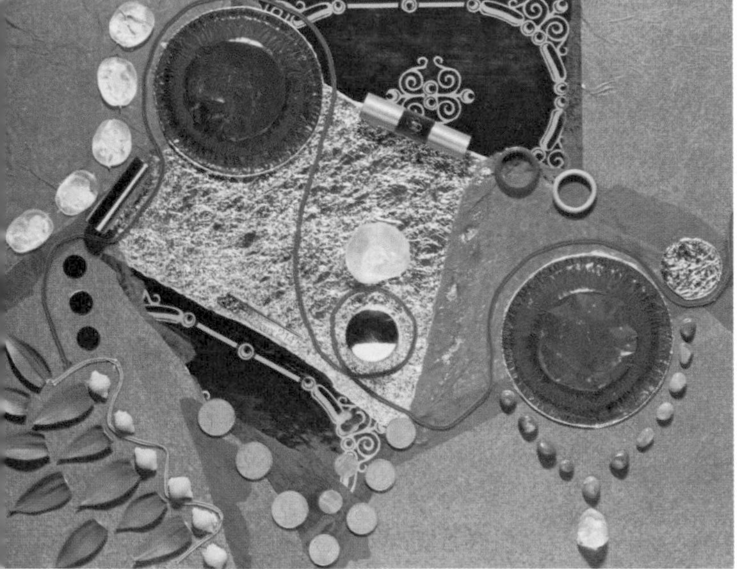

Fig. 18

Collage

The adhesive nature of acrylic colour makes it an ideal medium for collage work. The colour can be used as both a paint and an adhesive. However, there are transparent and colourless acrylic mediums on the market that can be used for gluing. One of them dries matt, the other gloss. Don't overload paint and mediums with materials such as sand or marble dust which might cause cracking in heavily loaded areas. Cracks rarely occur but if they do, they can be filled within a few hours of drying.

Texture Paste can be used to its full glory in collage work. In this context it is an ideal, thick, mouldable glue. It will hold anything in position, from a piece of paper to a lump of wood or plastic. The Texture Paste can be mixed with paint to colour it or it can be coloured when dry. In **fig. 17** (part of a finished collage work), Texture Paste has been put on the board first and heavy objects have been pressed in and left to dry. **Fig. 18** is a typical example of what can be created with acrylic colours and mediums. This delightful owl was designed and produced by my wife, using natural hessian as a support on hardboard. String, dried honesty seed pods, wool, dried parsley, barley, rice, monkey-tree leaves, lentils, shell, twigs and tin-foil were the other materials used.

Here is a more comprehensive list of materials that can be used for collage work – plastic, metal, glass, all kinds of paper, cardboard, cellophane, feathers, coloured foil and cork; all types of wood, from tree branches to sawdust; sequins, string, textiles and dried leaves. If materials used on a collage are covered with medium, they will be protected as well as sealed to the support.

Hard edge painting

Flow Formula colours have a high degree of opacity and may be easily brushed out to give flat, level areas of colour. These properties are ideal for a number of abstract techniques, hard edge painting being one of them. This is simply painting one flat colour against another with a crisp, hard edge. In **fig. 19**, masking tape was used to achieve the razor-edge sharpness between the colours. Make sure you press the edges of the tape down firmly to prevent paint seepage.

Fig. 19

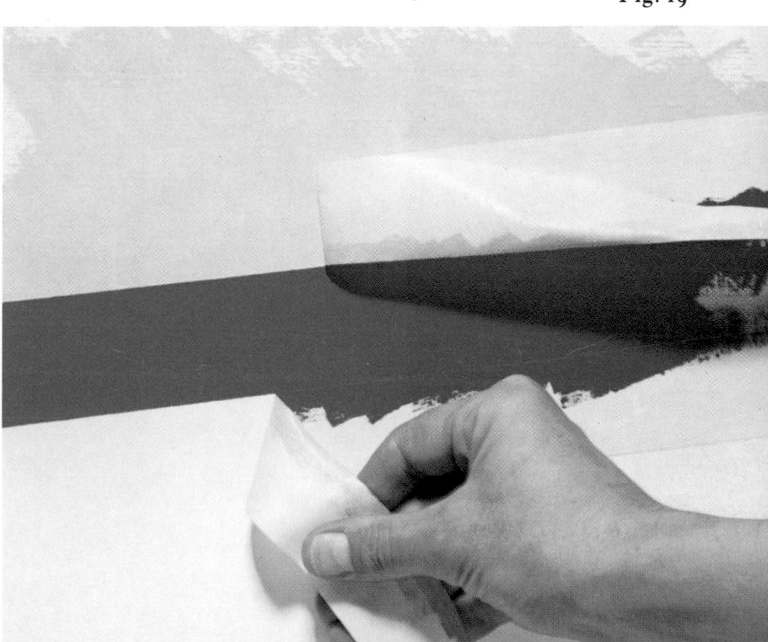

Fig. 20

Glazing

Acrylic colours will produce rich, transparent glazes when mixed with a glaze medium. The more glaze medium you add to your paint, the more transparent your glaze will be. A succession of thin glazes will produce soft colour gradations and the effect of colour fusion.

In **fig. 20**, the three primary colours were used, starting with yellow, then overpainted with red and finally with blue. This gives secondary colour effects where the primary ones have crossed each other. In this illustration, a mixture of one part colour to ten parts of glaze medium was used.

In **fig. 21**, a glaze was applied to a conventional painting to achieve the smoke effect. Use the brush as in the misty effect but this time, add glaze medium. This allows the paint to move better on the canvas because it is wet with the medium. It also makes sure that the paint is truly transparent. That part of the painting that has been glazed will look glossy and the rest will be matt. When you varnish your painting, this difference will disappear as the whole picture will be glossy or matt, depending on which varnish you use – a matt finish or gloss finish.

Fig. 21

Staining

Flow Formula colours can be diluted with water and painted into unprimed canvas to get an even, matt surface of colour. An acrylic, water tension breaker can be added (this is a medium for helping the flow of paint on to the canvas when very large areas are to be painted or the surface of the support is very, very porous and must stay that way, as in the unprimed canvas in this exercise). Water tension breaker, when added to the water, will give minimum dilution of the colour, at the same time retaining maximum colour intensity. This technique gives the appearance of a stained canvas, rather than a painted one (see **fig. 22**).

Fig. 22

Fig. 23

Murals

Acrylic colours are particularly suitable for mural painting and can be applied directly to plaster or masonry as well as to canvas without prior preparation of the surfaces. Depending upon the quality of plaster or cement, it is preferable to prime it with an acrylic primer, although this is not absolutely necessary. **Fig. 23** is a mural that my eighteen-year-old daughter painted on her bedroom wall; Flow Formula was used entirely for this painting.

Priming

Priming is a method of sealing absorbent surfaces before applying paint. Acrylic primer should always be used. Use a small, household brush to paint on the primer (**fig. 24**) or, for larger areas, a household squeezy painting pad. Try to avoid leaving brush strokes on the surface, brush them well out. Wash your brush out after use. I am often asked if paper should be primed: the answer is no.

Techniques - to sum up

In the foregoing pages I have tried to show you some of the basic methods of getting different results on canvas. If you can imagine all the brush strokes or painting knife strokes that occur during one painting – it must be tens of thousands – and all the variations that may occur, it must be obvious that I have only picked out the *basic* techniques. You will discover many of your own and you will add these to your reservoir of knowledge. Whatever you learn, either by accident or design, don't be afraid of using it if it helps your painting. If you stood on your head to paint and the result was disastrous, people would laugh at you but if the result was good, then people would marvel at you. Never worry *how* you paint it – *if* the result is good.

Fig. 24

EXERCISE ONE
FLOWERS

This first exercise is one that can be controlled to a large degree by the artist. The one main point to remember is that flowers change and eventually die. Therefore, any arrangement you prepare must be capable of outstaying your painting time. If you do not manage to finish in time, change the flowers for fresh ones: your painting should have progressed enough for you to improvise. Remember, it is an *impression* of a flower you are painting, not a *specific* one. A vase of different blooms, with exciting shapes and colours, can give tremendous inspiration and make a fine painting. It can also be very overpowering for the beginner, leading to disaster and disappointment. Study one flower at a time. Observe its characteristics, see how its petals are formed, their shape, how it grows from the stem and, just as important, study the leaves. Put this one flower against a plain and contrasting background, which will give it a clear, undisturbed shape. When you have mastered a certain flower put some in a vase and paint away. You will find it helpful, at times, to use other colours in addition to the ones on your palette, as the pigmentation of flowers is unlimited. For this exercise I have chosen flowers that can be painted with your normal palette (see the basic colours below).

First stage The light source here is coming from the left and from above. Draw the line between background and table top first, then the teapot and finally, the flowers and leaves. The large leaves, incidentally, are rhododendron and will last a long time. Using Raw Sienna, Cadmium Yellow, Crimson and White, paint the background; remember to paint thin where you want your drawing to show through.

Second stage For the leaves, mix three tones of dark, medium and light green on the palette, using Bright Green, Ultramarine, Cadmium Yellow and a little White (medium); add more White (light); add Crimson and more Ultramarine (dark). Paint the leaves with a size No. 4 nylon brush, wet on wet, working the brush into the centre, then down each side in turn, following the direction of the veins. With a mix of Cadmium Yellow, Crimson and a little White, paint the orange flowers with a size No. 4 nylon brush. Start at the centre and work the brush up and down to form petals, going round the centre and spreading out to the extreme edge of the flower. Remember: the centre of the flower is not necessarily the centre of the drawn flower shape. Continue in the same way with the yellow flowers, using Cadmium Yellow, Raw Umber, a little Crimson and White.

Third stage Now the table top: I have purposely used a non-shining surface, so you only have to contend with shadows and not reflections as well. Mix Raw Umber, Crimson, Raw Sienna and White; using a size No. 12 nylon brush, paint from the background down to the bottom of the canvas. Don't try to paint *up to* the teapot with your size No. 12 brush; let the brush go *over* the pencil lines; the excess will be covered when you paint the pot. Using a size No. 8 nylon brush, mix Burnt Umber, Crimson, Ultramarine and a little White, and start on the teapot. Keep your brush flat and move it down the pot. Bow the shape of the stroke as the pot is curved. Work in the lighter areas as you paint and add some orange and yellow for the flower reflections. The shadows on the background are the next stage. Use your size No. 4 nylon brush; mix Raw Umber, Crimson, Cadmium Yellow and White. The brush strokes should follow the direction of the cast shadow. Now the table top shadows: change to a size No. 8 nylon brush, mix

First stage

Second stage

Raw Umber, Ultramarine, Crimson and White. Keep your brush strokes horizontal to make the shadows look flat. Be *very* careful to meet the background shadows spot on. This helps to give the picture two definite planes, i.e. the perpendicular background and the horizontal plane of the table. Where the shadows have gone over the teapot, use your size No. 5 sable brush and paint the edge back on to the teapot. You can see where I did this on the bottom left edge of the spout.

Finished stage Start by working on the flowers. To achieve the appearance of hundreds of petals while showing only some, you should realize the importance of light against dark. Look at the top, right-hand flower. The dark shadow on the leaf underlines the shape of the light flower and the two bright petals against the dark petals beneath stress the bottom edge formation. However, the same flower has lost some of its contour into the background at the top and right-hand sides. This has been done to give depth to the flower: if sharp accents were everywhere they would cancel each other out and no accents at all would give a very flat picture. This secret of knowing what to put in or leave out, especially in painting flowers, will come from *observation* and practice. In the meantime, as you copy these flowers it will help you understand your first painting from life. You have already painted the light and dark areas; now, using a size No. 5 sable brush, mix Cadmium Yellow, Crimson and White, and add the light areas

Third stage

Finished stage

of the yellow blooms. Follow the shapes you have already painted in the second stage but this time, be more careful and precise with the petals. Work from the centre outwards: press the brush down, pull it towards you and slowly lift off; practise on some scrap paper, it's well worth it. Make sure you make some nice petal shapes against the teapot – light against dark! Do the same exercise with the orange flowers. Finish all flowers by adding some dark accents to help form the petal shapes (sable brush) and add some extra highlights by using Standard Formula. This will then stand in relief off the canvas and catch the light, providing those very important light accents. Now darken some of the leaves to give them form. Paint over the stems in the middle: this will give them tone, enabling them to recede. Paint in the fallen flower on the table now – watch for the light petals against dark. Glaze the teapot with a blend of Burnt Umber and Crimson, using your size No. 5 sable brush. When the glaze is dry, paint back the yellow reflection and the highlights and add some dark accents. When you have finished, it is advisable to leave the picture for twenty-four hours or so and come to it again with a fresh eye. You will then see things that you had not noticed before. You have only to correct these and then your painting is finished.

ALWYN CRAWSHAW

EXERCISE TWO
SEASCAPE

The sea has always fascinated artists. You will find that most of the stalwart landscape artists have had their fair share of painting the sea. Two of Britain's finest landscape artists, Constable and Turner, couldn't resist the call of the sea and in the eighteenth and nineteenth centuries, it wasn't just a case of jumping into a car after Saturday lunch and reaching the sea in a couple of hours. I think the sea holds its fascination by seeming endless: you can go around the world by leaving from the shore where you are painting. It is vast and restless; it has extremes of mood that range from the blissful and romantic to the simply terrifying. Like the sky, the sea changes its colour all the time and, of course, it is never still. This must be observed from life. Sit on the beach and watch wave after wave coming in and breaking on the shore. It is very valuable to learn how a wave is formed and how it breaks. Then try sketching with a 3B pencil, concentrating on the overall form of the wave. You can't draw the same wave, of course – it's only there for seconds – but there's another and another and another. You have to get a sort of retained image to carry on to the next wave, and that further image on to the next, and so on. Then you can have a go at painting from life. Remember that the horizon line must always be level otherwise the sea will appear to be falling off the canvas. If necessary, draw the horizon line with a ruler. The sky must belong to the sea in colour and tone. Generally speaking, use the same colours for both. To give more interest in composition and colour to a seascape we have cliffs, beaches, rocks and boats. Cliffs and headland give distance and perspective. Beaches and rocks give us the opportunity to paint crashing waves with spray and foam flying everywhere. In the picture prepared for the exercise I have painted rocks because they are a good subject for acrylics.

SKY–
ULTRAMARINE BLUE
CRIMSON
WHITE
CADMIUM YELLOW

DISTANT SEA –
ULTRAMARINE BLUE
CRIMSON
BRIGHT GREEN
WHITE

FOAM –
WHITE
ULTRAMARINE BLUE
CRIMSON
CADMIUM YELLOW

ROCKS
BURNT UMBER
BRIGHT GREEN
ULTRAMARINE BLUE
CADMIUM YELLOW
WHITE

First stage Draw the horizontal line with an HB pencil. Use a ruler to get it horizontal on the canvas. Then draw the rocks and waves. The bottom of the rocks is formed by the sea washing around them; therefore, it will follow the movement of the water and in most cases it will be level. Mix Ultramarine, Crimson and White for the top of the sky, add Cadmium Yellow with Crimson for the lighter clouds. Make this colour stronger (not as much White) on the right of the big rock. Paint this sky with a size No. 12 nylon brush and use Gel Retarder to paint wet on wet.

Second stage Paint the sea from the horizon to the big wave and rock. Use your size No. 4 nylon brush, mixing Ultramarine, Crimson, Bright Green and White. To the right of the rock add some more White with a touch of Cadmium Yellow as little highlights where the sun is coming through and catching the breaking waves. Under the top of the large breaking wave paint very thin (watery) Ultramarine and Bright Green. This will give the transparent colour of the wave where it is very thin. Now paint the shadow under the wave: this is the darker colour. The lighter colour is the foam that is running up the wave. Here, it is in shadow. The darker areas were achieved with Ultramarine, Crimson, Bright Green and a little White. The light foam was painted leaving dark areas and following the contour of the wave. Paint the side of the rock with Burnt Umber and Bright Green. Now, add much more White to the same wave colour and paint the rest of the wave – do not add too much White at this stage, leave some brightness up your sleeve. Lastly, paint the water breaking over the big rock. Keep this in shadow. Start at

First stage

Second stage

Third stage

the rock and work your brush up and away. Let the brush – and yourself – feel like spray bouncing off a rock, get excited about it and you will find the result will be worthwhile. Experiment on a piece of paper if you like.

Third stage All you have to do in this stage is paint the rest of the sea. This is treated as underpainting because finally, it will have foam added over it. The rocks have been left unpainted at this stage, as all the sides except the bottom of the rocks appear in front of the water: it is easier, therefore, to paint them when the majority of the sea is finished so that they will have a clean edge against the sea. Using your size No. 8 nylon brush, mix Ultramarine, Crimson, Bright Green and White and paint the sea, starting from underneath the large wave and working across and down the canvas. Keep the brush strokes horizontal to keep the water level. As you come nearer the foreground let your brush strokes loosen up, add lighter and darker tones and your brush will form movement in the water. Don't be too critical of yourself; remember, a lot of this area will be covered in the next stage.

Finished stage Now to paint the foam on the water. Use a size No. 4 nylon brush with White, Ultramarine, Crimson and Cadmium Yellow. Work the brush horizontally in short strokes, changing the tone and colour (very subtly) all the time. You will be working on this part of the sea until the picture is finished. For the finishing touches on this foam use sable brushes to enable you to paint the finer modelling. Next, work on the big, breaking wave: use your size No. 8 nylon brush loaded with White plus a little Cadmium Yellow and Crimson. Put the brush on the edge of the rock and then push it up and away to get the spray effect. If it

Finished stage

doesn't go right the first time, paint it dark again and have another go; or just practise on a piece of paper as you did in the second stage. Now retouch the big rock, just up to the wave and give it a clean edge. This part of the painting contains the darkest and lightest areas together, which produce a very sharp contrast. With the same brush and colour, paint some flying spume on the top of the large wave. Now dry the brush out and with a dry brush technique, using White and Ultramarine, work over the big rock and the bottom of the large wave by the rock; this will fuzz up the area around the rock and breaking wave, giving a feeling of misty spray. For the rocks you will need Texture Paste, Burnt Umber, Bright Green, Ultramarine, Cadmium Yellow and White. Use a size No. 8 nylon brush, don't mix the paint too much on the palette, let the mixing occur on the rocks. The Texture Paste and paint will thus make streaks of colour following the direction of your brush strokes and you will find that the rocks' contours are formed reasonably well, as long as your brush is worked in the direction of the rock surfaces. When this is nearly dry, add shadow to the dark side by dragging darker rock colour on to the rocks. You will find that it will drag up some of the existing paint in places: this again helps to show form and ruggedness. When the rocks are completely dry, with a dry brush add more colour – light and dark – to give even more texture. Finally, with a sable brush, pick out some shapes with dark or light colour. This is where you finish the large sea (foam) area. Work on this again, now that you have the tone of the rocks painted in and go over all your important highlights with Standard Formula White.

ALWYN CRAWSHAW

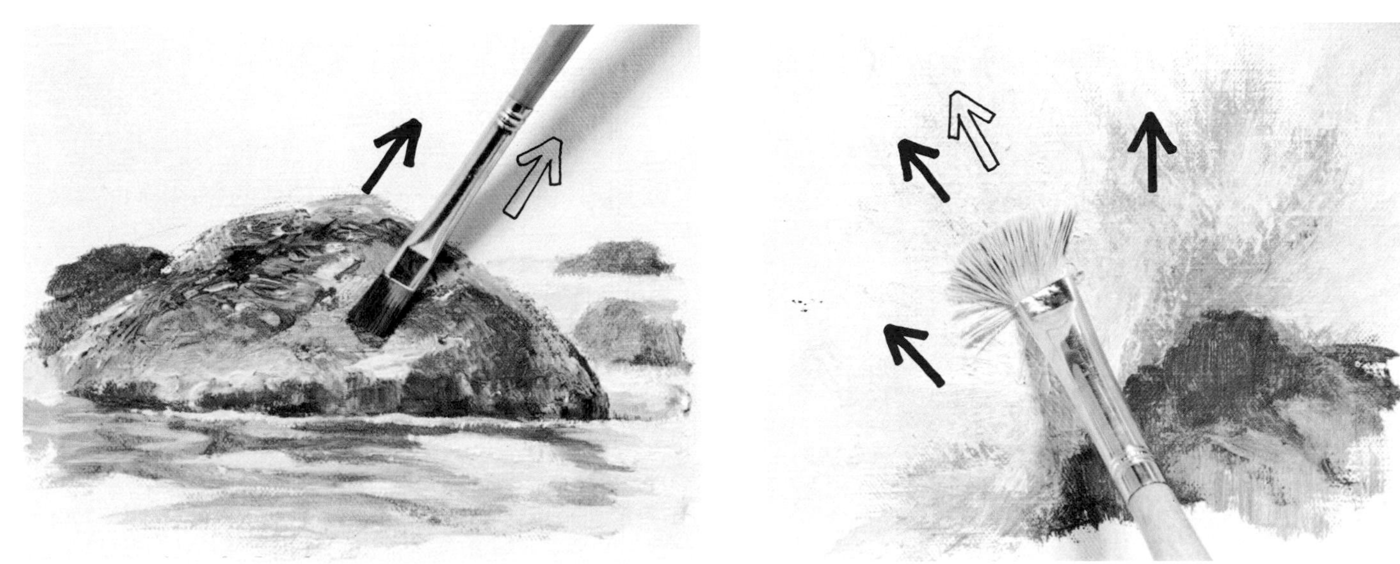

EXERCISE THREE
SNOW

In some parts of the world, snow is never seen. But, for those who experience it even for only short periods, it has a fascination all of its own. The stillness and quietness of a snowy landscape can be unbelievable. The clear rivers of the spring and summer turn to brown and the trees stand out in sharp silhouette. One of the problems with painting snow is obvious: you can't take the family out for a picnic in six centimetres of snow nor can you sit on the ground to paint. Above all, it would be very cold. If you are going to paint out-of-doors, then you must be able to accept and endure nature's conditions. Always put on more clothing than you think you need. Put your sketch book in a polythene bag so that if you drop it in the snow, it will stay dry. I once dropped mine in a pond – without polythene! The most important rule I can suggest, when painting snow, is never to use just White for any of it. It is only white in its purest form – just fallen – and even then, it reflects light and colour from all around. So even the whitest snow should have some colour. Add a little blue to cool the white paint or a little red or yellow to warm it up. Never be afraid to make snow dark in shadow areas. It can be as dark, in comparison to its surroundings, as a shadow in a non-snow landscape. The way to paint snow is to paint it in a low key: if we take our darkest shadow as number ten and our brightest snow as number one, with a natural gradation of tone in between, you should paint your snow in the range from eight to three. This will leave enough reserve up your sleeve to add darker shadows and brighter highlights.

SKY–
COERULEUM BLUE
CRIMSON
WHITE

BANK–
BURNT UMBER
CADMIUM YELLOW
ULTRAMARINE BLUE

SNOW–
WHITE
COERULEUM BLUE
CRIMSON
RAW SIENNA

SNOW HIGHLIGHTS–
WHITE
CADMIUM YELLOW
CRIMSON

First stage Use an HB pencil to draw the landscape, starting with the horizon. Next, draw the edge of the field with the two main trees on it, the other trees and the river banks. For the sky use Coeruleum, Crimson and White mixed with Gel Retarder. Half-way down the sky mix Cadmium Yellow, Crimson and White and paint back up into the wet 'blue' sky. Then paint down to the horizon, adding more Crimson as you go. This will give that lovely, luminous-sky effect.

Second stage With Coeruleum, Crimson, Cadmium Yellow and White, using a dry brush technique, paint the distant trees; then, with the same colours but much more White, paint the field underneath with a size No. 4 nylon brush. Paint the house with the same brush, the chimneys with your small sable brush. Put the highlight on the left of the house where the sun hits it. As in the landscape exercise, use a dry brush to paint the middle-distance trees and the hedge. Since the time is late afternoon, there is a warm glow in the sky and this should be reflected in the trees where the sun touches them: use more Crimson and Cadmium Yellow. Next, paint the snow on the lower field in the same way as the first one but make it very dark under the left-hand trees as this is in shadow. Next, paint the two main trees with Standard Formula colours Raw Umber, Burnt Umber, Bright Green, Ultramarine and Crimson.

Third stage Start by painting the feathery branches on both trees, using your size No. 8 nylon brush in a dry brush technique. Mix Cadmium Yellow, Crimson, Raw Umber and Ultramarine. Next, paint the hedge, using your size No. 4 nylon brush with Cadmium Yellow, Crimson and Ultramarine; use a dry brush and paint upwards. Now the water. This was painted as watercolour, i.e. using your size No. 8 nylon brush loaded with water and paint. You will find the paint runs down the canvas, which is how it should be. Use the brush flat on and run it down the canvas, starting each stroke at the top and at the side of the previous one. You will find the brush strokes will merge, giving a watery appearance. Use Burnt Umber, Crimson and Ultramarine.

First stage

Second stage

When the wash is absolutely dry, apply another over the top. If you look at the stage three illustration, you will see where my second wash came over the first one, which appears lighter. When the second wash is nearly dry, paint the reflections of the trees and bank. Use your size No. 4 nylon brush and start under the bank, bringing the brush down. You will find the paint mixes slightly with the second wash, giving a soft edge. Don't try to put all the branches in. Then, with horizontal strokes, paint the reflections under the river bank; keep your paint very watery.

Finished stage Paint the bank on both sides of the river: use your size No. 4 nylon brush and mix Burnt Umber, Cadmium Yellow and Ultramarine. The white area now left is going to be snow. Remember: paint from eight to three on your tone chart. Start under the trees, using White, Coeruleum, Crimson and Raw Sienna. Break up the line of snow under the hedge and change the tones and colours of the snow as you go, working down to the river bank. Drag the brush over the bank and into the painted bank areas. Now paint the trunks of the left-hand, middle-distance trees with your size No. 2 sable brush; use the paint thinly, working from the bottom of the trees upwards. With the same brush paint the small branches of the large trees, working downwards; for the left-hand one use warm colours as the sun is catching it. Notice the two small branches that have broken off and are in the hedge under the tree. Now you can finish the reflections in the water, using Burnt Umber, Ultramarine and Crimson with your

Third stage

Finished stage

size No. 5 sable brush; paint the reflections watery. You will have to repeat the wash over the area a few times as this will help to express the movement of water over the reflections. When this is dry, paint the highlights with White, Cadmium Yellow and a touch of Coeruleum (slightly watery). Remember to keep your brush strokes horizontal. With your size No. 4 nylon brush mix a snow shadow colour from Coeruleum, Crimson, Raw Sienna and White. Paint the shadows on the left bank and run the paint slightly over the bank colour. You now have to bring the snow to life by highlighting it. Mix Standard Formula White, Cadmium Yellow and Crimson, use your size No. 4 nylon brush (very clean) and drag in a dry brush technique over the sunlit areas. If you have painted the snow in the right low key, you will be surprised how white the highlights appear and how the snow seems to sparkle. Next, paint the gate and the fence, using your sable brush with Raw Umber, Bright Green and White. Finally, with your size No. 2 sable brush, paint in the winter grass and plants that show through the snow; they will add depth and perspective. Start your brush stroke at the bottom and work up and off the canvas. These must be confident strokes or they will not look real. Practise on paper and get used to the brush stroke. Finish by adding your light and dark accents.

ALWYN CRAWSHAW

EXERCISE FOUR
BOATS

We are back to the pull of the sea again. After all, boats are found on the sea and, therefore, the emotions we feel when painting boats are very similar to those we feel for the sea. However, I believe there is one difference. Boats make us feel more intimate with the sea; they reassure us about life on the sea by filling the emptiness of a vast expanse of water. In this painting of a Brittany harbour, your next exercise, we experience the intimacy of the scene: the boats give us a feeling of activity, while a friendly calm is conveyed by the very still, harbour water. More knowledge of drawing is needed to paint boats than to paint a landscape. For instance, if a branch of a tree you are copying is too low, it will still look fine in your painting but if a mast of a boat is leaning to one side, then the painting looks obviously wrong. A few days spent sketching all the bric-a-brac, natural and unnatural, of a small harbour – from an old wreck sticking out of a mud flat like the backbone of a great fish, down to an old piece of chain, all rusty and abandoned – would give you tremendous knowledge and make you familiar with boats and their surroundings.

SKY, WATER
ROOF-TOPS—
COERULEUM BLUE
CRIMSON
WHITE

RED BOAT–
CADMIUM RED
CRIMSON
BURNT UMBER
WHITE

BLUE BOAT–
COERULEUM BLUE
CRIMSON
RAW UMBER
WHITE

BEACH–
BURNT UMBER
BRIGHT GREEN
CRIMSON
CADMIUM YELLOW
WHITE

First stage I drew this harbour scene from a sketch and, therefore, had plenty of time to correct the drawing and make a careful study on the canvas in the studio. Had I painted this outside, the drawing would have been looser and I would have corrected it as I painted. First, draw the harbour wall; make sure the bottom is horizontal on the canvas. Next, draw the hill, a few of the main buildings in the distance and the middle-distance boats that have definite shapes. The other boats, which make this a bustling harbour, will be ad-libbed when you are painting. Finally, draw the main boat and the little one on the beach. The sky and water are exactly the same colour at this first stage. Using a size No. 12 nylon brush, mix Coeruleum, Crimson and White. Paint from the top, well over the hill and buildings, adding more Crimson as the sky disappears behind the hill. Using the same brush and paint, continue over the water to the beach.

Second stage Look at the picture: apart from the hill behind the harbour, which had Bright Green added to the previous colours, all the rest of the buildings in this stage were painted in Coeruleum, Crimson and White for the roof tops, adding Raw Sienna, Cadmium Yellow, Raw Umber and White for the walls. Again, it appears that a lot of colours were used but if you look closely, the real colour is Coeruleum for the roof tops and Raw Sienna for the rest. The other colours are there to be added sparingly, as I have said before. But remember, it is this *variation of colour* and tone that gives a painting life. Use your size No. 4 nylon brush, paint in the hill, then the roof tops and then the lower parts. Don't try to make every building just like mine, it would be impossible. It is an impression of buildings you want to achieve. They are in the distance, so paint them in low key. Put no more detail than the windows and shutters (only suggested) with a sable brush. On the right of the picture let the buildings merge even more to give distance. Paint the background inside the cabin windows when painting the buildings. For the main fishing boat use Cadmium Red, Burnt Umber, Crimson and White. Only add Crimson to the shadow areas and White to the light parts. Start with the cabin – leaving the window frames – then the hull. In my original, a size No. 4 nylon brush was almost plank size, which was ideal because you must paint the hull plank by plank, starting from the top. At the stern of the boat add White where the light catches the wood. Paint over the red with White, Coeruleum and Crimson in the spots where the paint has worn off the boat. Then add Cadmium Yellow to the white in the cabin framework.

First stage

Second stage

Third stage Use the colours that you adopted for the buildings and a very wet size No. 8 nylon brush to put in the reflections. Start underneath the harbour wall, using the brush flat, and work down, changing the colours slightly as you paint along the canvas. Paint over the drawing of boats. While the paint is still wet put in the window reflection. Now paint the boats: the secret is to give an impression of a harbour busy with small craft and to keep them in the distance so as not to overpower our fishing boat in the foreground. For your white paint now use Standard Formula colour to mix with the colours for the boats. Use your size No. 4 nylon brush and toned-down colours; with light colours paint oblong shapes to represent boats in the distance, then add some dark areas (cabins, ends of boats, etc.). Put in some masts with your small sable brush, some light and some dark. If you look closely at stage three illustration, you will see that the only real boats are the cabin cruiser on the right and the bows of the yacht to the left of the red boat. These you have to paint carefully as it is these that give the eye the impression that all the shapes and masts behind are boats. A little more detail will be put in at the final stage. Now add the old boat on the right. Use your size No. 4 nylon brush and paint it in planks as you did the red boat, using Coeruleum, Crimson, Raw Umber and White. When dry, drag over some darker paint in dry brush to give an ageing look. Finally, paint the front of the bows on the red boat.

Third stage

Finished stage

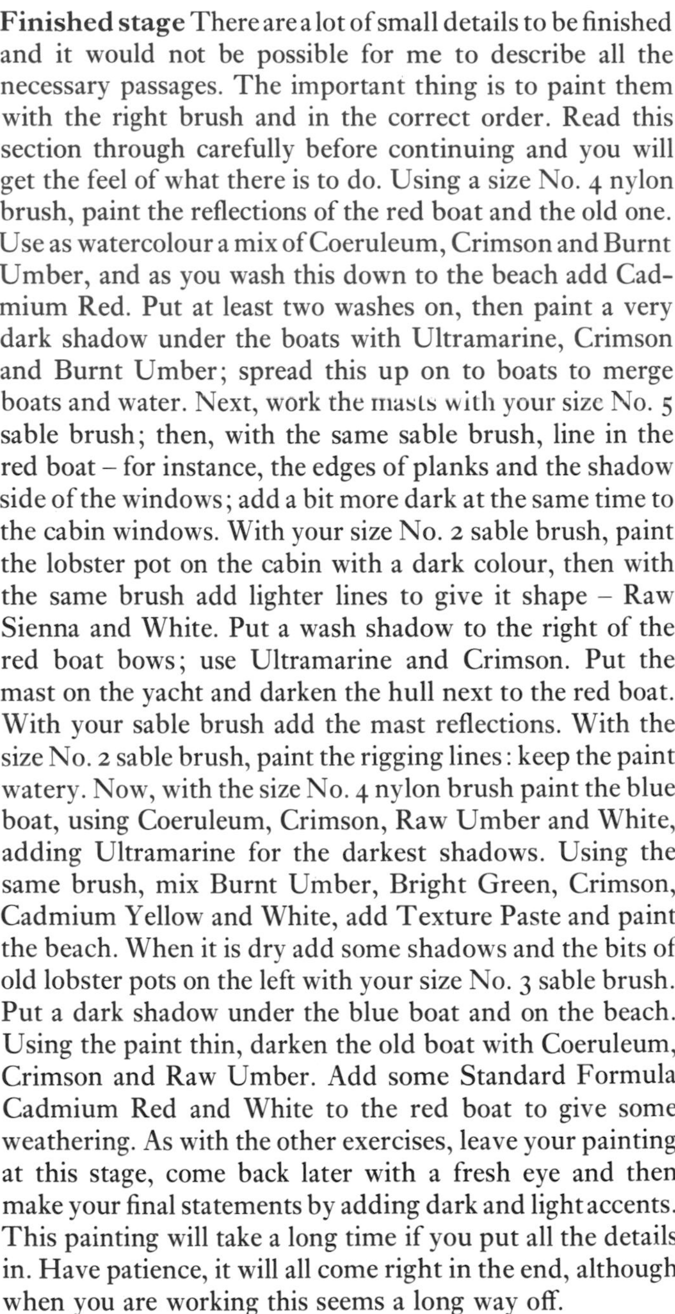

Finished stage There are a lot of small details to be finished and it would not be possible for me to describe all the necessary passages. The important thing is to paint them with the right brush and in the correct order. Read this section through carefully before continuing and you will get the feel of what there is to do. Using a size No. 4 nylon brush, paint the reflections of the red boat and the old one. Use as watercolour a mix of Coeruleum, Crimson and Burnt Umber, and as you wash this down to the beach add Cadmium Red. Put at least two washes on, then paint a very dark shadow under the boats with Ultramarine, Crimson and Burnt Umber; spread this up on to boats to merge boats and water. Next, work the masts with your size No. 5 sable brush; then, with the same sable brush, line in the red boat – for instance, the edges of planks and the shadow side of the windows; add a bit more dark at the same time to the cabin windows. With your size No. 2 sable brush, paint the lobster pot on the cabin with a dark colour, then with the same brush add lighter lines to give it shape – Raw Sienna and White. Put a wash shadow to the right of the red boat bows; use Ultramarine and Crimson. Put the mast on the yacht and darken the hull next to the red boat. With your sable brush add the mast reflections. With the size No. 2 sable brush, paint the rigging lines: keep the paint watery. Now, with the size No. 4 nylon brush paint the blue boat, using Coeruleum, Crimson, Raw Umber and White, adding Ultramarine for the darkest shadows. Using the same brush, mix Burnt Umber, Bright Green, Crimson, Cadmium Yellow and White, add Texture Paste and paint the beach. When it is dry add some shadows and the bits of old lobster pots on the left with your size No. 3 sable brush. Put a dark shadow under the blue boat and on the beach. Using the paint thin, darken the old boat with Coeruleum, Crimson and Raw Umber. Add some Standard Formula Cadmium Red and White to the red boat to give some weathering. As with the other exercises, leave your painting at this stage, come back later with a fresh eye and then make your final statements by adding dark and light accents. This painting will take a long time if you put all the details in. Have patience, it will all come right in the end, although when you are working this seems a long way off.

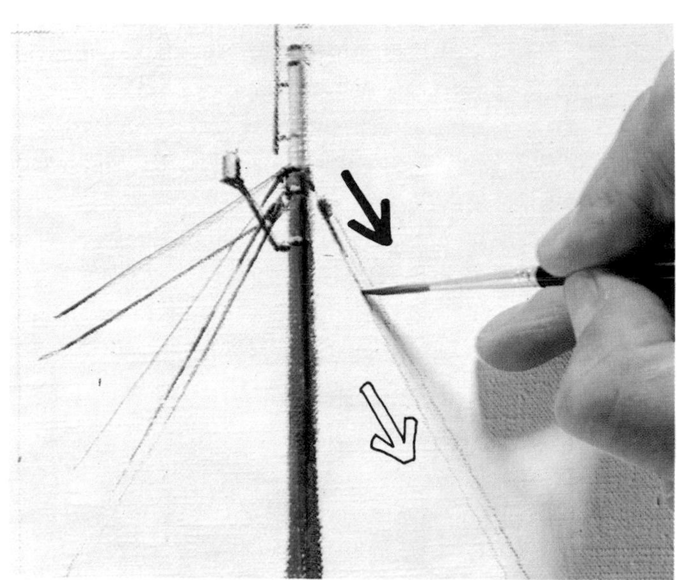

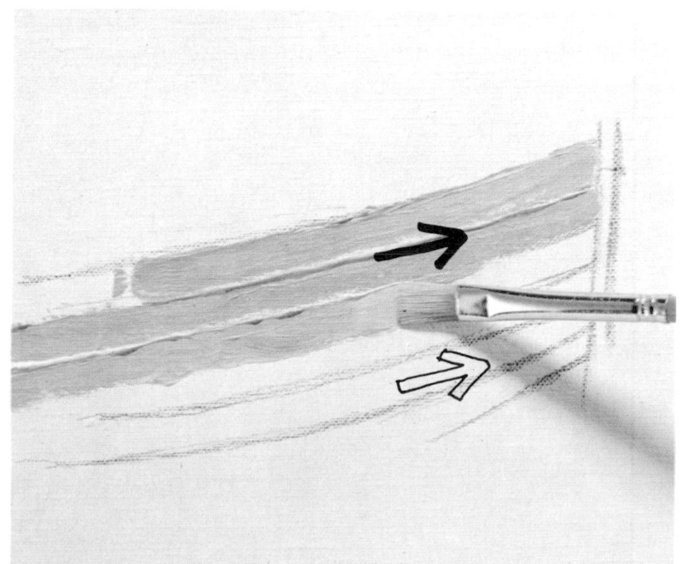